ZAGATSURVEY®

1999 UPDATE

CONNECTICUT SO. NY STATE RESTAURANTS

Edited by Valerie Foster
and Victoria Spencer

Updated by Julie Wilson
and Victoria Spencer

Published and distributed by
ZAGAT SURVEY, LLC
4 Columbus Circle
New York, New York 10019
Tel: 212 977 6000
E-mail: zagat@zagatsurvey.com

Acknowledgments

The editors wish to express their appreciation to Melanie Barnard, Kathy Bloomfield, Susan Cramer, Katharine Dunlop, Daria Foster, Stan Gurell, Lynne Hazlewood, Ruth Henderson, Jeremy Jones, Ira Levy, Judy and Kevin McEvoy, Ferdinand Metz, Joan and Sid Osofsky, and Michael Staats.

Contents

Introduction

This is not an all-new *Survey*. It is an *Update* reflecting significant developments since our last *Connecticut/ Southern New York State Restaurant Survey* was published. We have included a section of "1999 Additions" (see pages 19–25 for Connecticut, 147–153 for Southern New York State), covering 59 key places that were not in the previous *Survey*. We also have made changes throughout the book (excluding indexes) to show new addresses, phone numbers, chef changes, closings, etc.

As a whole, this *Update* covers over 940 restaurants with input from more than 1,800 people. We sincerely thank each participant. This book is really "theirs." By surveying large numbers of regular restaurant-goers, we think we have achieved a uniquely reliable guide. We hope you agree.

To help guide our readers to Connecticut's and Southern New York State's best meals and best buys, we have prepared a number of lists. See, for example, Connecticut's Favorite Restaurants (page 11), Top Ratings (pages 12–15) and Best Buys (pages 16–17) and Southern New York State's Favorite Restaurants (page 139), Top Ratings (pages 140–143) and Best Buys (pages 144–145). On the assumption that most people want a "quick fix" on the places at which they are considering eating, we have tried to be concise and to provide handy indexes.

We are particularly grateful to our editors, Valerie Foster, food editor for the *Stamford Advocate* and *Greenwich Time,* Julie Wilson, *Connecticut Magazine*'s former award-winning restaurant critic and now its travel columnist, and Victoria Spencer, restaurant reviewer for *Hudson Valley* and free-lance food editor and writer.

We invite you to be a reviewer in our next *Survey*. To do so, simply send a stamped, self-addressed, business-size envelope to ZAGAT SURVEY, 4 Columbus Circle, New York, NY 10019, so that we will be able to contact you. Each participant will receive a free copy of the next *Connecticut/ Southern New York State Survey* when it is published.

Your comments, suggestions and even criticisms of this *Survey* are also solicited. There is always room for improvement with your help.

New York, New York   Nina and Tim Zagat
May 22, 1998

Foreword

As has been true for some time, this year many of the top Connecticut restaurant openings are in Fairfield County and in the Litchfield Hills. The reason should be as obvious as it was to the enterprising Willie Sutton when asked why he robbed banks: "That's where the money is."

Recently, chefs such as Stonehenge's Christian Bertrand, Jean-Louis Gerin in Greenwich and the influential Steve Cavagnero at Cavey's set a standard giving Connecticut chefs a reputation equal to top toques in major urban areas. Increasingly, the state is home-growing its own chefs. They may graduate from Johnson & Wales in Providence or from Hyde Park's Culinary Institute of America, but they apprentice in Connecticut kitchens. And in increasing numbers, they are opening their own restaurants.

First Matthew Fahrner left the West Street Grill and opened Sharon's West Main Cafe in the Litchfield Hills and Bill Okesson (ex The Boulders Inn on Lake Waramaug) inaugurated John's Cafe in Woodbury. Then Riad Aamar departed Doc's for his own Oliva in New Preston, while Stephen Putnam (Spazzi, West Street Grill) premiered Canton's The Frog and The Peach. Christopher Wiersman (Avon Old Farms Inn) set his West Street in the rural fields of Ellington, while Cavey's-trained Tim Grills returned to his New London hometown to debut his namesake Timothy's.

Though the trend-setting chefs have opened mostly small, boutique cafes, there are other ways to go. Frederic Faveau (ex West Street Grill) became not only chef but also part of the management team at the ambitious Birches Inn on Lake Waramaug. Thomas Henkelmann (who actually came over the border from La Panetière in neighboring Rye, NY) bought the world-class Homestead Inn and, not surprisingly, renamed the dining room Restaurant Thomas Henkelmann at the Homestead. And amid all the chef shuffling, two very popular New Preston places closed: the fashionable Italian, Doc's, and the traditional American Inn on Lake Waramaug.

Whether they signal coming trends, or are merely cultural blips (as ephemeral as last year's brew pubs), this year's notables are cigar bars and beef. Oprah Winfrey notwithstanding, Connecticut likes its red meat, so steakhouses like J. Gilbert's in Glastonbury and Morton's of Chicago in

Stamford galloped across the state – some with prices (one hopes this is not a trend) that would make a cattle baron blink. Humidors abounded, and cigar nights became as popular in up-scale eateries as *Monday Night Football* in local bars.

But in Southern New York they weren't busy asking "where's the beef?", they were out trawling for fresh new seafood spots and a number of establishments opened to meet that need: The Bench & Bar (Newburgh), Down by the Bay (Mamaroneck), Gadaleto's Seafood Market & Restaurant (New Paltz), The Landau Grill (Woodstock) and The Mariner (Piermont) all make fish their focus.

Also in tandem with the trend toward keeping things light, grilling emerged as a restaurant theme. Grilling over a natural wood fire is the mainstay of Loretta Charles' in Ulster County. Even though pastas are available at the stylish Dolcigno Tuscan Grill in Cold Spring, grilled food is the focal point, as it is at Grill F/X in Port Chester, which appears to be the first South African eatery in our part of the world. And at the Brazilian Ipanema Grill in Bronxville, there's a never-ending supply of rotisserie-cooked *rodizio*.

But it is our own Contemporary American cuisine that is making the most sophisticated splash. Leading chef-owner Peter Kelly, who owns the No.1 and No.2 rated restaurants for food in the *SoNY Survey* – Xaviar's at Piermont and Xaviar's – has opened his latest and most ambitious venture, Restaurant X and Bully Boy Bar, in Congers. On a more modest scale, the Scarsdale Cafe also offers beautifully prepared and plated creative cuisine, which has earned chef-owner Connie Crupi kudos.

With all these offerings, it's no wonder that Connecticut and SoNYSers are eating out more often – an average of 3.7 times per week, despite the fact that the cost of an average meal in SoNY is $27.88, while it's $26.74 in Connecticut.

Each year the dining options for eating in Connecticut and the SoNYS area multiply and grow ever more exciting. We hope you'll use this guide to discover and delight in them.

Old Greenwich, CT
May 22, 1998

Julie Wilson
Victoria Spencer

Key to Ratings/Symbols

This sample entry identifies the various types of information contained in your Zagat Survey.

(1) Restaurant Name, Address & Phone Number

(2) Hours & Credit Cards

(3) ZAGAT Ratings

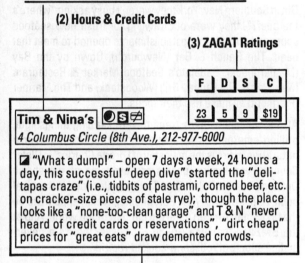

F	D	S	C
23	5	9	$19

Tim & Nina's ◐ Ⓢ ⌿

4 Columbus Circle (8th Ave.), 212-977-6000

▉ "What a dump!" – open 7 days a week, 24 hours a day, this successful "deep dive" started the "deli-tapas craze" (i.e., tidbits of pastrami, corned beef, etc. on cracker-size pieces of stale rye); though the place looks like a "none-too-clean garage" and T & N "never heard of credit cards or reservations", "dirt cheap" prices for "great eats" draw demented crowds.

(4) Surveyors' Commentary

The names of restaurants with the highest overall ratings, greatest popularity and importance are printed in **CAPITAL LETTERS**. Address and phone numbers are printed in *italics*.

(2) Hours & Credit Cards

After each restaurant name you will find the following courtesy information:

◐ .... *serving after 11 PM*

Ⓢ .... *open on Sunday*

⌿ .... *no credit cards accepted*

8

(3) ZAGAT Ratings

Food, Decor and **Service** are each rated on a scale of **0** to **30**:

F	D	S	C

F .... *Food*
D .... *Decor*
S .... *Service*
C .... *Cost*

23	5	9	$19

 0 - 9 .... *poor to fair*
10 - 15 .... *fair to good*
16 - 19 .... *good to very good*
20 - 25 .... *very good to excellent*
26 - 30 .... *extraordinary to perfection*

▽ 23	5	9	$19

▽ .... *Low number of votes/less reliable*

The **Cost (C)** column reflects the estimated price of a dinner with one drink and tip. Lunch usually costs 25% less.

A restaurant listed without ratings is either an important **newcomer** or a popular **write-in**. The estimated cost, with one drink and tip, is indicated by the following symbols.

–	–	–	VE

I .... *$15 and below*
M .... *$16 to $30*
E .... *$31 to $50*
VE .... *$51 or more*

(4) Surveyors' Commentary

Surveyors' comments are summarized, with literal comments shown in quotation marks. The following symbols indicate whether responses were mixed or uniform.

◨ .... *mixed*
■ .... *uniform*

Connecticut's Favorites

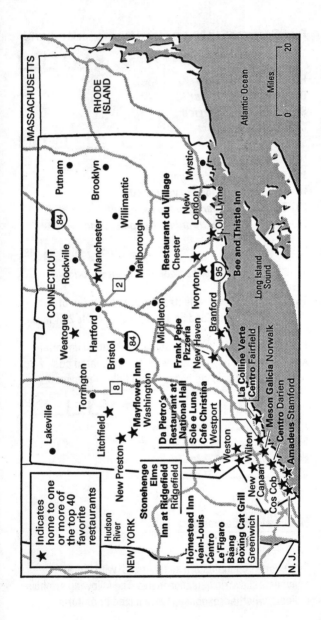

Indicates home to one or more of the top 40 favorite restaurants

MASSACHUSETTS
RHODE ISLAND
Atlantic Ocean
CONNECTICUT
NEW YORK
N.J.

Putnam
Brooklyn
Willimantic
Manchester
Rockville
Marlborough
Restaurant du Village
Chester
New London
Mystic
Old Lyme
Bee and Thistle Inn
Weatogue
Hartford
Bristol
Middleton
Ivoryton
Branford
Frank Pepe Pizzeria
New Haven
La Colline Verte
Centro Fairfield
Meson Galicia Norwalk
Centro Darien
Amadeus Stamford
Lakeville
Torrington
Litchfield
Mayflower Inn
Washington
New Preston
Da Pietro's
Restaurant at
National Hall
Sole e Luna
Cafe Christina
Westport
Weston
Wilton
New Canaan
Cos Cob
Stonehenge
Elms
Inn at Ridgefield
Ridgefield
Homestead Inn
Jean-Louis
Centro
Le Figaro
Bàang
Boxing Cat Grill
Greenwich
Hudson River
Long Island Sound
Miles
0   20

84
2
84
8
95

10

Connecticut's Favorite Restaurants

Each of our reviewers has been asked to name his or her five favorite restaurants. The 40 spots most frequently named, in order of their popularity, are:

1. Homestead Inn
2. Jean-Louis
3. Amadeus
4. Da Pietro's
5. Rest. at National Hall
6. Mayflower Inn
7. Stonehenge
8. Centro
9. Elms
10. Meson Galicia
11. La Colline Verte
12. Sole e Luna
13. Bee and Thistle Inn
14. Boxing Cat Grill
15. Inn at Ridgefield
16. Restaurant du Village
17. Le Figaro
18. Frank Pepe Pizzeria
19. Cafe Christina
20. Baang
21. Elm St. Oyster House
22. Bridge Café
23. West Street Grill
24. L'Abbee
25. Splash Pacific Rim Grill
26. Spazzi Trattoria
27. Copper Beech Inn
28. Le Petit Café
29. Cobb's Mill Inn
30. Terra Ristorante
31. La Bretagne
32. 64 Greenwich Avenue
33. Kathleen's
34. Hopkins Inn
35. Chart House
36. Cavey's
37. Mediterranean Grill
38. Il Falco
39. Pasta Nostra
40. Union League Cafe

It's obvious that many of the restaurants on the above list are among the most expensive, but Connecticut/Southern New York diners also love a bargain. Were popularity calibrated to price, we suspect that a number of other restaurants would join the above ranks. Thus, we have listed over 90 Best Buys on pages 16–17.

Top Ratings*

Top 40 Food Ranking

27 Cavey's
Jean-Louis
Restaurant du Village
Da Pietro's
26 Max Downtown
Homestead Inn
Frank Pepe Pizzeria
25 Mako of Japan
Stonehenge
L'Abbee
Meson Galicia
Copper Beech Inn
La Colline Verte
Sally's Apizza
Peppercorn's Grill
Frank Pepe's The Spot
Mayflower Inn
Max Amoré
Elms
Steve's Centerbrook

Le Petit Café
24 Ondine
Max-A-Mia
West Street Grill
Rest. at National Hall
Ann Howard's Apricots
Civic Cafe
Carole Peck's
Paci
Cheng Du
Inn at Ridgefield
Harry's Pizza
Baang
Aux Delices
23 Cafe Pika Tapas
Valbella!
Côte d'Azur
Pasta Nostra
Ruth's Chris

Top Spots by Cuisine

Top Additions
Adrienne
Birches Inn
Magnolia's
Oliva
Rebeccas

Top American (New)
26 Max Downtown
25 Mayflower Inn
Steve's Centerbrook
24 West Street Grill
Carole Peck's

Top American (Traditional)
25 Elms
23 Bee & Thistle Inn
21 Tavern on Main
Randall's Ordinary
20 Avon Old Farms Inn

Top Breakfast
23 Bee & Thistle Inn
22 Pantry
19 Rein's
18 Pat's Kountry Kitchen
17 Gail's Station Hse.

Top Brunch
26 Homestead Inn
25 Stonehenge
24 Ann Howard's Apricots
23 Bee & Thistle Inn
21 Cafe Christina

Top Chinese
24 Cheng Du
20 Bali of Greenwich
19 Chan's Choice
Little Kitchen
17 Tiger Bowl

---

* Excluding restaurants with low voting.

12

Top Continental
25 Stonehenge
24 Inn at Ridgefield
23 Amadeus
   Roger Sherman Inn
22 Hopkins Inn

Top French
27 Rest. du Village
26 Homestead Inn
25 Copper Beech Inn
   La Colline Verte
22 La Bretagne

Top French (New)
27 Cavey's
   Jean-Louis
25 Stonehenge
   L'Abbee
   Le Petit Café

Top Hotel Dining
26 Homestead Inn
   Stonehenge
24 Rest. at National Hall
23 Bee & Thistle Inn
   Roger Sherman Inn

Top Italian
27 Da Pietro's
25 Peppercorn's Grill
   Max Amoré
24 Max-A-Mia
   Paci

Top Japanese
25 Mako of Japan
21 Kotobuki
   Plum Tree
19 Abis
18 Kujaku

Top Lunch Spots
27 Cavey's (upstairs)
26 Max Downtown
25 Peppercorn's Grill
24 West Street Grill
   Carole Peck's

Top Mediterranean
25 Meson Galicia
23 Cafe Pika Tapas
22 Mediterranean Grill
   Barcelona Wine Bar
21 Bridge Café
   Mediterraneo

Top Miscellaneous
24 Baang/Cal-Asian
22 Splash/Pacific Rim
   La Maison Indochine/
      Vietnamese
21 Caffe Adulis/Eritrean
20 Lemon Grass/Thai

Top Pizza
26 Frank Pepe
25 Sally's Apizza
   Frank Pepe's The Spot
24 Harry's Pizza
23 First and Last Tavern

Top Seafood
23 Elm St. Oyster Hse.
22 Abbott's Lobster
22 Scribner's
21 Fiddler's
20 Lennie & Joe's Fishtale

Top Steakhouses
23 Ruth's Chris
21 Bennett's
18 Giovanni's
17 Mario's
   Manero's

Top Worth a Trip
25 Copper Beech Inn/Ivoryton
   Mayflower Inn/Washington
24 West Street Grill/Litchfield
   Ann Howard's Apricots/Farmington
   Carole Peck's/Woodbury

Top Yearlings/Rated
25 Elms
24 Paci
23 Cafe Pika Tapas
   Côte d'Azur
   Ivy

Top Yearlings Unrated
Dome
Promis
Restaurant Bricco
Savannah
Tigin

Top 40 Decor Ranking

28 Mayflower Inn
27 Stonehenge
26 Homestead Inn
  Rest. at National Hall
  Copper Beech Inn
  Tollgate Hill Inn
25 Simsbury 1820 House
  Water's Edge
  Max Downtown
  Paci
  Cobb's Mill Inn
  Bee and Thistle Inn
  Roger Sherman Inn
24 Hopkins Inn
  Boulders Inn
  Randall's Ordinary
  Inn at Ridgefield
  La Colline Verte
  Jean-Louis
  Union League Cafe

  Cavey's
  Silvermine Tavern
23 Ann Howard's Apricots
  Inn at Chester
  Le Figaro
  Restaurant du Village
  Griswold Inn
  Elms
  Spinning Wheel Inn
  Bank Street Brewing Co.
  White Hart Inn
  Dakota
  Avon Old Farms Inn
22 Amadeus
  Old Lyme Inn
  Cafe Pika Tapas
  Max Amoré
  Meson Galicia
  Bridge Café
  Ondine

Top Outdoor

Ann Howard's Apricots
Boulders Inn
Crab Shell

Hopkins Inn
Roger Sherman Inn
Silvermine Tavern

Top Romantic

Amadeus
Bee & Thistle Inn
Cobb's Mill Inn
Copper Beech Inn

Randall's Ordinary
Rest. at National Hall
Stonehenge
Tollgate Hill Inn

Top Rooms

Cafe Christina
Copper Beech Inn
Golden Lamb Buttery

Mayflower Inn
Rest. at National Hall
Restaurant du Village

Top Views

Abbott's Lobster
Boulders Inn
Chart House

Cobb's Mill Inn
Hopkins Inn
Mayflower Inn

Top 40 Service Ranking

26 Cavey's
Jean-Louis
La Colline Verte
25 Mayflower Inn
Stonehenge
Homestead Inn
24 Copper Beech Inn
Da Pietro's
Restaurant du Village
Inn at Ridgefield
23 Le Petit Café
Roger Sherman Inn
Elms
Max Downtown
Steve's Centerbrook
Meson Galicia
Bee and Thistle Inn
Inn at Chester
Simsbury 1820 House
Rest. at National Hall

Max Amoré
22 Cheng Du
Carbone's
Côte d'Azur
L'Abbee
White Hart Inn
Ann Howard's Apricots
Clemente's
Ondine
Paci
Civic Cafe
Amadeus
Cafe Pika Tapas
Peppercorn's Grill
Old Lyme Inn
La Bretagne
Gennaro's
Tollgate Hill Inn
West Street Grill
21 Valbella!

Best Buys

Top 50 Bangs For The Buck

This list reflects the best dining values in our *Survey*. It is produced by dividing the cost of a meal into the combined ratings for food, decor and service.

1. Firehouse Deli
2. Harry's Pizza
3. First and Last Tavern
4. Cheng Du
5. Mystic Pizza
6. Frank Pepe's The Spot
7. Congress Rotisserie
8. Frank Pepe Pizzeria
9. Pat's Kountry Kitchen
10. Boston Market
11. Bangkok Gardens
12. Sally's Apizza
13. Rein's NY Style Deli
14. Cafe Pika Tapas
15. Claire's Corner Copia
16. DeRosa's Firehouse
17. Lemon Grass Thai
18. Alforno Pizzeria
19. Lenny & Joe's Fishtale
20. Pantry
21. Caffe Adulis
22. Coach's Sports Bar
23. Sunrise Pizza Cafe
24. Oscar's
25. Max-A-Mia

26. Ash Creek Saloon
27. Sesame Seed
28. Dakota
29. Bertucci's
30. Bull's Head Diner
31. Bank St. Brewing Co.
32. Le Petit Café
33. Post Corner Pizza
34. Archie Moore's
35. Orem's Diner
36. Mario the Baker
37. Bricks'
38. Adriana's
39. Peppercorn's Grill
40. Gail's Station House
41. Magic Wok
42. Max Amoré
43. Simsbury 1820 House
44. Arizona Flats
45. Bloodroot
46. Eclisse
47. Hot Tomato's
48. Mackenzie's Grill
49. Abbott's Lobster
50. Saybrook Fish House

Additional Good Values
(A bit more expensive, but worth every penny)

Abis
Angelina's
Aux Delices
Avon Old Farms Inn
Bangkok
Barcelona
Bobby Valentine's
Bogey's Grille
Bonani
Boxcar Cantina
Breakaway
Brewhouse
Cafe Lulu
Cafe Morelli
Cannery
Capers
Civic Cafe
Côte d'Azur
David's
Fiddler's
Gaetano's

Gates
Gennaro's
Grappa
John Harvard's
Kotobuki
La Hacienda
Lime
MacKenzie's Roadhse.
Mako of Japan
Monica's
Onion Alley
Panda Pavilion
Quattro Pazzi
Sakura
Savannah
Scoozzi
Tiger Bowl
Tollgate Hill Inn
USS Chowder Pot
Via Sforza
Viva Zapata

Connecticut
1999 Additions

```
        R  = Recommendation Ratings
   ††††  = Don't Miss
    †††  = Very Good Bet
     ††  = Worth a Try, Not a Detour
      †  = Interesting, But No Big Deal
```

R | C |

Adrienne 🅂   ††† | E |
*218 Kent Rd. (bet. Boardman Bridge & Candlewood Lake Rd.),
New Milford, 860-354-6001*
This New Milford Contemporary American maiden with
colonial floorboards and fireplaces is the namesake of chef-
owner Adrienne Sussman, a former pastry chef at the
Waldorf's Peacock Alley, who does herself particularly
proud with desserts; located on Route 7, it's convenient
for denizens of Candlewood Lake and the Litchfield Hills.

Birches Inn 🅂   †††† | E |
233 W. Shore Rd. (Lake Waramaug), New Preston, 860-868-1735
Under new ownership, this venerable Alpine inn on the
shores of Lake Waramaug is making waves with chef
Frederic Faveau (ex West Street Grill) at the helm; his
French–New American dishes are as up-to-date as
tomorrow, and he plates each one like a picture; lake views
through the dining room windows – or from the outdoor
porch – add to the aesthetic appeal.

Cafe Angelique   †† | M |
30 Berlin Rd (91 N, exit 21), Cromwell, 860-632-8982
Devil-made-me-do-it desserts deserve their own display
case and get it at this romantic Cromwell cafe with angels
adorning the walls; loyal locals and travelers staying at
nearby hotels assuage cravings from the Eclectic menu,
then approach the confectionary case for sweet inspiration.

Cookhouse, The 🅂   †† | E |
31 Danbury Rd. (Rte. 7), New Milford, 860-355-4111
'Fat Tommy' and the family preside over this New Milford
BBQ barn where country cooking comes Louisiana-style;
citified weekend Cajuns amble down from the hills for their
fill of 'meat and three' (meaning meat, cornbread and side
dishes like collard greens) or fried catfish.

Costello's Clam Company 🅂   ††† | I |
140 Pearl St. (Noank Shipyard), Noank, 860-532-2779
Frying in the face of nutritional correctness, this nautical
Noank seafooder specializes in fish 'n chips and fried
bivalves, though bargain-priced steamed lobsters weigh-in
as well; it's BYOB, picnic-table dining with bracing views
of gulls and yachts; N.B. open Memorial Day – Labor Day.

Frog and The Peach, The 🅂   ₸₸₸   E
160 Albany Tpke. (Rte. 44), Canton, 860-693-6345
Serving only frog à la pêche or pêche à la frog, the
restaurant in a Peter Cook and Dudley Moore skit flopped;
but that didn't dissuade Stephen Putnam from adopting
the name for his new Canton BYO offering a varied New
American menu in a Victorian home near the town green;
reservations are a must at this peachy place.

GO FISH 🅂   ₸₸   E
Olde Mistick Village (1-95, exit 90), Mystic, 860-536-2662
Sole occupant of a former Mystic supermarket, this seafood
leviathan boasts a sushi bar, a raw bar, a raft of chowders, a
cargo of crustaceans and a flotilla of fish – fried, sautéed,
steamed or grilled – served up on pasta or under sauces; a
well-schooled staff keeps thing moving along swimmingly;
no doubt that Mystic Marinelife Aquarium, just across the
street, keeps an eye on its own inventory every night.

Hanna's Restaurant   ₸₸   M
72 Lake Ave. (I-84, exit 4), Danbury, 203-748-5713
Authentic dishes at this Lake Avenue Lebanese draw diners
to Danbury from as far away as Westchester and Waterbury;
the 12-item *maza* special is a Middle Eastern primer that's
popular for sharing and sampling.

Il Vigneto 🅂   ₸₸   E
Interlaken Inn, 74 Interlaken Rd. (Rte. 112), Lakeville, 860-435-9878
Diners seeking a respite from the rampant culinary one-
upmanship in the Litchfield Hills find it at this low-key
Lakeville restaurant at the Interlaken Inn; the Med-
Moroccan menu always satisfies, sometimes surprises;
post-prandial lakeside strolls are a plus.

J. Gilbert's 🅂   ₸₸₸   E
Somerset Sq., 185 Glastonbury Blvd. (Main St.), Glastonbury,
860-659-0409
In a new shopping center just a do-si-do off Main Street, this
Glastonbury steakhouse with a Southwestern-accent serves
up wood-fired steaks and chickens as well as skillet-seared
fish; flavors as bold as a Sedona sunset make for brisk sales
of microbrews and moderately-priced wines; smoke signals
signify that cigar puffing is allowed only in the lounge.

John's Cafe   ₸₸₸   E
693 Main St. S. (Rtes. 6 & 64), Woodbury, 203-263-0188
Bill Okesson (ex The Boulders Inn) has turned a Main Street
roadside eatery into a smart Contemporary American cafe;
pork comes from the nearby Egg and I Farm and produce
from other locals, while the excellent wine list comes with
enough crib notes to help even a diet soda devotee sound
like a plausible wine wonk.

Kazu ⑤ ⊞ E
64 N. Main St. (Washington St.), Norwalk, 203-866-7492
Superior sushi and an attractive, savvy staff make this
Norwalk newcomer a good bet to last in SoNo's traditionally
high-turnover neighborhood; the high-tech decor isn't
traditionally Japanese, but the four chefs' techniques are;
generous portions render this raw bar a relative bargain.

Lenny's Indian Head Inn ⑤⊟ ⊞ M
205 S. Montowese St. (Rte. 146), 203-488-1500
Pickup trucks and Cadillacs democratically bump along the
unpaved parking lot at this family-owned Branford shoreline
seafooder; the menu lists all the usual suspects – lobsters,
steamers, chowder, fish 'n chips – but they emerge as fresh
as a sea breeze here and in summertime the screened-in
porch seems to float on the green salt marsh.

Long Ridge Tavern ⑤ ⊞ E
*7635 Long Ridge Rd. (4 mi. north of Merritt Pkwy.),
Stamford, 203-329-7818*
Fair prices for Traditional American fare (with some trendy
twists) make this Back Country standby almost a club for
locals, while button-down Downtown business types come
up for lunches and 5PM – 7PM 'Corporate Life Relief' (known
as Happy Hour elsewhere); Bunyanesque fieldstone
fireplaces, pegged floorboards and brass lanterns lend a
'ye olde' air to this one-time horse trader's barn.

Magnolia's ⑤ ⊞ VE
55 Arch St. (I-95, exit 3), Greenwich, 203-552-9400
Fiddle-dee-dee, Miss Scarlett, it's the '50s again at this
Downtown Greenwich American-French flower where
they're serving Chateâubriand for two and de-boning Dover
Sole and tossing Caesar salads at tableside; however, de
rigeur amenities like a downstairs cigar bar and merger-
mogul prices place it firmly in the '90s; occupying a building
that's had more tenants than a boarding house, this
handsome, stylish restaurant just may bloom eternally.

Mill on the River ⑤ ⊞ E
*989 Ellington Rd. (2½ mi. from Buckland Mall), South Windsor,
860-289-7923*
On a pond off the Podunk River, this popular, capacious
South Windsor spot specializes in seafood (delivered from
Boston each morning), augmented by a Continental menu
ranging from tortellini Alfredo to sauerbraten; built around a
200-year-old grist mill, its groomed grounds and greenhouse
dining make it a great choice for marriage proposals or
Sunday brunch with Mom.

Morton's of Chicago S ††† VE

Swiss Bank Ctr., 377 N. State St. (bet. Atlantic & Washington Sts.), Stamford, 203-324-3939

Muscling its way onto the Downtown Stamford dining scene this year, this sophisticated steakhouse strode into the new Swiss Bank corporate headquarters with he-man sirloins, chilled martinis and retro ashtrays; though the expense-account prices make you realize why they opened in a bank, few have beefed about them so far.

Oliva S ††† E

18 E. Shore Rd. (Rte. 45), New Preston, 860-868-1787

Lest anyone miss the obvious, dishes of olives and cruets of olive oil on every table evoke the name of this New Preston cafe; chef-owner Riad Aamar originated the menu of bright Mediterranean dishes and pizzas at the late, lamented Doc's; overlooking the antiques shops of the picturesque village, it's a current darling of the weekend set, so reservations are suggested.

O'Rourke's S ⇏ †† I

728 Main St., Middletown, 860-346-6101

Deliverymen, insomniacs and Wesleyan students pulling all-nighters stagger sleepily into Middletown's landmark metal diner when the door opens at 4 AM (for weekend brunches, the line goes out that door); the third-generation owner makes fresh soups and breads daily, plus steamed cheeseburgers to order.

Polo Grille & Wine Bar S †† E

7 Elm St. (State St.), New Haven, 203-787-9000

Politicos, power brokers and silver-thatched lawyers hang out at this new New Haven Eclectic close to City Hall; the menu runs toward pasta and grilled items, the maps-and-mirrors decor is men's clubby, and the wine bar is cigar-friendly; the fun is in watching all the wheeling and dealing.

Prince of Wales S †† E

Norwich Inn & Spa, 607 W. Thames St. (Rte. 32), Norwich, 1-800-275-4772, ext. 630

Yes, the Prince of Wales (later Edward VIII) actually dined here and probably appreciated the plush Georgian decor of the Norwich Inn's dining room, but wouldn't recognize anything on today's half-traditional, half-spa cuisine menu; sybaritic celebs have been spotted splurging on sautéed sweet potato roesti.

Quattro's S   ††† | E

*Strawberry Hill Plaza, 1300 Boston Post Rd. (opposite
Bishop's Farm), Guilford, 203-453-6575*
The quartet of personable young owners of this aptly-named
Guilford bistro wear all the hats – they do the cooking and
greet the guests; the soft-hued, Tuscan-inspired decor
soothes, the traditional Italian menu comforts, the nightly
'New Italian' specials won the place its reputation.

Raffaello's S   ††† | E

*Mt. Carmel Shopping Ctr., 2977 Whitney Ave. (Rte. 10),
Hamden, 203-230-0228*
Beneath a formal facade, this homey Hamden family-owned
Italian is as warm as a summer sun; a cadre of repeat
customers comes for the daily fish specials and the 15,000-
bottle wine cellar; the prized tables are under the chandelier
in the small Crystal Room.

Rebeccas S   ††† | VE

265 Glenville Rd. (Riversville Rd.), Greenwich, 203-532-9270
Eponymous owner Rebecca Kirhoffer and her chef/husband
Kevin Khorshidi are successfully luring Greenwich
gourmands out to this Glenville gem where diners watch
the kitchen crew create some splendid Contemporary
American dishes behind a glass wall; reservations are a
must at this popular newcomer that's so hot it's lucky the
local fire station is across the street.

Sage S   ††† | VE

*363 Greenwich Ave. (bet. Fawcett Pl. & Railroad Ave.),
Greenwich, 203-622-5138*
In a nutshell: small restaurant, small menu, big flavors,
big success; this new Greenwich must hits all the New
American highlights with the high-style befitting its location
(in the former Rosy Tomatoes space); Sage ladies who
lunch find midday prices a bargain.

Taipan S   †† | E

Compo Shopping Ctr., 376 Post Rd. E., Westport, 203-227-7400
This Westport storefront stays serene even when jammed in
the early evening – maybe it's the trickling fountain; the
menu stops at every Asian port between Jakarta and
Singapore and pedestal dishes encourage sharing.

Timothy's   ††† | M

181 Bank St. (Pearl St.), New London, 860-437-0526
Views of the Thames through the windows and Coast Guard
Academy brass at the tables lend a surprisingly salty tang to
this Downtown Contemporary American housed in a 1913
drug store: behind a glass wall, chef-owner Tim Grills does,
and sautés and stirs as well; wines – tonier tonics than Lydia
Pinkham's – are displayed in the old pharmacy cases.

Tre Scalini ⑤   ⧺   M
100 Wooster St. (Franklin St.), New Haven, 203-777-3373
One of the Italian ristorantes on New Haven's famed
Wooster Street, this relative youngster eschews decorative
Neopolitan maroons for Tuscan spring colors; a lunchtime
business crowd gives way to couples and families in the
evening; the simpatico staff remembers who craves the
costolétta d'agnello, who raves about *risotto al frutti di mare.*

Tuscany Grill ⑤   ⧻   E
*120 College St. (bet. Broad & Main Sts.), Middletown,
860-340-7096*
The terra-cotta lobby of the old Middlesex Opera House is
the stage for Downtown Middletown's premier dining spot
where scene-stealing pastas and brick-oven pizzas star on
the Italian menu – rigatoni meet Rigoletto; yuppie singles
sip pinot grigio and order bowls of herbed mussels at
the circular bar.

West Street ⑤   ⧻   E
*Meadowview Plaza, 175 West Rd. (Rte. 83), Ellington,
860-870-1322*
It's a trek from almost anywhere to this Ellington bistro in a
small shopping plaza in the middle of farm fields, but trek
they do for bright and bold New American cuisine served by
an enthusiastic staff; coating chicken strips with honeyed
coconut, searing blackened ostrich, wrapping lobster in puff
pastry, chef Christopher Wiersman is a standout in his field

Alphabetical Directory of Connecticut Restaurants

Abbott's Lobster (Noank) S   22 13 12 $21
117 Pearl St. (Main St.), 860-536-7719
■ Bring the kids and "a bottle of wine" to this seasonal, outdoor picnic-style "lobster shack" that's "perfect for casual munching"; while there's very little in the way of decor, you can "watch the boats go by on the Mystic River" as you chow down on "excellent", "reasonably priced" seafood that's so fresh it "jumps from ocean to table"; P.S. "watch out for the seagulls."

Abis (Greenwich) S   19 16 17 $26
381 Greenwich Ave. (RR station), 203-862-9100
■ Expect a "wide variety" of "simple, "dependable-as-heck" Japanese in a "quiet", "friendly" "traditional" setting; it's a "great place to bring your two-year-old" because the fish pond "entertains"; P.S. the Sunday brunch reportedly rises to the level of "excellent"; detractors say "add liquor and it'll be a gem."

Abruzzi Kitchen (Norwalk) S   ▽ 18 10 18 $21
195 Liberty Sq. (behind the aquarium), 203-838-6776
■ This "inexpensive", "bare-bones" neighborhood Italian offers "solid but unspectacular" dishes such as "good pasta fagioli"; it does have its charms though, stemming from the Italian family that runs it; it's a good choice after a day at the Norwalk Aquarium.

Adriana's (New Haven)   21 13 19 $25
771 Grand Ave. (bet. Hamilton & Olive Sts.), 203-865-6474
■ A "basic", "cheap" New Haven Italian with a chef that everyone says is a "master of veal"; the setting is "homey", but the neighborhood is "out of the way" and iffy; expect service that's "more friendly than polished."

Aleia's Innovative Bistro   ▽ 21 17 18 $33
(Old Saybrook) S
1687 Boston Post Rd. (I-95, exit 66), 860-399-5050
■ Reviewers declare that the "imaginative" Italian at this Old Saybrook destination is so "surprisingly sophisticated" that it does "your Italian grandmother one better"; what's more, it's a "solid value" with "attentive" service and an "unhurried atmosphere."

Alforno Brick Oven Pizzeria   18 12 15 $17
(Old Saybrook) S
*Bennie's Shopping Ctr., 1654 Post Rd. (I-95, exit 66),
860-399-4166*
☑ "Good" brick-oven pizza, "Tuscan-style" pastas and walnut Gorgonzola salads make this Old Saybrook Italian a pleasant stop for a quick bite; however, some critics gripe it's "too hyped" and "way too pricey" for what they call "ordinary" pies.

28

Alla Bettola (Darien)   15 10 16 $23
*Good Wives Shopping Ctr., 25 Old Kings Hwy. N. (I-95, exit 12),
203-655-7010*
☑ "No surprises" await your visit to this strip mall Italian off
the Post Road that's "long on portions" and "value" and
"short" on charm; it's strictly a convenient "reliable" place
that's "good for a weeknight" dinner; but then some who
don't like to settle add: "why bother" – "tired."

Allen's Clam House (Westport) S 16 15 16 $30
191 Hillspoint Rd. (Greens Farms Rd.), 203-226-4411
☑ While there are no quibbles with the view of the pond, the
"basic '50s shore seafood" gets mixed reviews; boosters
applaud "fresh", "simply prepared" food that's "like an old
friend" while detractors insist the "cafeteria-style" place
is "the essence of a mediocre lobster restaurant" that's
"slowly slipping into the briny deep."

Altnaveigh Inn (Storrs) S   ▽ 22 24 23 $31
957 Storrs Rd. (Rte. 275), 860-429-4490
■ "Very New Englandy", this Continental is a favorite stop
on the way to UConn; expect "fuddy-duddy" (certainly not
"trendy") food that upstarts insist could be "seasoned" a bit
more; it's located in a "pretty", colonial-style house and the
"friendly" service creates a "warm" and "homey" feeling.

AMADEUS RESTAURANT   23 22 22 $40
(Stamford) S
201 Summer St. (bet. Broad & Main Sts.), 203-348-7775
■ A "formal", "old-world" Downtown Stamford locale
serving "reliable" Continental and Viennese cuisine in a
"sophisticated" "cocoon of mauve and mirrors"; nightly
piano music that "Mozart would have enjoyed" and
"professional" service make it popular for pre- and post-
theater dinners and business clients; save room for the
"to-die-for" chocolate desserts and check out the prix
fixe ($12) lunch that's a "steal."

Ambassador of India   ▽ 21 19 20 $23
(Glastonbury) S
2333 Main St. (Hebron Ave.), 860-659-2529
■ Reviewers say this "hard-to-spot" Indian in a Glastonbury
strip mall is worth the search for its "real McCoy" fare; it's
just the place to sample authentic curries and tandoori-
style dishes while enjoying sitar music (Sunday nights).

Amberjacks (South Norwalk) S 18 18 17 $29
99 Washington St. (bet. N. Main & Water Sts.), 203-853-4332
☑ A SoNo Contemporary American–seafooder with
"creative", "interesting combinations" that are "pleasing to
the eye"; it also doubles as a popular "singles haunt" with
a "happening" bar that attracts a "good-looking crowd";
detractors say it's "too noisy" with tables so close together
you'll be "eating your dinner on your neighbor's lap."

Amber Restaurant ▽ 17 | 10 | 16 | $19
(North Haven) **S**
132 Middletown Ave. (Quinnipiac Ave.), 203-239-4072
■ For three generations the DeMartino family has been serving barbecue in a "casual", "understated" "family place" off Route 17; despite just ok ratings, fans think they have the "best-in-the-state" ribs and "tasty" onion brick.

American Pie Company ▽ 19 | 14 | 17 | $17
(Sherman) **S**
29 Rte. 37 (Rte. 39), 860-350-0662
■ A "handy spot for soups and sandwiches", this Sherman Traditional American offers "huge portions of home-cooked fare" including baked goods made on the premises; it's located in a "down-home", "pleasant" country setting and has very "reasonable" prices that make it "worth the wait"; N.B. breakfast on Sunday is so good it moves some closer to God ("it's worth church going first").

Angelina's (Westport) **S** 14 | 7 | 13 | $17
Post Plaza, 1092 Post Rd. E. (Morningside St.), 203-227-0865
☑ This Westport "basic" Italian is considered convenient and "dependable" by moviegoers and the take-out crowd, however, those in a position to be more picky say "it's not worth the big wait at the door"; at least the price is right and everyone's welcome, even babies in strollers.

Angus (Fairfield) **S** 17 | 12 | 15 | $26
2133 Black Rock Tpke. (Merritt Pkwy., exit 44), 203-366-5902
☑ While "it's not up to the top steakhouses", the "decent" beef served at this "simple" strip mall locale on busy Black Rock Turnpike is "reliable" and "works fine" most of the time; the more demanding call it "high in cholesterol, high in grease, and low in ambiance" with "slow" service but hope that it will improve under the new partners.

ANN HOWARD'S APRICOTS 24 | 23 | 22 | $37
(Farmington) **S**
1593 Farmington Ave. (Rte. 4), 860-673-5903
■ Located in a "romantic" setting on the Farmington River, this Contemporary American "remains one of the standard-bearers" and is "holding up in spite of new competition"; upstairs it's "classy" and "pricey" with a "helpful", "attentive" staff; downstairs the pub menu attracts "wall-to-wall singles" nightly; weather permitting, head outdoors for drinks by the water.

Applausi (Old Greenwich) 18 | 17 | 18 | $34
199 S. Beach Ave. (Arcadia Rd.), 203-637-4447
☑ Some applaud this Italian for its "authentic", "solid" fare and proximity to the Old Greenwich RR station, which makes it a "convenient" whistle-stop for "very good daily specials"; but others call it "inconsistent" and "pricey for what you get"; the "friendly" staff can take a bow.

Archie Moore's Bar & Restaurant ◑ S   14 | 11 | 14 | $17 |
48 Sanford St. (Post Rd.), Fairfield, 203-256-9295
15 Factory Ln. (Milford Harbor), Milford, 203-876-5088
188 Willow St. (bet. Foster & Orange Sts.), New Haven, 203-773-9870
■ They're "crowded", "noisy" and filled with "second-hand smoke", just what you'd expect from '90s American saloons catering to the happy hour, game-watching crowd; while "it's hardly fine dining", imbibers say they're good for Buffalo wings and appetizer grazing.

Arizona Flats (Bridgeport) S   16 | 15 | 16 | $21 |
3001 Fairfield Ave. (Gilman St.), 203-334-8300
◪ While a few call it "a bright eating spot", others say this Southwestern in a "tough" Bridgeport neighborhood serves fare that's "flat" and "getting flatter", with service that ranges from "friendly" to "lousy" and decor that's "tired"; still, it's "always crowded on weekends", perhaps because it's near the multiplex on the Fairfield/Bridgeport line.

Arizona Grill & Cafe (Washington Depot) S (CLOSED)   ▽ 20 | 16 | 20 | $25 |
38 Bee Brook Rd. (Rte. 47), 860-868-2239
■ New and bigger digs for Woodbury's Arizona on Main – but chef-owner Todd Hauspurg (ex NYC's Arizona 206) is still in charge turning out "haute" Southwestern in the country; hopefuls say give it time and "it could be in the Top Five", once decor "catches up" with the food.

Ash Creek Saloon (Fairfield) S   20 | 18 | 17 | $21 |
93 Post Rd. (Grassmere Ave.), 203-255-5131
■ "The decor is relentlessly cowboy" so "wear spurs", "bring the earplugs" and hunker down for "solid" Traditional American–barbecue chow; it's a "good value" in a "relaxed" atmosphere that attracts an eclectic crowd – families to couples on dates; N.B. there's been a jump in ratings since our last *Survey,* so be sure to reserve for weekends.

Aspen Gardens (Litchfield) S   ▽ 13 | 11 | 18 | $19 |
51 West St. (across from the green), 860-567-9477
■ A "simple", "friendly", "cheap" Greek-Italian that's good for a sandwich or salad; however, reviewers stress "don't try anything fancy"; instead save your appetite for the people-watching from the outdoor terrace.

Atlantis (Greenwich) S   13 | 15 | 14 | $33 |
Greenwich Harbor Inn, 500 Steamboat Rd. (Arch St.), 203-861-SHIP
◪ For warm weather al fresco dining by the sea, you can't beat the view from this Greenwich seafooder; but "ok" food and "terrible" service at "shameful" prices leave some shaking their heads (it "could be terrific" with "lots of improvement"); the ever-optimistic say it's "trying hard."

Aux Delices Foods by
Debra Ponzek (Greenwich) S   24 | 16 | 17 | $29
1075 E. Putnam Ave. (Riverside Ln.), 203-698-1066

■ "What a delight" cheer enthusiasts of Debra Ponzek's (ex NYC's Montrachet) "quality" Contemporary French that "looks good" and keeps the restaurant's fifteen seats filled at breakfast and lunch; "if you have no time to cook" the convenient Post Road locale makes take-out dinners, with "fool-proof instructions", well worth it; however, a minority says the "pricey" concept "would only work in Greenwich."

Avon Old Farms Inn (Avon) S   20 | 23 | 21 | $32
1 Nod Rd. (bet. Rtes. 44 & 10), 860-677-2818

■ One of the twenty oldest restaurants in the country, this "fairly priced" Avon Traditional American in a colonial-style house has "maintained its high standards and is still an interesting place to go"; a "home away from home" for many, this inn with "sweet surroundings" is especially "cozy" and "beautiful" around the holidays; N.B. celebrity spotting bonus: "rub shoulders with Felix Rohatyn."

BAANG CAFÉ AND BAR   24 | 21 | 18 | $36
(Greenwich) S
1191 E. Putnam Ave. (I-95, exit 5), 203-637-2114

■ This Californian-Asian eatery on the Post Road is an "awesome experience" where every "zesty" dish is "bigger and livelier" than you expect; "pretty" people in a "chic", "crowded" setting and "unstuffy" help add up to a "warm", "wild" evening in the 'burbs; be warned: the noise level is "deafening" and waits can be long; P.S. "don't miss" dessert.

Bacco's Restaurant   ▽ 22 | 20 | 21 | $35
(Waterbury) S
1230 Thomaston Ave. (Chase Pkwy.), 203-755-0635

■ For over 60 years the Bacco family has been providing "big portions" and "outstanding service" at this classic Italian in a Downtown Waterbury neighborhood; and like its fine wine list surveyors say it keeps "improving"; N.B. it's "delightfully convenient" to the Rye Bridge movie theater.

Backstreet (Darien) S   17 | 13 | 16 | $27
22 Center St. (Post Rd.), 203-655-9944

■ A "reliable" Traditional American in Darien's center that's "good for a light bite" or "quick sustenance", although some gripe it's too "pricey"; the ambiance is laid-backstreet and "casual" with Gen Xers keeping the bar "cramped."

Bali of Greenwich (Greenwich) S   20 | 18 | 19 | $29
55 Arch St. (bet. Greenwich & Railroad Aves.), 203-629-0777

■ An "exotic" Greenwich Chinese-Indonesian that's usually "a treat to the palate and eyes" (rijsttafel) but can also be "inconsistent" with what some call "skimpy" portions; it's in a "lovely old house" that makes for "sedate", "relaxed" dining; most find the service "pleasant" and "well-paced."

Bamboo Grill   – – – I
50 Albany Tpke., Canton, 860-693-4144
875 Main St., Glastonbury, 860-633-3441
Vietnamese duo that we missed but reviewers insist has
deeply flavorful dishes at extremely reasonable prices;
the inside word is that the happy pancakes and crispy
whole-fried flounder in spicy sauce are the way to go.

Bangkok (Danbury) S   17 15 16 $23
Nutmeg Sq., 72 Newtown Rd. (I-84, exit 8), 203-791-0640
◪ While it's "cheap", "makes a nice change", is "one of
the few decent Thai places" around and "not what you
would expect from its strip mall location", not everyone is
won over – "tasteless"; a drop in food ratings since our
last *Survey* supports critics.

Bangkok Gardens (New Haven) S 20 15 18 $19
172 York St. (Chapel St.), 203-789-8684
■ A "comfortable", "tony" Thai "crammed" with "Yalies
and their parents"; the chow's "exceptionally tasty"
(winning peanut sauce) and the specials are always
"interesting"; "reasonable prices" and "quick service"
contribute to its success.

Bank Street Brewing Co.   16 23 18 $24
(Stamford) S
65 Bank St. (Atlantic St.), 203-325-2739
◪ Brew tanks have replaced money vaults in this turn-of-
the-century Downtown bank that's a "cool" place to hang
out despite the din; reactions to the Traditional American
fare range from "needs improvement" to "better-than-
average", but there are no quibbles about the decor
which is just "gorgeous."

Barcelona Wine Bar &   22 19 20 $31
Restaurant (South Norwalk) ◕S
63 N. Main St. (bet. Ann & Marshall Sts.), 203-899-0088
◪ "You forget you're in Connecticut" at this "authentic"
tapas bar that's a "neat" place for "joyous" Spanish-Med
food ("best paella I've ever had") and unusual wines by
the glass; some new to the "innovative concept" say the
"snack-food-sized" portions make it "expensive for what
you get" but the overwhelming majority likes the tastes and
calls it a "brilliant touch of Spain."

Barkie's Grill & Rotisserie   – – – M
(New Haven) S (CLOSED)
220 College St. (bet. Crown & Chapel Sts.), 203-752-1000
Traditional American in New Haven that was formerly
Bruxelles; those in the know say "not much has changed"
and that the townhouse setting is as lovely as ever; the
vittles are "not bad" and its proximity to Yale and the
Shubert Theater makes it a convenient stop; a few
grumble about "poor service."

Beach House (Westport) 🅂   19 | 20 | 17 | $34

233 Hillspoint Rd. (Old Mill Beach), 203-226-7005

◩ Ask for a table by the water at this "welcoming", "romantic" Caribbean with a daytime view of the Long Island Sound that's "worth the trip" – a good thing since comments about the cuisine suggest it can be "innovative" and "excellent, but not always."

BEE AND THISTLE INN   23 | 25 | 23 | $40
(Old Lyme) 🅂

100 Lyme St./Rte. 1 (I-95, exit 70), 860-434-1667

■ Fans make a beeline to this "always cute", "storybook New England" inn that serves "extremely fine" Traditional–Contemporary American cuisine; "friendly", "outstanding" service and a "romantic" atmosphere complete with a harpist playing in "grandmother's Victorian parlor" on Saturday night are more reasons it's "worth the trip" with many suggesting an overnight stay.

Bella Italia (Danbury) 🅂   17 | 13 | 18 | $29

2 Pandanaram Rd. (Hayes Town Ave.), 203-743-3828

◩ This "time-warp" Italian serves up "excellent" fresh pastas, "very good" pizzas and specials, amid lots of "red velvet and gold trim"; fans "don't understand why more people haven't discovered" it; detractors say they know why – it's just "ok."

Bellini (Hartford) 🅂   ▽ 20 | 18 | 20 | $40

438 Franklin Ave. (Brown St.), 860-296-2100

■ A "top-notch" Hartford Continental with "delicious", "beautifully presented" dishes and "super" service, but "you pay for it"; unusual packages include dinner and limo transport to and from the theater and monthly cigar-theme evenings.

Bennett's Steak & Fish House   21 | 18 | 21 | $37
(Stamford) 🅂

24-26 Spring St. (Summer St.), 203-978-7995

■ This "pricey" beef palace in the heart of Downtown Stamford is "a cut above" for its "wonderful" presentations, "attentive" service and traditional NYC steakhouse atmosphere; it's a place to "impress" offering lobster and seafood specialties as well; some find the "masculine" atmosphere so "dark" they "can barely read the menu."

Bentley's Restaurant   ▽ 20 | 20 | 21 | $28
(Danbury) 🅂⌀

1 Division St. (W. Wooster St.), 203-778-3637

■ Critics can't decide if the Italian menu is "inspiring" or "ordinary", but all agree the finished product is "well prepared"; it's conveniently located Downtown, has a "homey", "charming" ambiance, excellent service and fair prices that combined equal a "wonderful" dining experience.

Bertucci's 🅂   14 | 13 | 13 | $16
380 W. Main St. (Rte. 44), Avon, 860-676-1177
54 Post Rd. (I-95, exit 13), Darien, 203-655-4299
2882 Main St. (Rte. 44), Glastonbury, 860-633-2225
2929 Berlin Tpke. (Ames Plaza), Newington, 860-666-1949
330 N. Main St. (Asylum St.), West Hartford, 203-799-6828
833 Post Rd. (I-95, exit 18), Westport, 203-454-1559
☑ Kids love to play with the "blobs" of dough (a "positive distraction" for parents) given away at these "casual", "loud" pizza/pasta joints; opinions on the pies range from "surprisingly good" to "institutional" with the pastas pegged as "basic" but "plentiful"; overall they make for an "inexpensive night out" that's a step up from fast food.

Biscotti (Ridgefield) 🅂   ▽ 20 | 16 | 17 | $26
3 Big Shop Ln. (Main St. & Bailey Ave.), 203-431-3637
☑ A Ridgefield Italian that some think has "great home cooking" and others qualify as "looking good but lacking something"; the service can be "slow" and the decor could use "refinishing" but Sunday brunch, complete with entertainment, is hailed as the "best in Fairfield County"; N.B. they have a twelve-gun cruvinet (wine dispenser) that allows for "excellent" selections by the glass.

Bistro Café (New Milford) 🅂   20 | 17 | 18 | $30
31 Bank St. (Main St.), 860-355-3266
☑ A New Milford American bistro that still gets high marks for its "terrific" "skyscraper presentations" and "awesome chicken entrees", all at an "excellent value"; but while it's a "plus for the area" some grumble that the "menu is getting boring" with specials that "never seem to change."

Bistro East (Litchfield) 🅂   ▽ 20 | 16 | 18 | $30
Litchfield Inn, Rte. 202, 860-567-9040
☑ Still in its "shake-down phase", this "creative" New American, the sister of New Milford's Bistro Cafe, "needs polishing", particularly the "drab" decor that can "make the food seem less palatable than it really is"; critics add that the "staff needs an education."

Bistro on the Green (Guilford) 🅂 ▽ 18 | 14 | 16 | $23
25 Whitfield St. (Guilford green), 203-458-9059
■ The "casual", "relaxed" atmosphere at this "surprisingly good" Guilford Continental makes it perfect for long weekend breakfasts and "romantic" dinners: despite just ok ratings the service is called "friendly"; N.B. bring some extra cash because the paintings on the walls are for sale.

Black-Eyed Sally's   – | – | – | M
Barbecue & Blues (Hartford)
350 Asylum St. (bet. Ann & Allyn Sts.), 860-278-7427
Down-home ribs, smoked chicken and jambalaya keep fans and local politicians coming back to this Hartford barbecue joint with fair prices.

Black Goose Grille (Darien) ⑤   15 | 16 | 15 | $28
972 Post Rd. (Center St.), 203-655-7107
☑ This "dark", "smoky", "clubby" Darien locale officially serves Contemporary American fare but critics dismiss the "huge menu" as "typical", "less-than-ordinary" pub food; at least there's a "pretty" bar where "Muffy and Buffy do nachos"; regulars suggest that in winter you cozy up to the blazing fireplace and in spring try the patio garden.

Black Rock Castle (Bridgeport) ⑤   15 | 14 | 16 | $25
2895 Fairfield Ave. (Jetland St.), 203-336-3990
☑ The atmosphere and entertainment (Irish and rock 'n' roll bands on weekends) at this pub "outweigh" its food which can be good but should be kept simple; put it on your must-do list around St. Pat's Day to appease the "Irish in everyone."

Bloodroot (Bridgeport) ⑤⌿   19 | 11 | 10 | $18
85 Ferris St. (Harbor Ave.), 203-576-9168
☑ Tucked in an out-of-the-way locale overlooking Long Island Sound, this "one-of-a-kind" feminist-themed Vegetarian (with its own bookstore) has been quietly serving "fresh" ethnic fare for 20 years; it's cafeteria-style, bus-your-own tables, and while some find it "depressing" and "confrontational, even if you're a woman", others say it's a "favorite"; call for directions.

Bloomfield Seafood (Bloomfield) ▽   18 | 12 | 18 | $19
Bloomfield Mini-Mall, 8 Mountain Ave. (bet. Rtes. 189 & 178), 860-242-3474
■ It's the "fresh fish galore" – not the "unexciting" decor – that lures diners to this seafooder in a mini-mall that "does its thing well" and is a "great deal"; N.B. stop by the market in front to take home some seafood.

Bluewater Café (New Canaan) ⑤   19 | 16 | 17 | $27
15 Elm St. (bet. Main St. & South Ave.), 203-972-1799
☑ "Nice atmosphere" is the buzz at this "totally charming", "intimate" Italian smack in the middle of New Canaan that features "well-prepared" pasta and fish; the less-impressed say "you can hear what's going on at the table next to yours" and ask "what's all the fuss about?"

Bobby Valentine's Sports   11 | 12 | 14 | $18
Gallery Café ●⑤
280 Connecticut Ave. (I-95, exit 14), Norwalk, 203-854-9300
225 Main St. (Washington Blvd.), Stamford, 203-348-0010
■ With a "plethora of TV screens" and "lots of cheering", these "Taj Mahals of sports bars", owned by Stamford's own baseball hero Bobby Valentine, are "fun places" to root for the home team; the "tolerable" pub food is heavy on Tex-Mex and served by a "big-haired" "but down-to-earth" staff; they're also popular for a quick weekday lunch or an early "casual" dinner with the family.

Boccaccio (New Fairfield) S⊄ ▽ | 18 | 17 | 20 | $30
4 Cottontail Rd. (Rte. 37), 203-746-9900
☑ While we didn't receive Decameron-length comments on this New Fairfield "lots-of-garlic" Italian, we did hear that it's "very good", with "nice" atmosphere, "moderate" prices and above-average service; a few with a different story to tell say "disappointing."

Bogey's Grille & Tap Room | 15 | 16 | 16 | $23
(Westport) S
323 Main St. (Canal St.), 203-227-4653
☑ While some "expected an old film theme", this Westport Eclectic-American celebrates golf with dishes named for famous duffers; there's a "busy bar scene", especially on the weekends, but the grub gets mixed reviews; still, you won't be handicapped by trying the "good hamburgers."

Bombay Bar & Grill (Westport) S | – | – | – | M
316 Post Rd. E. (Rte. 1), 203-226-0211
A Westport "newcomer" that's "rapidly gaining in popularity" with "outstanding", "authentic" dishes that have quickly made it one of the "best Indian restaurants in Fairfield County"; non-rushed service and attractive decor also get high marks; it's tucked away at the end of a Post Road strip mall, south of the Sherwood Island connector, but apparently worth the search.

Bombay's Authentic ▽ | 18 | 11 | 16 | $19
Indian Cuisine (Hartford) S
89 Arch St. (bet. Columbus Blvd. & Main St.), 860-724-4282
☑ There "may be better" Indian restaurants but "not in Downtown Hartford"; given the context, they have "delicious" food, "excellent" service and an "inexpensive" tab, but the "simple", "plain" decor needs a spruce-up.

Bonani Indian Cuisine | 18 | 13 | 19 | $24
(Stamford) S
490 Summer St. (bet. Broad & North Sts.), 203-348-8138
☑ "Tasty flavors" of India shine through at this "consistently good" Downtowner with British clientele ("a good sign"), "caring" service and "pleasant" surroundings; a few gripe about "small" portions and a "menu that never changes" but for most it's "Indian comfort food"; N.B. try it for takeout.

Boston Market S | 13 | 7 | 11 | $11
232 W. Main St., Avon, 860-677-2899
Copaco Shopping Ctr., 395 Cottage Grove Rd. (Tyler St.), Bloomfield, 860-243-3400
45 Farmington Ave. (next to Bristol Commons), Bristol, 860-314-0102
61 Newtown Rd. (Plumtrees Rd.), Danbury, 203-792-4868
964 Post Rd. (opposite RR station), Darien, 203-655-9770
96 Frontage Rd. (I-95), East Haven, 203-467-4472
(Continues)

Boston Market (Cont.)
1982 Black Rock Tpke. (Stilson Rd.), Fairfield,
203-382-8090
2834 Main St. (Griswold St.), Glastonbury, 860-659-2850
597 Long Hill Rd. (Rte. 1), Groton, 860-448-3755
1542 Pleasant Valley Rd. (next to Buckland Hills Mall),
Manchester, 860-648-2471
755 E. Main St. (Swain Ave.), Meriden, 203-634-7677
Liberty Rock Shopping Ctr., 607 Bridgeport Ave., Milford,
203-874-6046
2495 Berlin Tpke. (Rte. 5), Newington, 860-665-7548
135 Washington Ave. (Rte. 5, off I-91), North Haven,
203-234-0188
1345 E. Putnam Ave. (Rte. 1), Old Greenwich, 203-637-4088
52 Danbury Rd./Rte. 35 (Rte. 7), Ridgefield, 203-438-1212
1780 Silas Dean Hwy. (Rte. 91), Rocky Hill, 860-529-8498
1081 High Ridge Rd. (Merritt Pkwy.), Stamford,
203-321-1410
935 Barnum Ave. (Main St.), Stratford, 203-378-8508
973 Wolcott St. (opposite Naugatuck Valley Mall),
Waterbury, 203-756-0009
1240 Farmington Ave. (near S. Main St., across from Stop
& Shop), West Hartford, 860-561-6150
2542 Albany Ave. (Bishops Corner), West Hartford,
860-586-7404
Compo Shopping Ctr., 390 Post Rd. E., Westport,
203-221-8733
◪ "Don't cook tonight – call Boston Market" urge fans of
the "high-quality fast food" "masquerading as home
cooking" at this ubiquitous American; but though its
chicken and other comfort fare "beat pizza and burgers"
and many "love those sides", foes claim "at these prices
you'd do better at your local diner"; still, most agree that
on a "lazy Sunday night" it's "perfectly fine."

BOULDERS INN (New Preston) S 22 24 20 $39
Boulders Inn, E. Shore Rd. (Rte. 45), 860-868-0541
◪ Dine in the "moonlight" over Lake Waramaug at this
"comfy", "romantic", "wonderful weekend getaway inn";
but since "you can't eat the view" you'll have to content
yourself with New American fare that can be "excellent"
but is more often "up and down."

Boxcar Cantina (Greenwich) S   19 17 17 $25
44 Old Field Point Rd., 203-661-4774
◪ A "friendly Albuquerque-bred owner" and her "fresh-
faced staff" will make you feel "welcome" at this Greenwich
Northern New Mexican housed in a boxcar; most find the
menu "different", "delicious" and a "good value", though
some insist it's "nothing special"; the "casual", "noisy"
setting is "kid-friendly" and "very crowded" but "lots of
fun"; P.S. there's a large margarita and tequila selection
that's "reason enough" to go.

BOXING CAT GRILL   21 | 19 | 18 | $32
(Old Greenwich) **S**
1392 E. Putnam Ave./Rte. 1 (bet. Havemeyer Rd. & Sound Beach Ave.), 203-698-1995
☑ This "noisy", "stylish" Southwestern has a "diverse", "eclectic" menu where you're certain to find "something to suit your taste"; and the "middle-aged Romeos" and "women looking for rich Greenwich men" are hoping for the same as they prowl the "smoky", "popular" bar; N.B. if you're more interested in eating than meeting critics say stick to a weekday lunch or brunch.

Brannigan's (Southington) **S**   – | – | – | M
176 Laning St. (I-84, exit 32), 860-621-9311
We missed it but our reviewers told us to head to this Traditional American for a rib-tickling experience; only gripe with this family favorite is service: "sometimes confused."

Breakaway (Fairfield) **S**   18 | 10 | 15 | $21
2316 Post Rd. (Sasco Hill), 203-255-0026
☑ A "cheap" and "cute" if "cramped" Fairfield New American burger joint that's popular with college kids and families; insiders say stick to the "dependable" salads, burgers, sandwiches and desserts, otherwise "break away at your own risk"; overall, it's "fun, but expect to wait."

Brewhouse Restaurant   15 | 20 | 17 | $24
(South Norwalk) **S**
New England Brewing Co., 13 Marshall St. (S. Main St.), 203-853-9110
☑ The New England Brewing Co. brews its beer on the premises of this "stunning" South Norwalk American-Continental-German; while the "excellent" pretzels, large selection of beers and accordion player win points, the chow's labeled "inconsistent" and "overpriced"; a few boosters insist that the "inventive cuisine" is simply "underappreciated."

Brick Oven Pizzeria Trattoria   ▽ 18 | 12 | 14 | $16
(Bridgeport) **S**
1581 Capital Ave. (Wood Ave.), 203-367-9958
■ Exactly what a "neighborhood Italian restaurant should be": "dependable", "nothing fancy", just a good place to relax and enjoy "terrific" pizza (especially the crust), pasta and focaccia; however, after seeing the "dingy surroundings" a few decide "to eat and run"; N.B. Friday takeout is so popular, it often means a one-hour wait.

Bricks, The (Norwalk) **S**   15 | 11 | 15 | $18
181 Main St. (Rte. 124), 203-846-0751
☑ Let your little ones watch the chefs toss the pies from the kids' station of this Norwalk Italian pizzeria; boosters say it's "underrated" and "worth a trip"; detractors throwing bricks say it's a step down from Bertucci's.

Bridge Café (Westport) **S**   21 | 22 | 19 | $34
5 Riverside Ave. (Rte. 33 & Post Rd./Rte. 1), 203-226-4800
■ A "trendy" American-Mediterranean in a "charming",
"country setting" where the warm-weather, al fresco dining
overlooking the Saugatuck river has patrons gushing
"location, location, location"; the "sophisticated"(some
say "too ambitious") fare includes "delicious pasta" and
"excellent seafood"; a few gripe about the difficulty parking.

Brookfield Bistro   22 | 13 | 18 | $29
(Brookfield) **S**
Colonial Shopping Ctr., 483 Federal Rd. (Rte. 133), 203-740-9555
■ New American–French bistro in Brookfield that "remains
innovative and committed to quality"; voters say the "very
tasty portions could be larger" and the "decor needs some
uplifting" but the "friendly" staff and "reasonable" tab
make it "worth the trip."

Brookside Bistro   20 | 20 | 19 | $33
(West Cornwall) **S** (CLOSED)
*416 Sharon Goshen Tpke. (bet. Rtes. 7 & 128 at the
covered bridge), 860-672-6601*
■ "Lunch or dinner on the terrace alongside the stream
is very charming" and "unbeatable in fair weather" say
visitors to this French bistro "hidden away" in Connecticut's
northwest corner; some insist the food's "solid", "even
adventurous" while others claim that if the chow "were
better it would be one of my favorites"; everyone likes
the "babbling brook."

Brookside Restaurant   – | – | – | M
(South Glastonbury) **S**
840 Main St. (Rte. 17), 860-633-2915
"Nothing fancy" at this South Glastonbury local joint: just
"very good" Italian-American dishes (many family recipes)
that have been packing 'em in for almost 50 years.

Bugaboo Creek Steak House   ▽ 16 | 18 | 18 | $18
(Manchester) **S**
1442 Pleasant Valley Rd. (Buckland Hills Plaza), 860-644-6100
■ Bring the kids to this "loud" Canadian mountain
lodge–inspired steakhouse set in a busy Manchester
shopping plaza; while some call it "food for people who
don't know any better" and wonder if the long waits are
for the grub or the "overdecorated" theme decor, others
find the meat "juicy" and think it's all "very entertaining."

Bull's Head Diner (Stamford) ◑**S** 13 | 10 | 14 | $15
43 High Ridge Rd. (I-95, exit 8), 203-961-1400
■ A few think this Stamford locale is what an "old-fashioned
Greek diner is about": a "huge menu", "plentiful" portions,
"inexpensive" prices, "quick" service and a "no-frills"
atmosphere; for others not even the "nostalgic setting"
charms because it's "too loud and bright."

Buon Appetito (Canton) **S**   ▽ 25 | 16 | 22 | $29
50 Albany Tpke./Rte.44 (Rte. 167), 860-693-2211
■ "What they lack in decor they make up for with interesting dishes" at this storefront Italian that's always a "fun place" to go with friends; expect service to match the "fine" food; regulars advise: "wear a sweater in the winter."

Buster's Bar-B-Que (Stamford) **S**   – | – | – | M
1308 E. Main St. (Rte. 1), 203-961-0799
"Fun" barbecue stop on the Stamford-Darien border; upstairs is a hopping bar scene where you'll find a large selection of microbrews; downstairs there's "succulent", "artery clogging" barbecue served cafeteria-style (no plates, you eat off paper mats on trays) and a "huge" selection of sides including "awesome" mashed potatoes; N.B. grab a handful of napkins.

Butterfly Chinese   ▽ 17 | 17 | 18 | $18
(West Hartford) **S**
831 Farmington Ave. (next to AAA Bldg.), 860-236-2816
☑ A "big" and "bright" Chinese in West Hartford that serves its dishes "with style and grace"; but the few surveyors who know it can't agree on whether the food is "excellent" with "tasty surprises" or "mediocre"; everyone agrees "you've got to love" the chocolate fortune cookies.

Cafe Allègre (Canton) **S**   ▽ 26 | 24 | 26 | $31
Gateway Office Pkwy., 50 Albany Tpke. (Rte. 177), 860-693-1009
■ A "super" American-French-Italian that's off the beaten path in northern Connecticut; the chef's "great new combinations", "open kitchen" and professional service make it an unqualified success; it's "small" (nine tables), gets "crowded" and can be "noisy", but nobody is complaining; N.B. reservations are a must.

CAFE CHRISTINA (Westport) **S**   21 | 21 | 19 | $33
1 Main St. (bet. Post Rd. & Rte. 1), 203-221-7950
☑ Despite its "soothing", "beautiful" location in a restored library with murals, this Eclectic in Downtown Westport is a "noisy", "always-packed", "see-and-be-seen" scene ("saw Joanne Woodward"); insiders say it's best for lunch for "reliable" soups, sandwiches and pasta; despite decent service ratings a few object to "attitude"; P.S. try the "outrageous" pot à la crème.

Café Lafayette (Madison) **S**   16 | 22 | 18 | $32
Inn at Café Lafayette, 725 Post Rd. (I-95, exit 61), 203-245-7773
☑ A "formal staff" serves the "ladies-who-lunch" crowd New American–French bistro fare in a "pretty", "pastel"-colored restored 19th-century church ("go to church without the sermon"); while some predict "it's destined to stick around" and insist they're "trying hard", detractors rain down on "overpriced" food and "slow" service.

Cafe Lulu (South Norwalk) S   18 | 16 | 16 | $25
70 N. Main St. (next to SoNo Crown Regent), 203-854-9688
■ Contemporary American that's "off to a good start" thanks to "reasonable prices", an "innovative menu" and a crew of "well-meaning rookie" servers "trying hard to create a friendly, pub atmosphere"; many "hope this place continues to grow" – "could be great if given a chance."

Cafe Morelli (Stamford) ◑S   18 | 15 | 17 | $26
269 Bedford St. (Forest St.), 203-353-3300
◪ An "upscale" Italian bistro in Downtown Stamford that elicits strong reactions: supporters say "super pizzas and pastas", "cute sidewalk" eating, "great people-watching" and atmosphere that "makes you feel like you're in Italy"; detractors say "cramped" and "smoky like a chimney", with "standard" dishes from a "limited menu."

Cafe Pika Tapas (New Haven)   23 | 22 | 22 | $25
39 High St. (bet. Chapel & Crown Sts.), 203-865-1933
■ "The best thing to happen to Downtown New Haven since Maya Lin", this "friendly", "interesting" unusual Spanish tapas eatery is applauded for "tantalizing tastes" in a "clean, bright, noisy place"; so once you get through the "long waits" sit back and order some paella, sip some sherry and "pretend you're a yuppie in NYC"; N.B. it's the sibling of Norwalk's highly rated Meson Galicia and Wilton's Mediterranean Grille.

Caffe Adulis (New Haven) S   21 | 20 | 20 | $23
228 College St. (bet. Chapel & Crown Sts.), 203-777-5081
■ Sure Eritrean food and communal-style seating "take some getting used to", but the "new" spices and "different flavors" will quickly "have your taste buds humming"; its "fun" "coffeehouse environment" and "knowledgeable", "friendly" staff are more pluses; live jazz Saturdays.

Calexico Mexican Grill   ▽ 11 | 9 | 10 | $14
(Greenwich) S
379 Greenwich Ave. (Railroad Ave.), 203-629-8989
◪ This Mexican prepares dishes from an open, "school cafeteria"–style kitchen as customers wait on line; despite very low ratings, some find it "casual", "fast" and "convenient" for a "quick bite before a movie"; detractors say the menu's "limited" and too "heavy on meat."

Cannery, The (Canaan) S   22 | 18 | 21 | $32
85 Main St. (Rtes. 7 & 44), 860-824-7333
◪ Enthusiasts of this New American with French influences in Canaan don't hold back saying the "ingenious" chef produces dishes "that rival any NYC or Fairfield restaurant"; they also gush about "simple but perfect decor" and a "warm, friendly atmosphere" that make it "well worth the stop on your way back from the Berkshires"; the less-blown-away say "good but precious and pretentious."

Capers (Brookfield) S   17 | 18 | 19 | $27 |
*Rolling Wood Plaza, 265 Federal Rd. (bet. Rte. 133 &
White Turkey Rd.), 203-775-1625*
☑ The "business crowd" finds the bar at this Brookfield
New American "a great place to watch a game", but for
more serious eating head to the dining room; there's a
"friendly" staff that's "good at what they do."

Carbone's Ristorante (Hartford)   22 | 19 | 22 | $35 |
588 Franklin Ave. (Goodrich St.), 860-296-9646
■ For 58 years the Carbone family has "proudly" watched
over this Italian "memory of what Hartford used to be"; the
"friendly" service and family-style portions of "great veal"
have made it a traditional celebration spot ("take mom for
her birthday"); to silence critics who say "time has passed
them by", they've brought in two new innovative co-chefs.

Carmela's Restaurante   ▽ 16 | 19 | 18 | $26 |
(New Milford) S
7 Main St. On-the-Green (bet. Bank & Bridge Sts.), 860-355-5000
■ "What they do they do well" at this "predictable but
satisfying" family Italian decorated with attractive hand-
painted murals; reviewers recommend the "gourmet pizza"
in the outdoor dining area with a view of the Green.

Carmen Anthony Steakhouse   – | – | – | E |
(Waterbury) S
496 Chase Ave. (Nottingham Terrace), 203-757-3040
Italian-style steaks, lobsters up to five pounds and desserts
made on the premises are some of the attractions at this
Waterbury locale that pleases the few familiar with it;
N.B. cigar dinners are scheduled regularly.

CAROLE PECK'S   24 | 17 | 19 | $36 |
GOOD NEWS CAFE (Woodbury) S
694 Main St. S. (Rtes. 6 & 64), 203-266-4663
☑ The good news, say the "artsy types" that frequent this
"cozy" but "lively" Woodbury locale, is that Carole Peck is
still turning out "dynamic", "amazingly innovative" healthy
Contemporary American–French that's the culinary "future
as it should be"; the bad news: staff has "serious attitude."

CAVEY'S RESTAURANTS   27 | 24 | 26 | $45 |
(Manchester)
45 E. Center St. (Main St.), 860-643-2751
■ With the highest food rating in the CT *Survey*, Steve
Cavagnero's shrine in Manchester is "a perennial first
choice" for two "exciting" restaurants in one; upstairs
you'll find a piano bar and Northern Italian at reasonable
prices, with pastas and risottos that change with the
seasons; downstairs is a "special-occasion" New French
that's "worth the price"; whether up or down expect
"professional" service and award-winning wine lists; "it
continues to set the standard."

Cedar's Steak House ▽ 23 | 21 | 25 | $39
(Ledyard) ◗⑤
Foxwoods Resort Casino (Rte. 2), 860-885-4252
■ Reviewers say this Foxwoods steakhouse is the casino's
only sure bet for "first-rate" beef; and, as with most casino
eateries, there's "excellent" service from a "very attentive"
staff; after a rough day gambling sweeten the pot with
one of the "fabulous desserts."

Center Grille – | – | – | M
(West Hartford) **(CLOSED)**
986 Farmington Ave., 860-236-6195
Chef Randy Nichols is starting to put this new West Hartford
Center American on the map; there's a nice mural over the
bar, and the service and price are just right.

CENTRO (Fairfield) ⑤ 19 | 19 | 18 | $28
1435 Post Rd. (Reef Rd.), 203-255-1210
CENTRO AT THE MILL (Greenwich) ⑤
328 Pemberwick Rd. (off Glenville Rd.), 203-531-5514
CENTRO RISTORANTE & BAR (Darien) ⑤
319 Post Rd., 203-655-4772
◪ Bring your little budding Michelangelo to these "casual",
"jam-packed", "hideously noisy" "brightly-decorated"
Italians where "kids love the crayons on the tables"; an
"attentive" staff serves "monster portions" of "fresh" pasta
and "stylish" pizzas at "a wide variety of prices"; although
for some it's a "constant in a changing world", others
worry that it's "slowly slipping into mediocrity"; N.B. the
Greenwich branch has a patio view of an old mill waterfall

Chale Ipanema (Hartford) ⑤ ▽ 23 | 17 | 18 | $24
342 Franklin Ave. (Bliss St.), 860-296-2120
■ Samba on down to this Brazilian Portuguese with some of
the "best feijoada on the East Coast"; although "it's unusual
fare for Hartford", a few live wires insist "it could even be
more daring"; there's "great live entertainment" on the
weekends when the bar becomes an "elegant pickup joint."

Chan's Choice (Norwalk) ⑤ 19 | 10 | 14 | $22
345 Main St./Rte.7 (Merritt Pkwy., exit 15), 203-846-3533
◪ You get a choice in how your Chinese is prepared at this
"healthy" (no MSG, no food colors, etc.) Asian in Norwalk
with readers insisting that the "fresh seafood" is the
way to go; on the downside, as ratings suggest, service is
"unconscious" and the place is a little "cramped."

Char Koon Restaurant ▽ 28 | 14 | 23 | $20
(South Glastonbury) ⑤
882 Main St. (Rte. 17), 860-657-3656
■ A red-brick-and-bamboo decorated Pacific Rim–noodle
shop in the Hartford suburbs that's called "new", "fresh"
and a "hidden gem" for "delicately prepared" "really
innovative Asian cooking."

Charley's Place　　　　▽ 13 | 12 | 16 | $20
(West Hartford) **S**
445 S. Main St. (New Britain Ave.), 860-521-8679
◪ Many say this West Hartford steakhouse is "getting long
in the tooth", but the "casual", "friendly" atmosphere plus
a "better-than-average" salad bar ("one of the few good
ones left") keep it popular with families; foes growl "no self-
respecting Charley would admit to owning this place."

Chart House, The **S**　　17 | 20 | 17 | $32
129 W. Main St. (Rte. 9), Chester, 860-526-9898
3 River Rd. (Post Rd.), Cos Cob, 203-661-2128
100 S. Water St. (Howard Ave.), New Haven, 203-787-3466
4 Hartford Rd. (Rte. 10), Weatogue, 860-658-1118
◪ Sure they have a "romantic" atmosphere, "great" views
and decent prime rib, roast beef and mud pie, but overall
this Traditional American chain leaves many shaking their
heads wondering "why do restaurants on the water think
they can serve mundane food and charge a lot?"; some take
advantage of the settings while avoiding the "formulaic"
food – "strictly for drinks."

Chef Eugene's (Hartford) **S**　　– | – | – | M
428 Franklin Ave. (Brown St.), 860-296-4540
Light, bright Hartford Italian newcomer with soaring food
and ceiling, and a view from the no-smoking section that's
worth giving up your habit; those who've found this place
say it "feels like home" right down to the moderate prices.

CHENG DU CUISINE OF CHINA　24 | 19 | 22 | $19
(West Hartford) **S**
923 Farmington Ave. (Trout Brook Dr.), 860-232-6455
■ "Innovative and delicious" multiregional Chinese fare
and an "attentive owner" draw kudos for this "well-run"
West Hartford locale; though a few insist it's "not quite
excellent", they agree "it will please most diners" and
"the specials are always, well, special."

Cherry Street East　　　15 | 12 | 14 | $21
(New Canaan) **S**
45 East Ave. (Cherry St.), 203-966-2100
◪ A "fun", "casual" neighborhood pub in "hotsy totsy" New
Canaan that's good for large portions of "great burgers" and
"excellent fries"; it's the kind of place you try for a quick bite
with the family before or after a movie; otherwise, "nothing
special" and there are "other options" in the area.

Chez Noüe (Ridgefield) **S**　19 | 19 | 18 | $39
3 Big Shop Ln. (Main St. & Bailey Ave.), 203-894-8522
◪ A Ridgefield "jazzed-up" storefront serving French
country fare draws decent ratings but very mixed comments:
"wonderful" and "will return again" vs. "consistently
unremarkable" with "poor service from youngsters who
are not trained"; your call.

Chez Pierre (Stafford Spring) ▽ 21 | 21 | 20 | $48
111 W. Main St./Rte. 190 (Rte. 32), 860-684-5826
☑ This Classic French "joy in the culinary wilderness" with
lots of "fresh flowers" "could be the best" of its kind in the
area; but even admirers reserve it for "special occasions"
due to the tab; a few say it's "not performing at its peak."

China Pavilion (Orange) S ▽ 20 | 17 | 20 | $21
185 Post Rd. (I-95, exit 41), 203-795-3555
☑ "Oh, the wonders that lie behind strip malls" enthuse
boosters of this Szechuan Chinese; others dis "typical
middle-America" fare that can be "greasy"; weekend
reservations are recommended, so it's pleasing somebody.

Christopher Martin's 16 | 14 | 17 | $26
(New Haven) ● S
860 State St. (bet. Clark & Humphrey Sts.), 203-776-8835
☑ A New Haven Italian-Continental with an "inventive"
menu that's sometimes "marvelous" and other times
"doesn't work" (if you're going to play it conservatively try
the steaks and sandwiches); there's a separate entrance
for the "noisy", "overcrowded" bar that's good for "dreamy
cocktails" and live music on the weekends.

Christopher's (Brookfield) S 17 | 20 | 18 | $30
834 Federal Rd./Rte.7 (Rte. 25), 203-775-4409
☑ The consensus on this Brookfield Center Traditional
American set in an "old house" is that it's a "quaint",
"comfortable" spot with "courteous service"; it's especially
attractive on a "fall day" or during the winter holidays when
the fireplaces are roaring; diners caution the "food has
been better" but it's "ok for a burger."

Chuck's Steak House S 17 | 14 | 17 | $26
1340 Post Rd. (I-95, exit 11), Darien, 203-655-2254
788 Farmington Ave (I-84, exit 39), Farmington, 860-677-7677
1 Civic Ctr. Plaza (I-91, exit 32), Hartford, 860-241-9100
250 Pequot Ave. (I-95, exit 75), New London, 860-443-1323
2199 Silas Deane Hwy. (I-91, exit 24), Rocky Hill, 860-529-0222
1003 Orange Ave. (Meloy Rd.), West Haven, 203-934-5300
Rte. 32 (I-84), Mansfield Depot, 860-429-1900
☑ Family-oriented steakhouses whose fans say they're
"like 10-year-old Weejuns" – "comfy" and "dependable"
with "no surprises" ("solid steaks" and a "great" salad bar)
at a "decent value"; those for whom the shoe doesn't fit
bemoan "average fare that's slipping", "slow" service
and a no-reservation policy that means "long waits."

Ciao! Cafe and Wine Bar – | – | – | M
(Danbury) S
2B Ives St. (White St.), 203-791-0404
Over 35 wines by the glass keep this Danbury Downtowner
hopping, and the modern black and white decor is just the
place to enjoy creative Italian fare.

Cinzano's (Fairfield) S   16   15   17 $27
1920 Black Rock Tpke. (I-95, exit 24), 203-367-1199
☑ While "good specials keep the menu interesting" at this Italian in north Fairfield, overall it's "nothing special" with "atmosphere that needs a face-lift"; but you can have another Cinzano on the rocks because the vittles are "reasonably priced for the portions."

Citron (Greenwich) ●S (CLOSED)   15   14   15 $30
18 W. Putnam Ave. (Greenwich Ave.), 203-869-8383
☑ "Despite a new name and new menu" this "basic" Eclectic-American "local hangout" "is still ordinary"; it's a "noisy bar" that's fine for "the good happy hour."

CIVIC CAFE (Hartford) S   24   21   22 $32
150 Trumbull St. (bet. Asylum & Pearl Sts.), 860-493-7412
■ "Can this be Hartford?" ask incredulous visitors to this "hip", "innovative" Eclectic that has everyone hoping that it "will last a long time"; look for "beautiful presentations", "scrumptious tastes" and "large" portions; N.B. there's a big "singles bar" scene that can be "overpoweringly noisy."

Claire's Corner Copia   16   10   10 $13
(New Haven) S⊟
1000 Chapel St. (College St.), 203-562-3888
☑ "You must like your first name" to eat at this "earthy", "healthy", cafeteria-style Vegetarian in the center of New Haven; the reason: "they call it out when" you can pick up your order; it's a favorite with Yalies looking for "eats on the cheap" but be warned a number think the chow's "bland."

ClearWaters (Monroe) S   ∇ 21   12   21 $31
Tollgate Plaza, 838 Main St. (Rte. 25), 203-268-7734
■ A New American–seafooder that's known for its fresh fish, "very generous portions" and friendliness toward children; "it's probably the best Monroe ("that restaurant hotbed") has to offer"; N.B. "decorators beware", the decor "needs some sprucing up."

Clemente's (Westport) S   21   19   22 $35
Colonial Green, 256 Post Rd., 203-222-8955
■ A "very, very personable" staff will "make anything you want" at this "tiny" Italian that has big portions, big heart; while the majority says "excellent", "one of the best meals of the year" a tiny minority sighs "service is great but I wish everything else were better."

Coach's Sports Bar & Grill   13   17   15 $18
(Hartford) S
187 Allen St. (Union Pl.), 860-522-6224
☑ Go Huskies! – UConn's men's basketball coach Jim Calhoun owns this bar so it's no surprise what the theme decor is; it's really "not an eating establishment" but a "loud" sports joint that's a good place to hang out, eat some wings and drink some beers.

COBB'S MILL INN (Weston) S   17 | 25 | 19 | $34 |
12 Old Mill Rd. (Rtes. 53 & 57), 203-227-7221

☑ "You must go once" to this "picture-perfect", "romantic" Traditional American for the "magnificent" waterfall and fowl (ducks); you can have faith in the staff that "takes the time to make sure you're satisfied" and "knows what they're doing"; but many ask the $64,000 question – "why doesn't someone do something to upgrade the food?"

Colonial Tymes (Hamden) ◐S ▽ 20 | 21 | 18 | $31 |
2389 Dixwell Ave., 203-230-2301

☑ When this American-Continental in Hamden is good, it's "great", but critics say it can be "inconsistent" and a few pine for "some vegetarian dishes"; but rebels and Tories unite on the colonial home: "beautiful."

Columbus Park   21 | 14 | 17 | $30 |
Trattoria Italiana (Stamford)
205 Main St. (Washington Blvd.), 203-967-9191

■ It "feels, smells and tastes" like Italy at this family-owned "gem" in Downtown Stamford with "very authentic" dishes, "particularly the risotto" and "don't-miss" tiramisu; the luncheon business crowd makes it "hard to get a table", but once in, it's "non-rush comfortable" (although "loud") with "considerate" service from real paesani.

Congress Rotisserie   17 | 10 | 14 | $13 |
333 N. Main St. (Albany Ave.), Bishops Corner, 860-231-7454 S
208 Trumbull St. (Asylum St.), Hartford, 860-525-5141
274 Farmington Ave. (Woodland St.), West Hartford, 860-278-7711 S

☑ "Big, hearty, imaginative" sandwiches and "juicy" rotisserie chicken served in "generous" portions place this chain a "cut above its competitors"; although there are a few squawks that it's "going downhill", the majority insists "it does its thing well."

COPPER BEECH INN (Ivoryton) S 25 | 26 | 24 | $45 |
46 Main St. (Rte. 9, exit 3), 860-767-0330

■ Expect "excellent" country French fare and a "great wine list" at this "elegant", "beautiful", antique-filled landmark near the Goodspeed Opera House; it's "still a favorite" with the "older crowds" who set their watches by the "efficient" staff; while a few find the "formal" setting "stuffy", it's usually a "lovely all-around" experience.

Costa Del Sol (Hartford) S   ▽ 22 | 18 | 22 | $29 |
Monte Carlo Plaza, 901 Wethersfield Ave. (I-91, exit 27), 860-296-1714

☑ A Downtown Hartford Spanish that some cherish as an "unknown treasure" for "paella from heaven" but others insist "doesn't quite capture the Spanish idiom"; those with enough sangria may not notice the "sterile", less-than-sunny decor.

Côte d'Azur (Norwalk)　　　23 ｜ 20 ｜ 22 ｜ $34 ｜
86 Washington St. (Water & N. Main Sts.),
203-855-8900

■ "They really know what to do with food" marvel fans of this "instantly popular" New French bistro on SoNo's restaurant row; expect "spectacular" dishes and a "friendly" staff in a "charming" setting; toss in "reasonable" prices and you see why everyone's "grateful" for this "little gem"; N.B. word's out so make reservations.

County Seat on the Green　　–｜–｜–｜ I ｜
(Litchfield) S
3 West St. (on the corner of South & West Sts.),
860-567-8069

This hub in lovely Litchfield is a relaxing, inexpensive coffeehouse and New American restaurant perfect for hanging out all day in overstuffed chairs or listening to jazz on the weekends.

Crab Shell (Stamford)　　　13 ｜ 15 ｜ 14 ｜ $26 ｜
Stamford Landing, 46 Southfield Ave., 203-967-7229

■ The "great view" and "outside bar" at this waterfront American-seafooder attract huge crowds of "lively" twentysomethings "summer trolling" for partners; if you're going to eat the "so-so" grub, stick to the lobster, chowder and salads; N.B. be prepared for "long" waits and a steep tab for what you get.

Cuckoo's Nest (Old Saybrook) S ▽ 15 ｜ 16 ｜ 15 ｜ $21 ｜
1712 Boston Post Rd. (Rtes. 1 & 166), 860-399-9060

■ For 20 years this "always-crowded" Mexican has been giving customers "big" portions at reasonable prices; and while some say it's "wonderful", others note that "there's not much to compare it to in CT"; it's still a "great summer hangout", especially on the patio.

Curtis House (Woodbury) S ▽ 14 ｜ 18 ｜ 16 ｜ $28 ｜
Curtis House, 506 Main St. S. (Rte. 6), 203-263-2101

■ A Woodbury Traditional American housed in the oldest inn (1736) in Connecticut, which for history buffs is "reason" enough to make a visit; while some rate the fare and service "good" and like the "comfortable" and "homey" feel of the place, others shrug "olde inn, olde food."

Dakota (Avon) S　　　　21 ｜ 23 ｜ 21 ｜ $25 ｜
225 W. Main St./Rte. 44, 860-677-4311

■ "An inspired log cabin setting", "friendly service" and a salad bar that will test the borders of your plate are the trademarks of this "formula, upscale" seafood-steakhouse where both the beef and the Sunday brunch are singled out for special notice; a few quibblers say it "falls short of lofty expectations."

DA PIETRO'S (Westport)   27 | 19 | 24 | $47
36 Riverside Ave. (bet. Cross St. & Post Rd.), 203-454-1213
■ "They're always trying new menus" at this Northern
Italian–Southern French "little jewel" that turns out "in-a-
class-by-itself" food from "a shoe box of a kitchen"; "you'll
feel like family" as the "stylish" staff "pampers" in an
intimate setting that's "great for eavesdropping"; a tiny
minority finds it "too claustrophobic for comfort" but
"it's tough to get a reservation, and it should be."

David's American Food & Drink   15 | 12 | 16 | $21
(Stamford) S (CLOSED)
108 Prospect St. (North St.), 203-324-5724
■ Despite unimpressive ratings, the lawyers from the
court house who frequent this Traditional American argue
on its behalf citing "huge salads", "great hamburgers" and
"carbonara to die for" "at a reasonable tab"; add to the
record that the staff provides a "personal touch."

Da Vincenzo Bistro   ∇ 18 | 19 | 18 | $26
(Stamford) S
222 Summer St. (Broad St. & Columbus Park), 203-353-9555
■ You'll "always be able to get a table" at this "quiet"
Stamford Italian with "very good prices for the type of
atmosphere and amount of food"; ho-hummers say the
food's "served slowly" and "nothing special."

Da Vinci's (Greenwich) S   – | – | – | E
(fka Mare e Monte)
235 Greenwich Ave. (E. Elm St.), 203-661-5831
It's too soon for a verdict on this new Greenwich restaurant
that's replaced Mare e Monte on the Avenue; specializing
in Northern Italian, they'll do Southern if asked, and takeout
is available for the too-busy-to-cook crowd.

DeRosa's Firehouse Pizza   16 | 15 | 16 | $16
(Westport) S
6 Wilton Rd. (Rtes. 1 & 33), 203-221-1769
■ Situated in a restored antique firehouse in Westport,
this festive pizzeria is the "most kid-friendly" spot in town
thanks to the design-your-own-pizza menu and a popular
Friday and Saturday night magician; as for the actual pies,
the range of opinion is from "standard" to "excellent"
depending on your age; it's great for birthday parties
for the little ones.

DeRosa's Italian Restaurant   16 | 13 | 15 | $26
(Westport) S
577 Riverside Ave. (I-95, exit 17), 203-227-7596
▨ "Bring Advil and Alka-Seltzer" 'cause it's "noisy" and
there are long waits for the generous portions of "garlicky",
"basic" Italian at this yuppie and family institution near
the Westport train station; while the decor could use
some work, the Gorgonzola salad is said to be a winner.

Diana (Groton) 🅂　　　　－|－|－| M
Fashion Plaza, 970 Poquonnock Rd./Rte.1 (across from Hoyt's Cinema), 860-449-8468
Don't let the "unlikely shopping center locale" stop you from discovering this Lebanese-Mediterranean; voters recommend any lamb dish and chicken with hot peppers to start your exploration; the "helpful" staff will steer you in the right direction at this "different" experience.

Diorio Restaurant & Bar Inc.　▽ 23 | 23 | 22 | $36
(Waterbury)
231 Bank St. (Grand St.), 203-754-5111
■ Waterbury's Downtown "power place" for "knockout" Italian food, "wonderful" decor and "upscale" service; old friends like to meet at the "beautiful" old bar and those-in-the-know suggest capping off this "fine dining" experience with a chocolate crème brûlée.

Doc's (New Preston) 🅂⊘ (CLOSED) 23 | 12 | 18 | $29
62 Flirtation Ave. (Rte. 45), 860-868-9415
☒ It's difficult to get a reservation at this "small", "cozy" "very NY-trendy" BYO Italian in rural New Preston; the reason: "memorable", "experimental" dishes using "superfresh ingredients"; a few heretics claim that "it's slipped", falling prey to the "revolving chef" syndrome.

Dolce Vita (Danbury) 🅂　　　▽ 17 | 16 | 15 | $31
52 ½ Pembroke Rd./Rte. 37, 203-746-0037
■ Situated in a white-shingled house with a series of cozy dining rooms, this Danbury Italian is a nice place to enjoy a good meal at a reasonable price (the prix fixe is $16.50); it attracts the pre-theater Candlewood Playhouse crowd, and come warm weather the outdoor patio is just the ticket.

Dolphins Cove Marina　　　　▽ 15 | 13 | 15 | $25
Restaurant (Bridgeport) 🅂
Dolphins Cove Marina, 421 Seaview Ave., 203-335-3301
☒ Located in a "rough" Bridgeport neighborhood but right on the marina, this Portuguese seafooder is known for its Brazilian music and busy bar scene; those who say the chow's "tasty" are countered by others who say "routine and boring"; N.B. the outdoor deck is a big draw.

Dome (Greenwich) 🅂　　　　－|－|－| E
253 Greenwich Ave. (E. Elm St.), 203-661-3443
First reports on this Contemporary American–International in a light, bright, gothic-ceilinged, renovated old bank building are that it's a welcome addition to Greenwich's restaurant row; look for unusual combinations of world cuisines prepared with an all-American flair; the huge menu includes such far-reaching dishes as seared rare lacquered tuna and spicy tuna roll with papaya mint salad and wakame.

Don Juan's ▽ 15 | 11 | 12 | $21
(New London) **(CLOSED)**
403 Williams St. (Rte. 32 & Broad St.), 860-437-3791
■ The few surveyors who've tried this "funky", "quirky"
New Londoner praise the "electric" Eclectic fare that's
"great for lovers of hot and spicy"; since it's reportedly
"like nowhere else", it may be worth a try.

Drawbridge Inne (Mystic) S ▽ 20 | 19 | 18 | $27
*Drawbridge Inne, 34 W. Main St./Rte.1 (bet. Gravel &
Pearl Sts.), 860-536-9653*
■ This "pretty" Mystic inn has always been popular with
tourists, but locals also give a thumbs-up to the Continental
fare, "friendly" staff and "comfortable atmosphere."

Eastside Restaurant ▽ 19 | 15 | 22 | $21
(New Britain) S
131 Dwight St. (Stanley St.), 860-223-1188
☑ For 62 years this German-American has been turning out
hearty fare at its New Britain location; if a few complain
that it's "not up to the standards of good German cooking",
plenty of others still show up for the home-cooked tastes –
fat calories be damned.

Eclisse (Stamford) S 19 | 16 | 17 | $24
700 Canal St. (south of I-95), 203-325-3773
■ This Stamford Italian, known for "megaportions" and
"noisy" atmosphere, is a "pasta lover's fantasy" for "fresh"
and "flavorful" dishes such as "outrageous" Penne Eclisse;
since the price is right it's a good choice for families, but
you must also like children because on weekends there
are a lot of them running around.

El Inca (Stamford) S ▽ 21 | 15 | 21 | $25
21 Atlantic St. (bet. Broad & Main Sts.), 203-324-9872
■ For the adventurous this "pricey" Peruvian in Downtown
Stamford is a "wonderful surprise" serving "distinct",
"interesting" dishes (especially the shrimp); while the staff
may be "nice" and upbeat the decor is most definitely not
("stolid and cheerless").

Elizabeth's (Tariffville) S – | – | – | M
(fka Cracker Barrel Pub)
28 Main St. (off Rte. 187 N.), 860-658-1618
This recently opened eatery in an 1800s brick building
is an "after-work gathering place" with Traditional
American-Italian pub fare that caters to all ages; in summer
head for the outdoor deck or if you're a stay-at-home type
takeout is available.

ELMS RESTAURANT   25 | 23 | 23 | $44
& TAVERN (Ridgefield) S
500 Main St. (Gilbert St.), 203-438-9206
■ Celeb-chef Brendan Walsh's (ex NYC's Arizona 206) "great resuscitation" of this Ridgefield landmark has our reviewers crying "bravo!" for "big-time" Traditional American food ("great venison") in a "small town inn"; there's "charming" colonial decor and a "warm, welcoming atmosphere", including a staff that gets the "highest praise"; a few gripe "overpriced" and "still trying to get their feet off the ground" but more say "finally a NYC-quality restaurant in the area."

Elm Street Oyster House   23 | 18 | 19 | $35
(Greenwich) S
11 W. Elm St. (Greenwich Ave.), 203-629-5795
■ A "classy", "oyster lover's must" for "huge" servings of beautifully presented "superb" fish and the namesake bivalve in many varieties; it's clearly "the best seafood in Greenwich" and in the *Survey* but many find the "long waits" and no reservations for less than five frustrating; N.B. if you don't like crowds, "forget" it on the weekends.

Eric & Michael's Steak House   17 | 17 | 19 | $33
(Wilton) S
205 Wilton Town Green (Wilton Ctr.), 203-834-2000
☑ "Men's club decor" and "crowds" await you at this "NYC steakhouse wanna-be" that's "consistent" and "ok if you're in the area"; but even those who find the steaks tender have difficulty sinking their teeth into the prices – "much too much for this stuff"; P.S. call about their cigar dinners.

Ettorucci's (Stamford) S   16 | 15 | 16 | $28
559 Newfield Ave. (next to Newfield Green Shopping Ctr.), 203-348-4616
☑ A local Italian that's child-friendly and perfect for "last-minute" dining; you'll find some "reliable" "hits" (pasta fagioli and "like-butter" veal) and some "misses" on the large menu; overall "nothing special" but the "price is right."

Fat Cat (Avon) S   – | – | – | M
136 Simsbury Rd. (Rte. 44), 860-674-1310
An Avon Southern French–Northern Italian set in a Nantucket-looking cottage complete with flowering window boxes; first reports indicate that it's elegant but casual, and living up to its motto, "fine dining, no whining."

Fiddler's Seafood Restaurant   21 | 17 | 21 | $31
(Chester) **S**
4 Water St. (W. Main St.), 860-526-3210
◪ "Nicely prepared", always fresh and "delicious" fish is the catch at this American-Continental seafooder; the pre-theater prix fixe menu appeals to the Goodspeed Opera House crowd that takes advantage en masse; expect "warm", "professional" service from a "pleasant" staff.

Firehouse Deli (Fairfield) **S**   19 | 12 | 16 | $10
22 Reef Rd. (Post Rd.), 203-255-5527
◼ A "sandwich/salad staple" in Fairfield Center across from the Gazebo, this "excellent" deli is a favorite spot to sit outside and "people-watch" while enjoying "solid", "dependable" breakfasts and lunches; its popularity often means "a long wait" (and some say crowds make it feel "like a Japanese subway"), but they all keep coming back for the "great fresh sandwiches."

First and Last Tavern **S**   23 | 19 | 20 | $17
26 W. Main St. (Rte. 44), Avon, 860-676-2000
939 Maple Ave. (Linnmore St.), Hartford, 860-956-6000
◼ "Lively tavern atmosphere" is part of the charm at this "always crowded" family-friendly pizza and pasta duo; while locals uniformly praise the Hartford flagship, some claim the Avon offshoot is a bit "uneven."

500 Blake Street Cafe   20 | 19 | 20 | $31
(New Haven) **S**
500 Blake St. (Whalley Ave.), 203-387-0500
◪ An "old establishment", neighborhood New Haven Italian with a "convivial", "dark, woody" piano bar and a "lovely", "romantic" dining room that's great for a date; most are pleased by a menu filled with winning "sauces" and "seasonings" but a few shrug "like any other Italian"; N.B. the "Sunday brunch is a Roman banquet."

Fjord Fisheries   19 | 13 | 17 | $30
(Stamford) **S** **(CLOSED)**
Sportsplex, 49 Brownhouse Rd. (Selleck St.), 203-325-0255
◪ A Scandinavian seafooder that, despite a "dreary" ambiance and a "thumping" sound from the attached health club, stays afloat because of fish "so fresh you'll think you caught it yourself"; try the chowders, stews, herring and the midweek "outstanding smorgasbord."

Flanders Fish   ▽ 23 | 14 | 20 | $21
Market & Restaurant
(East Lyme) **S**
22 Chesterfield Rd. (Rte. 161), 860-739-8866
◼ When you get a hankering for seafood, this is "just what you want": a "wonderful variety" of "very tasty" "fresh" fish along with fine service and an "informal" setting "near the shore"; P.S. they ship lobsters anywhere in the U.S.

Flood Tide (Mystic) **S**   ▽ 21 | 22 | 20 | $38 |
Inn at Mystic, jct. Rtes. 1 & 27, 860-536-8140
☑ A "pretty" but "aging beauty queen", this New England–
Continental has "excellent rack of lamb and grilled fish", but
a few think it's "inconsistent" and "resting on its laurels";
even if you're not eating you're welcome to take a tour of the
lovely grounds that include a turn-of-the-century mansion.

Fortune Village Restaurant   ▽ 21 | 14 | 17 | $18 |
(Branford) **S**
120 N. Main St. (Cedar St.), 203-481-3568
■ An "above-average", "local surprise" Chinese in Branford
that gets the nod for its green beans and cold sesame
noodles; expect "friendly" waiters watched over by an
owner "who demands service from his staff."

FRANK PEPE PIZZERIA   26 | 12 | 13 | $15 |
(New Haven) **S**⇗
157 Wooster St. (bet. Brown & Olive Sts.), 203-865-5762
■ "The gold standard" proclaim devotees of this Wooster
Street landmark that's been turning out "unbeatable" pies
since 1925; although partisans draw swords over whether
Pepe's or Sally's is "the king of the pizza wars", you can
count on the "legendary" white clam and plain tomato
varieties, as well as "horrendous" waits, "nonexistent"
decor and a staff that "doesn't give a damn"; no matter,
say fans, "the memory of these pies will smolder in you."

FRANK PEPE'S THE SPOT   25 | 10 | 13 | $14 |
(New Haven) **S**⇗
163 Wooster St. (bet. Brown & Olive Sts.), 203-865-7602
■ The new kid on Wooster Street (only 17 years young),
this "quicker, smaller" pizza joint is right next door to
Pepe's "mother ship"; aficionados swear it serves the
"same great pizza with less hassle" – sometimes there's
even a "chance at getting a table."

Gaetano's (Hartford)   21 | 18 | 20 | $31 |
*Hartford Civic Ctr. Mall, 1 Civic Ctr. Plaza (Trumbull St.),
860-249-1629*
☑ Popular with the Hartford Civic Center lunch crowd, this
Italian is a "busy meeting place" that fits the bill "if you're in
a hurry"; but while the well-rated food gets a few nods as
"always excellent", others find it uninspiring.

Gail's Station House   17 | 12 | 15 | $20 |
(Ridgefield) **S**
378 Main St., 203-438-9775
■ "Every New England Main Street should have a Gail's" cry
devotees who come in droves for the "reasonably priced"
healthy Eclectic fare; while they do serve lunch, and dinner
on certain days, purists insist "it's breakfast all day with
awesome corn and cheddar pancakes"; have your morning
coffee before coming 'cause there are "long waits."

Gates (New Canaan) S   17 | 18 | 18 | $25

10 Forest St. (bet. East & Locust Aves.), 203-966-8666

☑ "All the locals go" to this "casual" Continental that's a "meeting place" when "browsing through" New Canaan; they advise: "stick to" the burgers, soups and sandwiches and add that it's "time to turn over the menu."

Gathering, The (Milford) S   14 | 14 | 15 | $23

989 Post Rd., Rte. 1 (Cherry St.), 203-878-6537

☑ Regulars have been gathering at this "popular", "friendly" Milford family-style Traditional American for close to 30 years; while enthusiasts defend the fare ("no bells and whistles", just "simply prepared meats" and an "above-average" salad bar), most are "disappointed" with the chow and think the place "needs to be refurbished."

Gelston House (East Haddam) S   17 | 21 | 18 | $37

8 Main St. (Goodspeed Opera House), 860-873-1411

☑ A "pretty" riverfront location next to the Goodspeed Opera House makes this Continental a pleasant and convenient spot for dinner before a show, especially because the "accommodating" staffers "get you out on time"; a small bump in food and service ratings indicates the new management's "trying."

Gennaro's Ristorante d'Amalfi   23 | 21 | 22 | $33
(New Haven)

937 State St. (bet. Bishops & Humphrey Sts.), 203-777-5490

■ "Mom and pop" provide the "personal touch" at this "classic" New Haven Italian that "will cook to order"; factor in "pleasant", "comfortable" and "knowledgeable" servers who provide "impeccable service" and you see why some wonder – "why go to Italy?"

Giovanni's Serious Steak House S   18 | 13 | 17 | $30

2748 Post Rd., Darien, 203-325-9979
1297 Long Ridge Rd. (Merritt Pkwy., exit 34N), Stamford, 203-322-8870

☑ These "casual", "no-frills" seafood-steakhouses stand out for their serious portions, which "meet the expectations" of locals (the beef's "solid" and "dependable" and the lobsters a "good value"); outsiders think "routine."

Golden Lamb Buttery, The   ▽ 24 | 26 | 24 | $53
(Brooklyn) ⊅

499 Wolf Den Rd. (Bush Hill Rd.), 860-774-4423

■ "Romantic" hay rides before dinner, views of deer frolicking on the 1,000-acre farm, tableside "love songs" by guitarists and delicious Traditional American fare make a visit to this definitely-not-NYC Brooklyn xanadu a "magical experience"; while it may feel "like being a guest on a friend's country estate" "you pay a premium for the ambiance" and so "reserve it for that special day."

Golden Pagoda (Bristol) S　　　－ － － M
Bristol Farms Plaza, 1235 Farmington Ave. (bet. Stafford Ave. & Camp St.), 860-583-9514
Sure it's in a shopping mall, but the few surveyors familiar with this Bristol multiregional Chinese unanimously gush that it's "great" and "better than NYC" counterparts; let us know if it lives up to its acclaim.

G.P. Cheffields (Newtown) S　　　－ － － E
97 S. Main St. (1 mi. south of Rtes. 302 & 25), 203-270-6717
A new Newtown American-Mediterranean-seafooder family operation (two brothers are the chef-owners) that's currently "very good" with "not too far to go" before "excellent"; it already has a good following, especially on Thursday and Friday nights for cigars and jazz.

Grappa (Litchfield) S　　　19 17 16 $27
Litchfield Commons, 26 Commons Dr. (Rte. 202), 860-567-1616
■ An "upscale" crowd attracted to this Litchfield Italian's "civilized", "artsy" setting and "mouthwatering creations" calls it "my kind of pizza place"; most say management "takes its food seriously" with pies that are "unbeatable"; N.B. try the namesake drink.

Great Taste (New Britain) S　　▽ 25 19 24 $17
597 W. Main St. (Corbin Ave.), 860-827-8988
■ Don't let the "pancake house exterior" stop you from stepping inside this "authentic" Chinese; its admirers consider it one of the most "delicious" and "hospitable" multiregional Chinese restaurants in the state.

Greenwoods Market & Cafe　　　－ － － I
(Norfolk) S
32 Greenwoods Rd. W., 860-542-1551
A Norfolk self-service cafe/deli with a wide range of American and Middle Eastern specialties; it's quickly become a hit with locals looking for soups, sandwiches and salads on the run; come summer, the outdoor deck is a nice spot to enjoy rural Connecticut's countryside.

Grist Mill Restaurant　　　▽ 20 23 19 $32
(Farmington) S
44 Mill Ln. (Rte. 10 S. & I-84, exit 39), 860-676-8855
■ While this Farmington Mediterranean is well rated by those who know it, and there's praise for the "incomparable" setting overlooking a waterfall, food and service comments are grist for the mill; aside from "superb" Dover sole, the kitchen's called "erratic", and "condescending", "imperious" management makes some wonder "why they do business."

Griswold Inn (Essex) S   18 │ 23 │ 19 │ $34
Griswold Inn, 36 Main St., 860-767-1776
▨ This Traditional American in a 200-year-old inn is a
"comfy" place to warm up with "excellent" prime rib, a
few beers and a "slice of Connecticut history"; the interior is
"brought to life" by banjo players and memorabilia including
a gun collection that NRA types salivate over ("better than
the food"); modern taste buds say menu needs a revamp.

G.W. Tavern   – │ – │ – │ M
(Washington Depot) S
20 Bee Brook Rd., 860-868-6633
Townies "welcome" this Washington Depot newcomer
for its New England "comfort" fare including superb fish;
the "comforting" and "casual" interior includes murals.

Harry's Pizza (West Hartford) S⇄   24 │ 16 │ 20 │ $14
1003 Farmington Ave. (west of Main St.), 860-231-7166
▧ The "reasonable" pies are "always good and hot" at
this "fun, upscale" West Hartford "scene" serving "super
wines at fair prices"; no wonder it has "cult appeal."

Hawthorne Inn (Berlin) S   ▽ 20 │ 15 │ 19 │ $31
2421 Wilbur Cross Hwy., 860-828-3571
▨ Traditional American in Berlin that serves lots of beef to
a loyal following: most mavens say it's "the place to go"
for "very good" prime rib, steak and roast beef; dissenters
complain about too "many banquets."

Hearth Cafe, The (Westport) S   17 │ 17 │ 17 │ $31
Westport Inn, 1595 Post Rd. (Maple Ave.), 203-259-3189
▨ Boosters of this "cozy" and "quiet" Continental in the
Westport Inn say the grub's "better than its local reputation";
others admit it's "not bad for a hotel" if you don't mind
contending with "old-fashioned heavy" food.

Hogan's Miguels   – │ – │ – │ M
(Woodbury) (CLOSED)
757 Main St. S. (Rtes. 6 & 64), 203-263-0002
This SW-Mexican Woodbury newcomer has reviewers
shouting olé, bring on the "excellent" fajitas and "great"
chips and salsa; it's a welcome addition to Woodbury.

HOMESTEAD INN (Greenwich) S   26 │ 26 │ 25 │ $49
(nka Restaurant Thomas Henkelmann
at the Homestead Inn)
*Homestead Inn, 420 Field Point Rd. (bet. Bush Ave. &
Horseneck Ln.), 203-869-7500*
▧ Thomas Henkelmann (ex La Panetière) is now the chef/
co-owner of this famed Greenwich "romantic" New England
country inn for the "moneyed"; but Classic French and
"professional service" still reign supreme, so "get dressed
up" and prepare to enjoy new signature dishes such as
seared Hudson Valley Duck foie gras and jumbo sea scallops
in puff pastry with sherry vinegar sauce.

HOPKINS INN (New Preston) 🈂🚭 22 | 24 | 21 | $38
22 Hopkins Rd. (½ mi. west of Rte. 45N), 860-868-7295
■ The summer terrace of this 50-year-old New Preston Continental inn has a "spectacular", "memorable" ("I remember it when I was a pup") view of Lake Waramaug that makes it one of the "prettiest spots" in rural Connecticut for a "relaxing dinner"; count on very good "old-world cooking" and "pleasant", "careful" service.

Hot Tomato's (Hartford) 🈂 19 | 16 | 18 | $25
1 Union Station (Asylum St.), 860-249-5100
■ "You'll smell the garlic two blocks away" at this "affordable", "inventive" "friendly" Italian with portions so large that carrying them could "give you a hernia"; those cool to the concept say "not so hot tomatoes" – "garlic covers a lot of sins."

Hunan Harmony – | – | – | M
(South Norwalk) 🈂
13 Washington St. (across from post office), 203-838-6669
Diners "welcome" this newcomer to SoNo's restaurant row that serves a little bit of everything Asian: Chinese, dim sum, Hunan, Szechuan and Japanese; fans pray the harmony continues since the fare is "excellent."

Il Falco (Stamford) 23 | 19 | 21 | $37
59 Broad St. (bet. Summer St. & Washington Blvd.), 203-327-0002
■ Serving classic Italian on Downtown Stamford's restaurant row, this place to "take out-of-towners to impress them" or a "midpoint to meet NYC friends" features a kitchen that "knows its arugula"; the service is "pleasant" and "accommodating" though some think the place is "short on atmosphere."

Il Mulino (Stamford) 22 | 15 | 19 | $34
Springdale Shopping Ctr., 1078 Hope St., 203-322-3300
■ While it may never compare to the NYC restaurant of the same name, this "casual", "no decor" Stamford Italian in a strip mall is labeled a "surprising find" for "reliable" "high-quality" fare; it's a favorite with the older crowd.

Inn at Chester (Chester) 🈂 23 | 23 | 23 | $40
318 W. Main St. (Rtes. 145 & 81), 860-526-9541
■ A "quaint" and "cozy" antique-filled early American inn serving Contemporary American fare that's "ideal winter country dining" ("look for the lamb sausage"); the "attentive, efficient" staff and "quiet setting provide a good backdrop" for conversation; since "romance is happening here" some suggest climaxing the evening with a stay in one of the "charming" rooms.

INN AT RIDGEFIELD (Ridgefield) S 24 24 24 $44
20 West Ln. (Rtes. 35 & 33), 203-438-8282
■ "The gray-haired group" loves the "cozy elegance" of this "formal but not snobby" New England inn with "romantic" candlelight and fireside dining that's "perfect" on a cold winter's night; service is "tops" and the new lighter Continental menu is "a hit"; P.S. spend some time at the piano bar and try to make the Sunday brunch.

Inn at Woodstock Hill – – – E
(South Woodstock) S
94 Plaine Hill Rd. (Rtes. 169 & 171), 860-928-0528
A charming rural estate provides the setting for this converted carriage house Continental in Connecticut's quiet NE corner; it's a favorite stop while antiquing, and summer patio dining affords a great view of the surrounding countryside; the main complaint – "overpriced."

Inn on Lake Waramaug 19 23 21 $36
(New Preston) S **(CLOSED)**
107 North Shore Rd. (1 mi. west of Rte. 45), 860-868-0563
◪ Set in a "lovely", "traditional" New England inn "for all seasons", this "informal", "chic" New Preston New American has "to die for" views of Lake Waramaug; while the food is good ("breakfast is the best meal") some "prefer to go for drinks" at sunset during the summer.

It's Only Natural ▽ 22 14 19 $14
(Middletown) S
686 Main St., 860-346-9210
■ It's only natural that this Middletown Vegetarian wins kudos from its core followers who think it's "great" and "worth going out of the way for", although a few dissenters point out that tofu sausages are not for everyone; N.B. chef Mark Shadle gives monthly natural foods classes.

Ivy Restaurant & Bar, The 23 21 19 $44
(Greenwich) S
554 Old Post Rd. No. 3 (W. Putnam Ave.), 203-661-3200
◪ A "promising" New American–Continental newcomer in an "attractive" stone house with "simple" decor and "well-spaced" tables adds up to a "bit of glamour, Greenwich-style"; the food's "superb" and they're "trying" so most agree that despite "inexperienced" staff and "long waits", it "should make the grade."

Japanica (Farmington) S ▽ 19 20 20 $23
Exchange Bldg., 270 Farmington Ave. (Rte. 84 W, exit 39), 860-677-5633
◪ "Super sushi", "appealing" decor and "friendly", "attentive service" combine to make this Japanese a "pleasant", "authentic" experience in Farmington; it's "very good" but sticklers say "not the best in the area"; P.S. karaoke on weekends is another draw.

Jasmine (Westport) **S**   15 | 15 | 16 | $22
60 Charles St. (I-95, exit 17), 203-221-7777
Serving Hunan-Szechuan specialties and sushi, this "nice addition to the Asian scene" is "quickly becoming a favorite" for its "reasonable prices" and a "pretty fish tank" that's "wonderful for children"; however, as ratings suggest, some find it "equally as poor as its predecessor."

JEAN-LOUIS (Greenwich)   27 | 24 | 26 | $56
61 Lewis St. (Greenwich Ave. & Mason St.), 203-622-8450
It's "Lutèce in New England" at this Greenwich New French where chef Jean-Louis Gerin creates "memorable" "rich", "beautifully presented" creations in a "small", "simple" and "intimate" setting; while it's already a "mecca for foodies" that's "exciting every time", the kitchen keeps "striving for perfection"; P.S. try the Celebration tasting menu.

Jimmy's Seaside (Stamford) ◐S   15 | 12 | 15 | $22
891 Cove Rd. (Seaside Ave.), 203-964-9225
Locals prize this "true" neighborhood "beer drinking" "hangout" where everyone knows your name; the American seafood is "not bad" and "not expensive" but for many the place is "too noisy", has "too many tables" and is getting tired.

John Harvard's Brew House   – | – | – | M
(Manchester) **S**
1487 Pleasant Valley Rd. (Buckland Ave.), 860-644-2739
Chic microbrewery offering an array of interesting beers and a menu large enough to appeal to both foodies and their children; expect burgers, salads, meat loaf and more sophisticated dishes such as fennel chicken sausage with pasta; N.B. a no-reservations policy means come early if you want to get a seat on the weekend.

Kathleen's (Stamford) **S**   23 | 19 | 20 | $34
25 Bank St. (Washington Blvd.), 203-323-7785
A Downtown Stamford New American that's a favorite with the business and pre-theater crowd for "esoteric", "innovative" fare using a "wide variety of spices"; the staff is "friendly" and "helpful" making it a "pleasant" "weekend date" place; "they get things right over and over."

Khan's Mongolian Garden   16 | 11 | 13 | $20
(Stamford) **S**
135 Bedford St. (bet. Broad & Spring Sts.), 203-975-0209
"Everyone should try the Mongolian BBQ" once at this "cheap" Downtown Stamford Chinese where you either choose from a buffet or "pick raw ingredients, spices and sauces and watch the chef stir-fry it up"; it's a "fun" place to go with a group or kids, but even with their input many admit the final product is only "satisfactory".

King and I (Bridgeport) 🅂   ▽ 24 │ 14 │ 19 │ $23 │
545 Broadbridge Rd. (Huntington Tpke.), 203-374-2081
■ Thai crown "jewel" in a Bridgeport strip mall; the reasonably priced fare is "simple" but with a "spark" that prompts admirers to "take Thais there because it's real and tops"; N.B. it does a busy take-out trade.

Kismet (Ridgefield) 🅂 **(CLOSED)**   19 │ 10 │ 18 │ $27 │
296 Ethan Allen Hwy. (Rte. 7), 203-431-1211
☑ A "popular" Ridgefield Indian on busy Rte. 7 "that looks like a hotel"; most agree it's "consistently better than most" which means "as good as Indian can get in WASPville with prices to match."

Kotobuki Japanese Cuisine   21 │ 13 │ 19 │ $27 │
(Stamford) 🅂
457 Summer St., 203-359-4747
☑ "Crowded", "busy", "very small", this Japanese in Downtown Stamford earns applause for "beautifully" presented sushi and other "surprisingly good" food.

Kujaku (Stamford) 🅂   18 │ 13 │ 16 │ $25 │
84 W. Park Pl. (Summer St.), 203-357-0281
☑ For "fresh" sushi, "great" tempura, and "decent" hibachi in your own tatami room, head to this large Japanese in Downtown Stamford; even those who don't usually have a yen for this type of food admit "not my thing, but this one's pretty good"; N.B. reservations recommended.

L'ABBEE (New Canaan) 🅂   25 │ 20 │ 22 │ $46 │
62 Main St. (Locust St.), 203-972-6181
☑ The "skinny and wealthy" enjoy "excellent", "creative" Contemporary French at this New Canaan eatery that can feel very "cozy" vs. "cramped" and "attentive" vs. "snobby" depending on your state of mind; although ratings side with those who say it "deserves more attention", a vocal minority insists it's "overrated."

La Bretagne (Stamford)   22 │ 17 │ 22 │ $42 │
2010 W. Main St. (bet. exits 5 & 6 off I-95), 203-324-9539
■ A "sleeper" on the Greenwich/Stamford border serving "consistently satisfying" "heavy" Classic French ("the greatest duck") the "way it was before nouvelle"; there's "a good loyal staff" that will deliver your meal with "grace" but the "tired", "'70s" decor draws yawns.

LA COLLINE VERTE (Fairfield) 🅂   25 │ 24 │ 26 │ $47 │
Greenfield Hill Shopping Ctr., 75 Hillside Rd. (Bronson Rd.), 203-256-9242
☑ "Everyone's trying to please" at this "high-quality" Fairfield Classic French; despite being tucked away in a tiny shopping center in Greenfield Hill there's a "sophisticated" but "cozy" atmosphere and "excellent" food; a few grumble about "high prices" and "inconsistent" fare, but most agree that it's "one of the best for real French."

La Hacienda (Stamford) **S**　　　16 | 16 | 17 | $24 |
(fka Hacienda Don Emilio)
222 Summer St. (bet. Broad & Main Sts.), 203-324-0577
☑ Those who shout "si" for this Stamford "traditional" Mexican insist it's "the best for miles around", "more handsome than most" and has a "welcoming" staff; those who give it a resounding "no" consider it "proof there is no good Mexican food in Fairfield county."

La Maison Indochine　　　22 | 15 | 20 | $35 |
(Greenwich) **S**
107-109 Greenwich Ave. (Lewis St.), 203-869-2689
■ This Greenwich Vietnamese may be located in a difficult-to-find, "unimpressive", second floor, back-entrance locale, but the food is "solid" to "sensational"; while the staff's "solicitous" some warn: if "you put yourselves in their hands they will make sure you spend."

La Taverna (Norwalk) **S**　　▽ 22 | 14 | 19 | $30 |
Broad River Corner Shopping Ctr., 130 New Canaan Ave. (I-95, exit 15, Rte. 7, exit 2), 203-849-8879
■ An "up-and-coming" Southern Italian in Norwalk serving "good", "reasonably" priced food in a setting that some say has "no ambiance" but others label as "lovely, old-world"; N.B. takeout available.

La Trattoria (West Redding) **S**　▽ 21 | 22 | 22 | $39 |
4 Long Ridge Rd. (RR station), 203-938-9160
■ A "pretty", "upscale" West Redding Northern Italian at a whistle-stop on the Metro North line; it's reliable for "attentive service" and for "meeting friends in a quiet atmosphere"; try the "Saturday prix fixe" but be prepared for "too much food."

La Villa Restaurant (Westport)　▽ 18 | 12 | 18 | $30 |
3 Bay St. (Post Rd. & Rte. 1), 203-454-1312
☑ "Reasonably priced" Westport Italian ("good veal") in a "comfortable", "pleasant" setting; as always, a few grouse "nothing special"; N.B. if you don't see what you want on the menu, just ask – they will prepare it for you.

Le Bistro des Amis (Westport)　　23 | 19 | 21 | $37 |
Sconset Sq., 15 Myrtle Ave. (Post Rd.), 203-226-2647
■ "Edith Piaf would be proud to sing" at this "warm", "charming", "romantic" French bistro "tucked away" in Westport; devotees say they serve a mean steak frites and that ordering dessert is a "great decision."

Le Bon Coin (New Preston) **S**　▽ 20 | 18 | 17 | $37 |
223 Litchfield Tpke., 860-868-7763
☑ A "lovely little" New Preston Classic French in the "middle of nowhere" that "continues to please" loyalists with "innovative" and "carefully prepared" fare in a "comforting" country setting; while a few critics call it "lackluster" others feel "it deserves greater patronage."

LE FIGARO BISTRO DE PARIS   21 | 23 | 20 | $40 |
(Greenwich) **S**
372 Greenwich Ave. (Railroad Ave.), 203-622-0018
☑ A "beautifully appointed", "stylish" belle epoque–style Greenwich French bistro with a "well-trained" staff, "peppy crowd" and "good portions" of "dependable" "très bien" fare; although pricey, a few exaggerate – "the charm of a French bistro but prices of a three-star Michelin."

Lemon Grass Thai Cuisine   20 | 17 | 19 | $20 |
(West Hartford) **S**
7 S. Main St. (Farmington Ave.), 860-233-4405
■ A "solid" "tasty", "spicy" Thai that's a "nice addition to the dull West Hartford food scene" with a staff that makes "an effort" to "please"; but what some call "tiny" servings can leave a hankering for more.

Lenny & Joe's Fishtale **S**   20 | 12 | 15 | $17 |
1301 Post Rd., Madison, 860-245-7289
86 Boston Post Rd. (I-95, exit 64), Westbrook, 860-669-0767 ⊟
■ These "eat-with-your-fingers" seafooders have been reeling in patrons for almost three decades with "fast, fresh, fried fish that's the standard" on the shoreline; be on your toes because they're "crowded" and with self-seating at the Madison location it's "every man for himself"; N.B. regulars love the fried clams and chips.

Leon's Restaurant (Hamden) **S**   20 | 16 | 17 | $28 |
1640 Whitney Ave. (Park St.), 203-281-5366
☑ Loyal customers applaud this 59-year-old Italian's move to a "safe" locale in Hamden ("great not to have to wear my bullet-proof vest") and say the "homestyle" food is "fabulous again"(especially "imaginative appetizers"); while there are a few gripes about service (plan on "a lot of time"), "the menu's still large" and "you'll still have leftovers."

LE PETIT CAFÉ (Branford) **S**   25 | 20 | 23 | $29 |
225 Montowese St. (Main St., across from town green), 203-483-9791
■ Enjoy "wonderful", "no-frills, no-attitude" French bistro fare that's a "stupendous" bargain at this Branford locale that'll "make you feel like you're in France"(you're actually looking at the town green); be forewarned, dinner is always prix fixe; and at $21.50 it's a "madhouse" on Saturday night; "all the foodies say this is paradise."

Lily's of the Valley (Simsbury) **S** ▽ 21 | 19 | 20 | $22 |
142 Hopmeadow St. (Rte. 44 E.), Simsbury, 860-651-3676
☑ There's "big-appetite food" at this Simsbury Traditional American with "mouthwatering potatoes" that taste like "real home cooking"; while a few gripe about "so-so" eats most say it's "worth going just for the biscuits."

Lime Restaurant (Norwalk) S 18 10 17 $21
168 Main Ave. (Center Ave.), 203-846-9240
■ This "small", "informal" Eclectic is "healthy" "heaven", especially for the number of vegetarian selections; there's a "charming" staff and "fun" atmosphere so you can see why many call this Norwalk mainstay "an old friend"; a few dissenters cite "some hits, some misses."

Li's Brothers Inn (Darien) S ▽ 14 12 14 $23
Goodwives Shopping Ctr., 25-48 Old King's Hwy. N., 203-656-3550
☑ A Darien "shopping center" Chinese that a few claim serves "fresh" and "consistently good" fare while others grouse "pretty ordinary" and "overpriced"; your call.

Little Kitchen, The (Westport) S 19 8 14 $21
47 Main St. (Post Rd.), 203-454-5540
☑ A Westport Chinese-Indonesian known for "interesting" combos labeled "excellent" "even by NYC standards"; plan on takeout or a delivery because there are only eight seats.

Little Mark's Big BBQ (Vernon) S ▽ 23 8 12 $18
226 Talcottville Rd. (Rte. 83), 860-872-1410
■ "Lip-smacking" sauces are served with the "amazing" "dependable" ribs at this Vernon Traditional American and BBQ shop; but that's where the charm ends because critics say you feel like you're "dining in someone's shack" and the hosts are "arrogant."

Lotus Restaurant (Vernon) ▽ 26 19 21 $20
409 Hartford Tpke./Rte. 30 (Merline Rd.), 860-871-8962
■ Surveyors appreciate the "authentic", "painstakingly prepared" Vietnamese at this former Vernon post office; since everything's in the family don't be surprised if you're served by one of owner Hong Nguyen's children.

Luigi's Restaurant
(Old Saybrook) S ▽ 21 15 21 $20
1295 Boston Post Rd. (Rte. 1 & Schoolhouse Rd.), 860-388-9190
■ It's "like coming home" say enthusiasts of this 40-year-old family-run Old Saybrook Italian serving "hearty portions" of "tasty", "homey" dishes; those in the know say try anything with the clam sauce or order a tuna hero.

Luna Pizza S ▽ 23 8 15 $14
Farmington Valley Mall, 530 Bushy Hill Rd. (Rte. 44), Simsbury, 860-651-1820 ⊟
999 Farmington Ave. (LaSalle Rd.), West Hartford, 860-233-1625
■ Regulars of these Southern Italian pizzerias wonder when they're going to stop being a "well-kept secret"; you reportedly "get your money's worth" for "excellent clam pies" so why are they "often half empty"?; N.B. the West Hartford parlor has replaced the closed Hartford branch.

Mackenzie's Grill & Tap Room   ▽ 13 12 13 $24
(Fairfield) **S**
*4180 Black Rock Tpke. (Merritt Pkwy., exit 44 or 45),
203-256-8686*
◪ A "glorified bar scene" awaits you at this "smoky"
Fairfield American with "humdrum food"; it attracts a
"young crowd" but even "younger service."

MacKenzie's Redding   17 20 18 $25
Roadhouse (Redding) **S**
406 Redding Rd./Rte. 53 (Rte. 107), 203-938-3388
◪ A Redding sibling of the Fairfield locale with a more
upscale menu and dining room; it too has a huge bar scene
with live music, making it a "great neighborhood hangout
even if it's not your neighborhood."

Madd Hatter Bakery & Café   ▽ 19 17 16 $23
(Chester) **S**
23 Main St. (Spring St.), 860-526-2156
◪ A "funky", "artsy" outpost in Chester serving New
American–Mediterranean fare and bread baked on the
premises; some find it "always inspired", others "standard"
but in any case it's a safe bet for breakfast on weekends –
try one of the "light", "fluffy" chocolate pastries; N.B.
they do seasonal wine and beer prix fixe dinners.

Magic Wok (New Canaan) **S**   17 13 18 $22
73 Elm St. (next to New Canaan Playhouse), 203-966-8830
◪ A convenient "too-tired-to-cook" Chinese next door to
the New Canaan Playhouse; enthusiasts recommend the
spicy dumplings and say the dishes are "delicate" and
"adequate in all respects"; detractors say "gluey, all
tastes the same."

Maiden Lane Restaurant   – – – E
(Sherman) **S**✝ **(CLOSED)**
*Sherman Common, 1 Rte. 37 E. (junction 39N & 37E),
860-355-2225*
We just found out about this maiden in the Sherman
countryside, serving an International menu of classic
cuisines catering to special diets, including vegetarian;
two prix fixes are offered: one at $27.95 (three course)
and the other at $42.00 (six course); N.B. dinner is served
Thursday–Sunday only.

Main & Hopewell   – – – E
(South Glastonbury)
2 Hopewell Rd. (Rte. 17), 860-633-8698
While we didn't hear from too many surveyors on this
Contemporary American, those who did respond say the
"hearty, inspired, imaginative fare" is putting this "suburban
retreat" in South Glastonbury "on the map"; the re-do of
what was once a 200-year-old former bootery makes it a
neat place to unwind.

MAKO OF JAPAN (Fairfield)   25 | 11 | 20 | $28
941 Black Rock Tpke. (I-95, exit 24), 203-367-5319
■ The exterior may need a makeover but this tiny strip mall Japanese serves "authentic", "truly outstanding" sushi that many say is the "best" in Fairfield County; even those who don't like this type of food say they "enjoyed" it since you "can taste the quality."

Manero's (Greenwich) 🅂   17 | 12 | 16 | $29
559 Steamboat Rd. (I-95, exit 3), 203-869-0049
☑ A "favorite", "loud and informal" Greenwich seafood-steakhouse "institution" for families celebrating birthdays (serenading waiters add to the din); loyalists cheer the "fabulous" onion rings and Gorgonzola salads "to die for"; detractors find it "tired" and "mediocre."

Mansion Clam House (Westport) 🅂   17 | 12 | 16 | $29
541 Riverside Ave. (Bridge St.), 203-454-7979
☑ This Westport Traditional American "lobster shack" may have "dreary and depressing" decor but it's been a local "staple for seafood" for almost 40 years, and some swear it's still "as good as ever"; others say it "has seen better days" and note that "things can really add up."

Margaritas (Canton) 🅂   ▽ 16 | 17 | 18 | $22
144 Albany Tpke. (Rtes. 44 & 177), 860-693-8237
☑ A long-running Canton Mexican that's a favorite with families and the take-out trade; it's "typical" but fine if you're "looking for a margarita and taco fix."

Maria's Trattoria (Norwalk)   23 | 11 | 18 | $27
172 Main St. (Rte. 7, exit 2), 203-847-5166
■ "Everything's made from scratch" at this "tiny" Norwalk Italian in the "middle of nowhere" that's "still wonderful after all these years"; N.B. since there are only 40 seats the unofficial waiting room is the bar next door.

Mario's Place (Westport) 🅂   17 | 11 | 15 | $26
36 Railroad Pl. (opposite RR station), 203-226-0308
☑ A "lively", "friendly" Westport Italian-American across from the train station that's a great place for "unwinding" and feeling "like a native"; while "foodies shouldn't bother going" supporters say it's a "miniclassic for the basics" meaning "large" portions of beef, pastas and martinis.

Mario the Baker (Stamford) 🅂⊘   16 | 8 | 14 | $16
864 High Ridge Rd. (Vine Rd.), 203-329-0440
☑ A Stamford Italian known for pizza that some think is "not Sally's but the best thin-crust in the area" and others insist is only "so-so"; as for the other dishes they're called "lacking in imagination."

Marisa's Ristorante   ▽ 24 | 16 | 22 | $24 |
(Trumbull) **S**
6540 Main St., 203-459-4225
■ A move from a "touch-and-go" Bridgeport neighborhood
to new digs in Trumbull is good news to reviewers of this
"cheerful" Southern Italian; expect "scrumptious" fare
but "be prepared for lots of garlic and oil"; a highly-regarded
staff ensures that it remains a "real treat."

Marlborough Tavern   – | – | – | M |
(Marlborough) **S**
Marlborough Tavern Green, 3-5 E. Hampton Rd./Rte. 66,
860-295-8229
A 256-year-old New England country tavern with "small
private rooms" and "attentively served", "moderately
good" Traditional American fare; history buffs take note:
Presidents Madison and Jackson dined here.

MAX-A-MIA (Avon) **S**   24 | 19 | 21 | $24 |
70 E. Main St./Rte. 44, 860-677-6299
■ A "yummy", "inspired" Italian in Avon known for
"wonderful bread", "huge salads" and "delicious pasta";
it's "noisy, noisy, noisy" and "lively" so even the "kids
love it"; the only complaint is that it's "hard to get in", but
once you do the "price is right" and you're in for a "treat."

MAX AMORÉ RISTORANTE   24 | 19 | 21 | $25 |
(Glastonbury) **S**
Somerset Sq., 140 Glastonbury Blvd., 860-659-2819
■ A "yuppies" fave, some say this Glastonbury locale is
the "best" of the three Max's with "first-rate", "consistently
good" Italian fare (especially the Tuscan pastas, pizzas and
chicken with mashed potatoes), a "bustling" atmosphere
and a "top-notch" staff; N.B. "bring earplugs."

MAX DOWNTOWN (Hartford) **S**   26 | 25 | 23 | $38 |
185 Asylum St. (Trumbull & Ann Sts.), 860-522-2530
■ Reviewers say "right on" to this Downtown Hartford
Contemporary American Max; while the menu changes
monthly you can always expect "fabulous" food and a
"nice wine selection" in "sophisticated digs" that create
a "warm", "clubby" "NYC ambiance"; it's "wonderful,
especially when totally packed."

Max Steaks and BBQ   – | – | – | M |
(Greenwich) **S**
2 S. Water St. (I-95 N., exit 2), 203-532-9651
For hearty portions of good, basic food at reasonable
prices head for this new kid in Greenwich; it's a steak
place with a twist – besides the usual beefy offerings
you'll find BBQ ribs and chicken, pork chops and some
interesting fish dishes.

MAYFLOWER INN, THE   25 28 25 $51
(Washington) **S**
118 Woodbury Rd. (Rtes. 47 & 199), 860-868-9466
■ A "posh", "stately" Litchfield County inn that receives
the highest decor ranking in the *Survey*; "walk through
the gardens", have "lunch on the porch", "coffee in the
library" or drinks in the "cozy bar and lounge area"; the
"top-notch" staff skillfully serves well-rated New England
fare that has its critics ("boring"), but is "good for an inn."

Mediterranean Grill (Wilton) **S**   22 21 21 $33
*Stop & Shop Plaza, 5 River Road (bet. Rte. 33 & Wolfpit),
203-762-8484*
■ This Wilton Mediterranean makes a "nice alternative"
"if you're too tired to schlep to Meson Galicia", its sister
restaurant; expect "efficient service", "innovative, tasty
dishes, from appetizers through desserts", and "splashy",
"sleek" California decor that "lifts the spirits"; "it's strip
mall dining at its best."

Mediterraneo (Greenwich) **S**   21 20 18 $36
366 Greenwich Ave. (Grigg Ave.), 203-629-4747
☑ A "chic", "trendy scene" in an "attractive space" and
"interesting, well-put together" Mediterranean fare make
this Greenwich locale a "popular" spot "to impress a date";
however, be prepared for "small portions" and "high prices"
and service that's fine "if you can stay the week."

Meera Cuisine of India (Stamford) **S**   19 12 19 $25
227 Summer St. (bet. Broad & Main Sts.), 203-975-0477
☑ This Stamford locale may genuinely be the "best Indian"
around but it's still only the "typical suburban" variety; but
reviewers are quick to note that there's a "nice tandoori
oven" and a "favorite palak paneer recipe"; P.S. it's a
stress-free experience – "easy to be seated", "pleasant
people" running it.

MESON GALICIA RESTAURANT   25 22 23 $39
(Norwalk) **S**
10 Wall St. (bet. High & Knight Sts.), 203-866-8800
■ People come to Downtown Norwalk "from miles around"
for the "glorious" Spanish dishes (grilled squid, paella, tapas)
that come out of this "relentlessly inventive" kitchen; it's
"spacious", "romantic" and "elegant in a quiet way" with
a "solicitous" staff and an owner who "personally welcomes"
each diner; despite the NYC prices many "feel fortunate
to have this restaurant in the area."

Métro bís (Simsbury) **S**   ▽ 23 23 21 $32
928 Hopmeadow St., 860-651-1908
■ A "favorite" Simsbury French bistro–Eclectic with
something for everyone; fans say it's "always superb"
with "beautiful presentations."

Metropolitan (Bridgeport)   – – – M
Wright Investors Bldg., 1000 Lafayette Blvd., 11th fl. (I-95, exit 27), 203-331-9701
"Enjoy the view" of Long Island Sound from the top of the Wright Investors office building because the American-Eclectic fare "isn't coming soon"; but the food "isn't bad" and there's "plenty" of it at "reasonable prices" so it just "might overcome the stigma of Downtown Bridgeport."

Mhai Thai Restaurant   19 16 17 $32
(Greenwich) S
280 Railroad Ave., 203-625-2602
☑ "Delicious", "spicy", "fresh" Thai in Downtown Greenwich that's the "best" in the area primarily because of "wonderful", "to-die-for" sauces (especially the green curry); dissenters say it's "lost its creative edge" and is still serving "small portions" at "high prices."

Miguel's (Woodbury) (CLOSED)   – – – M
757 Main St. South (Jct. of 6 & 64), 203-263-0002
This sibling of Mount Kisco's popular Casa Miguel has our reviewers shouting olé!: bring on the "excellent" fajitas and "great" chips and salsa; a few complain about "overpriced" Tex-Mex and lack of decor, but all-in-all it's a welcome addition to Woodbury.

Mill Pond Café (Cos Cob) S   16 16 17 $27
Mill Pond Village, 203 E. Putnam Ave. (bet. Strickland Rd. & Replay Pl.), 203-629-9029
■ "Watch the water birds" from the interior or the patio of this Cos Cob hole-in-the-wall with "big portions" of "basic" American fare ("great burgers"); the "gracious" staff is another reason boosters think it's a "cut above."

Mona Lisa (Stamford)   21 17 19 $32
133 Atlantic St. (Main St.), 203-348-1070
☑ "Even La Gioconda would smile" over this Stamford Italian where "proud" chef-owner Luciano Magliulo's cooks all the "unconventional" entrees and "visits every table"; it's "low-key", "pleasant" and a block from the theaters.

Monica's Restaurant (Stamford)   18 8 18 $23
323 Shippan Ave., 203-359-0678
■ Forget the "diner-like" looks, it's a "friendly" Stamford Italian with a "wide selection" of "wonderful", "fresh" pastas made on the premises; higher prices at night prompt budget-watchers to call it "great for lunch."

Moody's Bar & Grill (Darien) S   – – – E
390 Post Rd. (I-95, exit 13), 203-655-6549
A new breed of steakhouse with the usual beef lineup but also lighter fare such as grilled poultry, veal dishes and fish specialties; first reports are calling it "another high star" in Fairfield County; N.B. a few get moody after seeing the "prices" of some entrees.

Mooring, The (Mystic) ⑤   ▽ 16 | 18 | 17 | $29 |
Mystic Hilton, 20 Coogan Blvd. (I-95, exit 90), 860-572-0731
◼ A Mystic Traditional American– seafooder frequented
by hotel guests and families; there's a "great view" and
"central location" that make up for fare that's mostly "typical"
aside from standout "lobster"; "it gets rather noisy in the
bar area" where you can hear piano music on weekends.

Mumbo Jumbo (New Canaan) ⑤   – | – | – | M |
12-14 Forest St. (East Ave.), 203-966-5303
A New Canaan eatery with wild and crazy decor and a
melange of Italian offerings from standard pizzas and
meatballs and spaghetti, to such grown-up favorites as
penne alla vodka and baked goat cheese salad.

Murasaki (Simsbury) ⑤   – | – | – | M |
Fiddler's Green, 10 Wilcox St. (Rte. 10), 860-651-7929
For "innovative" sushi and sashimi this Japanese is the
"very best" Simsbury has to offer; it can be "inconsistent"
but it's still "better" and "less expensive" than competitors.

Museum Cafe at the   – | – | – | M |
Wadsworth Atheneum
(Hartford) ⑤
600 Main St. (Atheneum Sq. N.), 860-728-5989
For a winning combo spend the day perusing the galleries
at the Wadsworth, America's oldest public art museum, and
then stop by the cafe where you'll find a tricultural blend
of American, European and Asian cuisines.

Mystic Pizza (Mystic) ⑤   16 | 12 | 16 | $13 |
56 W. Main St. (Bank St.), Mystic, 860-536-3700
Mystic Pizza 2 (N. Stonington) ⑤
Rte. 184 (I-95, exit 92), 860-599-5126
◼ "Stick to the movie" advise those "disappointed" with this
"touristy" pizzeria that's nevertheless been "hyped" enough
to spawn a second parlor in North Stonington; while a few
give at least one thumb up for "very good" pies, more agree
they're just "so-so" – although the "curious" film fan may
have "fun" at this "joint with pictures of Julia Roberts."

Netto's (Mansfield Depot) ⑤   – | – | – | M |
57 Middle Tpke./Rte. 44, 860-429-3663
This "neat" restored authentic caboose situated in a former
Vermont train depot makes a perfect whistle-stop in the
state's quiet corner for "above-average" American-Italian
served by a "friendly" staff.

Nistico's Red Barn (Westport) ⑤   13 | 18 | 15 | $31 |
292 Wilton Rd. (Merritt Pkwy., exit 41), 203-222-9549
◼ "Sit by the fire in winter" at this Westport Continental
"loaded with charm" and "Yankee decor"; but aside from
a few nods for the "Sunday brunch", the fare is labeled
"boring", "mediocre" and "overpriced for what you get";
"pity, with such an attractive setting."

North Cove Express (Essex)   – | – | – | E
Valley RR Station (Rte. 9), 800-398-7427
All aboard for a train trip along the Connecticut River from Essex north to Gilette's Castle; along the way you'll dine on Traditional American fare prepared fresh in the kitchen car while enjoying the views, taking part in a murder mystery or listening to a barbershop quartet; call ahead for seasonal schedule and departure times.

Oasis Diner (Hartford) ◐⧆   ▽ 18 | 18 | 19 | $18
267 Farmington Ave. (Laurel St.), 860-241-8200
■ "Betty and Veronica" would feel right at home in this "upscale" Hartford diner styled with '50s iconography; it's good for a relaxing, "nostalgic" "Sunday dinner" of meat loaf and vegetables or a "late-night bowl of mashed potatoes"; N.B. in the basement is Pancho's, a Mexican restaurant by the same owner.

Old Lyme Inn (Old Lyme) ⧆   22 | 22 | 22 | $39
85 Lyme St./Rte. 1 (Halls Rd.), 860-434-2600
■ "Grandpa would love" this "quiet", "quaint" Old Lyme New England inn ("where the men lunch") for its "big portions" of "no-nonsense", "simply presented" American cooking; the "luscious" desserts leave some insisting it's worth a detour off I-95.

Oliver's Taverne (Essex) ⧆   ▽ 13 | 14 | 15 | $20
Rte. 153 (I-95, exit 65), 860-767-2633
■ The late-night menu and Essex locale make this pub "convenient" for "standard" burgers, sandwiches and chile; there's a "noisy" sports bar upstairs.

Olive Tree, The (Woodbury) ⧆   ▽ 20 | 19 | 19 | $30
Barclay Sq., 20 Sherman Hill Rd. (Rtes. 6 & 64),
203-263-4555
■ A Woodbury Continental with "pleasant" decor, "creative sandwiches" and "moderate prices"; critics say give the prime rib a try.

ONDINE (Danbury) ⧆   24 | 22 | 22 | $40
69 Pembroke Rd./Rte. 37 (Wheeler Dr.), 203-746-4900
■ For an "unexpected" "knockout", reviewers suggest trying this "pretty" Danbury Contemporary French with a prix fixe ($42) that's a "great value"; it's a "very old-fashioned" dining experience that could "compete with NYC's best" and is "a safe bet in a city with few choices."

One Way Fare (Simsbury) ◐⧆   ▽ 18 | 20 | 15 | $16
4 Railroad St. (Iron Horse Blvd.), 860-658-4477
◪ Located in an old Simsbury train station, this "noisy", "comfy", "real local's place" serves "heavy" Traditional American fare and "pub grub" like "great chile burgers"; another way is "go to drink."

Onion Alley (Westport) S   15 | 15 | 15 | $22
42 Main St. (Post Rd.), 203-226-0794
◪ A Downtown Westport Traditional American that's a
"convenient", "casual lunch spot" for a "solid", "energizing"
"quick bite"; more demanding types gripe about "greasy"
food and "inattentive", "local kids" as servers.

Orem's Diner (Wilton) S   13 | 8 | 14 | $15
209 Danbury Rd./Rte. 7 (Rte. 33), 203-762-7370
◪ A Wilton Greek diner that's been around since the '20s;
boosters think it "should go on forever" for "plain cooking
done very well" (omelets, french fries, egg salad); detractors
say it's "typical" so "why bother unless you're desperate."

Osaka (West Hartford) S   – | – | – | M
962A Farmington Ave., 860-233-1877
Blue and mauve decor and cherry wood tables create a
soft, soothing environment at this West Hartford Center
Japanese with a wide selection of sushi; P.S. we hear
high praise for the fried ice cream.

Oscar's (Westport) S⊟   16 | 8 | 11 | $14
159 Main St. (Rte. 1), 203-227-3705
◪ A "cramped" kosher-style deli in Westport that's
well-positioned for "people-watching" on Main Street;
the bagels and cream cheese and Hebrew National hot
dogs are praised but the decor "needs a renovation" as
does the "NY-style" service.

Oxford House (Oxford) S   ▽ 14 | 17 | 14 | $27
441 Oxford Rd./Rte. 67 (Rte. 8, exit 22 or Rte. 84, exit 15),
203-888-6241
◪ "Comfortable gentry charm" awaits you at this landmark
Oxford inn (1795) serving Continental fare; the consensus
is that you go for the "New England setting" and not the
"decent" but "typical banquet" vittles.

Oyster House   18 | 16 | 17 | $29
(Rowayton) S (CLOSED)
148 Rowayton Ave. (Rte. 136), 203-855-0025
◪ Located in a small Cape Cod–like town on the river, this
American seafooder is called "more bar than food"; while
"there's not much ambiance" it's a "good meeting place"
especially for "informal lunches"; if you're going to get
serious with the menu, readers recommend one of the
"trendy pastas or fish specials" and the apple crisp.

PACI RESTAURANT (Southport) S   24 | 25 | 22 | $39
96 Station St. (Pequot Ave.), 203-259-9600
◼ One of the "best new spots" in Fairfield County, this
Italian "gem" in a "very open" restored railroad terminal
("Philippe Starck–style", "gorgeous blonde wood") has
"outstanding" fish dishes and desserts; fans "even like the
trains running by", however a few say it's too expensive.

Panda Pavilion ⑤   16 | 14 | 16 | $22
Grand Union Shopping Ctr., 923 Post Rd. (I-95, exit 22),
Fairfield, 203-259-9777
137 W. Putnam Ave. (bet. Deerfield & Broadside Drs.),
Greenwich, 203-869-1111
370 Main Ave./Rte. 7 (Merritt Pkwy., exit 40), Norwalk,
203-846-4253
1300 Post Rd. E. (Morningside Dr.), Westport, 203-255-3988
■ A minichain serving what most think is "reliable" if
"formula" Chinese that's "just what you expect for the
prices"; regulars say bring the kids and "sit by the fish
tanks" but don't get too comfortable because service
tends to be rushed; N.B. they're popular for "on-time"
delivery and takeout.

Pane Vino (Westport) ⑤   21 | 16 | 20 | $34
1431 Post Rd. E. (bet. Turkey Hill Rd. & Maple Ave.),
203-255-1153
■ For "delicious", "well-seasoned" "pasta, pasta, pasta",
and "attentive" service, reviewers say head to this "small",
"crowded" Italian bistro in Westport that's "worth the
squeeze"; it's "modest" but "pleasing."

Pantry, The (Washington Depot)   22 | 17 | 17 | $21
5 Titus Rd. (Rte. 47), 860-868-0258
■ The "Litchfield horsey set" enjoys the "excellent"
breakfasts and lunches at this American-Eclectic that oozes
"NYC sophistication in the country"; "since the baked goods
always smell delicious" many grab a few to go; N.B. be
prepared to sit among "kitchen tchotchkes" that are for sale.

Paradise Bar & Grille   ▽ 18 | 23 | 16 | $26
(Stamford) ⑤
78 Southfield Ave., 203-323-1116
■ A Stamford Contemporary American with a "wonderful"
waterside location and harbor view; while it's a "hot spot"
in summer for its "vacation" ambiance, a few gripe that the
menu "needs to be more varied and the chef more creative."

Pasta Garden (Stamford) ⑤   17 | 14 | 15 | $25
20 Summer St. (Main St.), 203-324-5071
■ A "family-style" Italian where "Bill Clinton had lunch"
during a campaign stop in Stamford; they serve "huge
portions" at "reasonable prices" in a "warm", "comfortable"
setting that's "great for kids or a group"; Republicans still
sour over the election sniff "you get what you pay for."

Pasta Nostra (Norwalk)   23 | 11 | 15 | $32
116 Washington St. (bet. Main & Water Sts.), 203-854-9700
■ Norwalk Italian with homemade pastas and "superb
sauces" in a "busy" no-decor, deli-like setting ("fluorescent
lighting"); while everyone says the food's "fabulous" some
question whether it's worth dealing with the limited hours
(Wednesday–Saturday nights) and "attitude."

Pasta Vera (Greenwich) **S**　　20　13　17　$25
48 Greenwich Ave. (W. Putnam Ave.), 203-661-9705
☑ "Interesting", "innovative" fresh pastas are the lure
at this "very casual", "friendly" Greenwich Italian in a
"phone booth"–sized setting; those less impressed say
"not earth shattering, but acceptable"; N.B. takeout is
a popular option.

Pat's Kountry Kitchen　　18　16　19　$17
(Old Saybrook) **S**
70 Mill Rock Rd. E. (Rte.1), 860-388-4784
■ This "best road stop between New York and Boston" is
a "too-kute-for-words", "moderately priced" American
serving three squares a day of "basic home cooking";
although there are a few warnings about "mediocre lunch
and dinner", the "great breakfasts", complete with legendary
hash, are "not to be missed."

Pearl of Budapest (Fairfield) **S** ▽ 21　18　20　$26
57 Unquowa Rd. (Post Rd. & RR station), 203-259-4777
■ A Fairfield "family-run" Hungarian with "authentic",
"stick-to-your-ribs" fare that's "lovingly prepared" and
"elegantly served" by a "friendly" staff in a "quaint",
"charming" "walk-back-in-time" setting; it's a "welcome
addition" to Fairfield Center.

Pellicci's (Stamford) ●**S**　　16　10　16　$24
96-98 Stillwater Ave. (bet. Rte. 1 & Broad St.), 203-323-2542
☑ This "loud" and "boisterous" "mom and pop" Italian
pizzeria has been serving "family-style" portions for 50
years; while most praise "real home cooking" that's a
"good value", especially for families, dissenters argue it's
"past its prime" and there's "too much competition."

PEPPERCORN'S GRILL　　25　21　22　$31
(Hartford) **S**
*357 Main St. (bet. Capital Ave. & Buckingham St.),
860-547-1714*
☑ A "busy", "informal" Downtown Hartford Italian "small
gem" that's a "consistent" performer for "delightfully
different", "creative" fare from a "strong nouvelle kitchen";
everyone applauds the "friendly staff" and "handsome"
renovation that "must have cost a fortune" but a few find
the "noise" a "drawback"; N.B. they reportedly have a
"great wine" list.

Peppermill (Westport) **S**　　16　14　17　$25
*1700 Boston Post Rd. (border of Fairfield & Westport),
203-259-8155*
☑ An "ages-old" seafood-steakhouse in Westport that
serves "huge quantities" of "typical" but "reliable" dishes;
there's a "warm and pleasant" staff plus "reasonable"
prices that make it "even more delicious"; the "shabby"
decor could use a sprucing up.

Pequot Grill (Ledyard) ◐S   – – – M
Foxwoods Casino, Rte. 2, 860-885-3176
It's a sure bet that this American at the Foxwoods Casino
is a good breather between gambling binges; critics say
"creative chefs" serve "ample" portions at "fair" prices
in a "lovely" setting; the wait is "long" but once seated,
you're "never rushed."

Per Bacco! Ristorante (Wilton)   20 16 19 $37
142 Old Ridgefield Rd. (opp. Wilton Library), 203-762-5777
■ A Wilton "hard-to-find" Italian in a "quiet" storefront
setting that's "warm" and "cozy"; the fare's called
"delightful, delicious, delovely" and worth searching out.

Piccolo Arancio (Farmington)   ▽ 24 19 22 $35
819 Farmington Ave. (Rtes. 4 & 10), 860-674-1224
☑ This sibling of Peppercorn's, a "creative" Farmington
Italian, has a loyal following for its "out-of-this-world"
veal and tuna dishes; the "stylish" interior is "handsomely
refurbished", with added seating; throw in a staff that's
"caring" and you see why it makes a "special treat."

Pierpont's (Hartford) S   ▽ 24 25 23 $38
*Goodwin Hotel, 1 Haynes St. (bet. Anne & Asylum Sts.),
860-522-4935*
■ A Contemporary American menu in a "luxurious",
Downtown Hartford hotel dining room wins praise for
"beautifully prepared", "interesting choices" including
"healthy options"; service is "exceptional."

Playwright Restaurant, The   ▽ 16 15 17 $23
(Stamford) S
488 Summer St. (bet. Broad & Spring Sts.), 203-353-1120
■ Our own authors say this "large", "friendly, Irish-style
pub" in Downtown Stamford has lots of "noise", "smoke"
and "typical appetizer" grub; the "youthful clientele"
sees it as a place to "hang out", listen to bands, and have
"good times" with friends.

Plum Tree Japanese Restaurant   21 20 16 $30
(New Canaan) S
70 Main St. (Locust St.), 203-966-8050
☑ A "delightful", "delicious" surprise awaits sushi lovers
in New Canaan at this "elegant" Japanese complete with
outdoor rock and bamboo garden and indoor fish pond
with Japanese koi; the only gripes are over service which
is fine "if you have hours to wait."

Portofino (Wilton) S⇗   19 17 18 $28
10 Center St. (Rte. 106), 203-761-9115
■ No reservations and no credit cards can't keep the
"family" crowd away from this "reliable" Italian in Wilton,
known for "well-priced", "tasty" food; some say the menu
is "too limited", but add that the "friendly" staff makes it a
"fun place" to eat and drink; N.B. "great take-out pizza."

Post Corner Pizza (Darien) ◐⑤   16 | 10 | 14 | $16 |
847 Post Rd. (Mansfield Ave.), 203-655-7721
Post Corner Pizza III (Westport) ◐⑤ 18 | 16 | 16 | $29 |
1495 Post Rd. E., 203-256-1575
☑ Packed nightly, these Med-Greek pizzerias are a
"serviceable" "port in a storm" for tot-toters ("more high
chairs than pizza toppings") looking for "great pies" and
"big salads"; expect "plain decor", weak service and an
early evening rush; N.B. takeout is an option.

Prezzo (New Canaan) ⑤   18 | 16 | 16 | $29 |
2 Forest St. (East Ave. & Main St.), 203-972-7666
■ A "cool", "smart-looking" too "noisy" Italian in New
Canaan with "enormous servings" from an "innovative"
menu, and solid standards such as thin-crust pizzas and
spaghetti with clam sauce.

Prince of Wales (Norwich) ⑤   – | – | – | E |
Norwich Inn & Spa, 607 W. Thames St./Rte. 32, 860-886-2401
Not many reviewers know about this Continental located
in a luxurious inn and health spa in NE Connecticut; the
healthy food from the spa menu and beautiful setting will
hasten your rejuvenation.

Promis (Westport)   – | – | – | M |
1563 Post Rd. E., 203-256-3309
It has promise, say locals of this recently opened Continental
on the Westport/Fairfield border; while "every plate is a
work of art" a few grumble about the lack of decor and
service that varies; "give it time" to work out the kinks.

Pub and Restaurant, The   ▽ 19 | 21 | 18 | $22 |
(Norfolk) ⑤
Station Pl. (Rte. 8 N. & Rte. 44 W.), 860-542-5716
■ A local watering hole in rural Connecticut that seems to
have it all: "fine" American food, lots of "beautiful" brick
and stained glass, "friendly" owners and the area's greatest
beer selection (200 brews); it's all "really good."

Quattro Pazzi ⑤   23 | 13 | 17 | $27 |
1599 Post Rd. (Reef Rd. & Ruane St.), Fairfield, 203-259-7417
245 Hope St. (Rockspring & Colonial), Stamford, 203-964-1801
■ "They're heavy into pastas" at this Italian where "long
waits", a "limited menu", "mediocre service" and "a clumsy
seating arrangement" are outweighed by "huge portions"
of "quality" dishes from an "accommodating cook", at a
"reasonable cost"; P.S. the Fairfield location is new.

Ragamont Inn (Salisbury) ⑤⇗   22 | 19 | 21 | $37 |
8 Main St./Rte. 44 (Rte. 22, 5 mi. west of Millerton), 860-435-2372
☑ The building housing this "quaint" country inn has been
a Salisbury landmark for almost 200 years, and although a
few say it's "tired" and could use a "spiffing up" all agree
the Swiss-German fare is "excellent", the service "prompt"
and summer dining on the patio "delightful."

Ralph 'n' Rich's (Bridgeport)   ▽ 23 | 17 | 20 | $29
121 Wall St. (bet. Main & Middle Sts.), 203-366-3597
■ Forget the "terrible" Downtown Bridgeport neighborhood and "plain dining room" and embrace the "surprisingly good" Italian-Continental that a few think is some of the best in town; throw in "great" service and you see why it's recommended as a "good choice" for the theater crowd.

RANDALL'S ORDINARY   21 | 24 | 21 | $36
(N. Stonington) S
Rte. 2 (I-95, exit 92), 860-599-4540
■ There's nothing ordinary about this national landmark inn (1685) and Traditional American in North Stonington where the staff wears period costumes and the "authentic" Colonial American fare is cooked over an original open hearth; despite a "limited menu" it's a "unique experience not to be missed"; N.B. dinner is a "reasonable" ($30) prix fixe and, for extra fun, call ahead to get the hayride schedule.

Rattlesnake Southwestern Grill S 13 | 15 | 15 | $20
106 Federal Rd. (I-84, exit 7), Danbury, 203-794-1000
2-4 S. Main St. (I-95, exit 4), South Norwalk, 203-852-1716
◩ Slither in for a "large" menu of "gimmicky" SW-American in a "kid-friendly" environment (crayons provided); a handful call it "innovative" but more hiss at "inexperienced" help serving chow that's "dry and tough as a rattlesnake"; N.B. the theme bar is called a "kitschy pick-up joint."

Red Lion Belzoni Grill   ▽ 13 | 14 | 13 | $27
(Ridgefield) S
619 Danbury Rd. (Rtes. 35 & 7), 203-438-7454
◩ A "big" and "noisy" Italian conveniently located along Route 7 that's very "family-oriented", right down to the kiddie menu; defenders say "once past the red decor – decent"; bashers say "pedestrian" and "forget it."

Rein's NY Style Deli-Restaurant   19 | 10 | 16 | $15
(Vernon) ◕ S
Shops at 30 Plaza, 435 Hartford Tpke. (I-84, exit 65), 860-875-1344
■ "Jewish road food" is offered at this "noisy" Vernon "last outpost of deli-dom" for I-84 travelers heading north; it gets a "steady stream of New Yorkers" craving "big" portions of "real" deli fare, and is "well worth a stop off the highway."

RESTAURANT AT   24 | 26 | 23 | $48
NATIONAL HALL (Westport) S
(fka Restaurant Zanghi)
Inn at National Hall, 2 Post Rd. W. (Rte. 33), 203-221-7572
■ "Watch for Redford and Newman" at this Contemporary American–French on the shores of the Saugatuck River in Westport; it "dazzles" diners with "serious", "fantastic", "imaginative" fare, "impeccable" service and a "romantic" setting that's "refined" ("wear your finery") "without being pretentious"; a few gripe about an "inconsistent" kitchen.

Restaurant Bravo Bravo   ▽ | 26 | 19 | 22 | $35 |
(Mystic) **S**
Whaler's Inn, 18 E. Main St., 860-536-3228
■ "Quaint" Italian-seafood "gem" in Mystic that uses "fresh" ingredients in "interesting" combos; it "can get noisy" and the "wait" can be "long" but reviewers claim it's "like the best of NYC without the pretension."

Restaurant Bricco | – | – | – | M |
(West Hartford) **S**
78 LaSalle Rd. (Farmington Ave.), 860-233-0220
There are lines out the door to sample chef Billy Grant's Mediterranean fare at this West Hartford locale; expect a lively atmosphere, people-watching and an open kitchen.

RESTAURANT DU VILLAGE | 27 | 23 | 24 | $49 |
(Chester) **S**
59 Main St. (Maple St.), 860-526-5301
☑ An "integral part of why Chester couldn't be more charming", this "tiny" (40 seats) French has "excellent" classic and contemporary dishes, a "good wine list", "fine and knowledgeable" service and "personal touches" that make for an "elegant" evening; "a treasure", though there was a small contingent that said "overpriced."

Rib House (East Haven) **S**   ▽ | 20 | 11 | 17 | $20 |
16 Main St. (I-95, exit 51), 203-468-6695
■ East Haven barbecue joint with "great" ribs that make "good, messy eatin'"; a few suggest it's "not as good as it once was" but the staff is "helpful" and the price is still right.

Roberto's Restaurant   ▽ | 17 | 15 | 17 | $22 |
(Monroe) **S**
505 Main St., 203-268-5723
■ Take a "picturesque drive" "in the back country" to this Monroe "basic" Italian that's a "nice place to be taken care of"; families especially enjoy the "big" portions from a wide menu – "love that free broccoli bread."

Rocco's Restaurant (Westport) **S** | 17 | 15 | 18 | $32 |
1330 Post Rd. E., 203-255-1017
☑ A Westport "upscale" Italian that's "been around for a long time"; loyalists appreciate the "excellent selection of veal dishes" and "helpful", "friendly staff"; foes call it "overpriced" and "tired, including the waiters."

ROGER SHERMAN INN | 23 | 25 | 23 | $43 |
(New Canaan) **S**
Roger Sherman Inn, 195 Oenoke Ridge (Homewood Ln.), 203-966-4541
☑ A "formal" New Canaan mainstay, this "plush", "elegant old inn" (1740) has "fresh", "precisely prepared" Continental fare, "first-class" service, a "great porch" and a "romantic" piano bar where you can smoke cigars and sip cognac; a few grumble about food that "should be better" but most think it's "the country inn motif at its best."

Rosy Tomatoes
17 | 14 | 15 | $21
(Greenwich) 🅂 **(CLOSED)**
363 Greenwich Ave. (Fawcett Pl.), 203-622-5138
■ "You pick out your own antipasti" and "design your own pizza" at this "accommodating" and "friendly" Italian with Caesar salads so large "one is enough for two"; the less rosy say "crowded" and "not worth the discomfort"; N.B. the BYO policy makes it "the best dollar value in Greenwich."

Rudy's Restaurant
▽ 19 | 19 | 21 | $31
(New Milford) 🅂🗗
122 Litchfield Rd. (Rte. 202), 860-354-7727
☑ Friendly "Swiss maids" serve a "mature crowd" "quality" food at "fair" prices in an "earthy", "hearty" atmosphere; it's "always a safe bet" and therefore busy on weekends; the less-impressed gibe "if you're silent you can hear the greasy gratin closing your arteries."

Russell's Ribs (Groton) 🅂
– | – | – | M
214 Rte. 12 (I-95, exit 86), 860-445-8849
Most "love" the "greasy" ribs served up at this Groton barbecue joint but a few say just "ok"; when you need a fix they do fine.

Rusty Scupper 🅂
14 | 17 | 15 | $26
501 Long Wharf Dr. (Rte. 91 & I-95, exit 46), New Haven, 203-777-5711
183 Harbor Dr., Stamford, 203-964-1235 **(CLOSED)**
■ Waterfront seafood chain with "great views" eliciting comments such as "with this location, and these crowds, you'd think they could afford a real chef"; nonetheless, the "young crowd" finds them "lots of fun for drinks and appetizers" and the "extensive" Sunday brunch is "ok for your 90-year-old aunt."

Ruth's Chris Steak House
23 | 18 | 21 | $41
(Newington) 🅂
2513 Berlin Tpke. (Kitts Ln.), 860-666-2202
☑ "Buttery", "melt in your mouth" steaks, "great salads", a "good wine list" and service that's "professional to a T" are the draws at this high-end, "cholesterol city" steakhouse; reviewers are less enthusiastic about the "sterile decor", but overall you're getting one of the "best steaks in CT."

Sadler's Ordinary
– | – | – | M
(Marlborough) 🅂
Marlborough Country Barn, 61 N. Main St. (Rte. 66), 860-295-0006
Get "comfortable" in front of one of the roaring fireplaces at this Marlborough locale with both Traditional and Contemporary American fare; it's a "comfy sandwich spot" with an on-premises bakery and a Sunday breakfast that will give you enough energy to visit the repro 19th-century stores surrounding the eatery.

Sakura Japanese Restaurant   19 | 17 | 18 | $28 |
(Westport) S
680 Post Rd. E. (Roseville Ave.), 203-222-0802
☒ Kids love watching the "food showmanship" at the "fun",
"grill tables" of this "always jammed" Westport Japanese
with decor that some call "traditional" and others "ersatz";
there's "good sushi", too

SALLY'S APIZZA (New Haven) S⌀   25 | 9 | 13 | $16 |
237 Wooster St. (Olive St.), 203-624-5271
■ "Best pizza in the universe but the staff treats you like
dirt" sums up the highs and lows of this venerable New
Haven institution and arch rival of Pepe's serving "fantastic
pies" with "luscious tomato sauce" "for purists"; many
note "lines are a problem", but resigned fanatics shrug:
"be prepared to wait but know it's the real thing."

San Miguel Restaurant   ▽ 15 | 15 | 15 | $28 |
(Bethel) S
8 P. T. Barnum Sq. (Greenwood Ave./Rte. 302), 203-748-2396
☒ Our reviewers can't agree on whether it's "really good
Mexican" or just "so-so" but it's been in Bethel for almost
20 years so they must be doing something right; there's
live music on Fridays.

Savannah (Hartford) S   – | – | – | E |
391 Main St. (Capital Ave.), 860-278-2020
You might think Georgia, but this Hartford newcomer is
thinking globally with an Eclectic fusion of cuisines that
equals a "world-class" experience; although "pricey", the
"big-enough-to-share" portions and "inventive", "exciting"
fare make it all worth it.

Saybrook Fish House S   18 | 16 | 17 | $25 |
460 Albany Tpke./Rte. 44 (Rtes. 202 & 179), Canton, 860-693-0034
4137 Whitney Ave. (Rte. 10), Hamden, 203-230-8088
99 Essex Road, Old Saybrook, 860-388-4836
2165 Silas Deane Hwy. (Rte. 91, exit 24), Rocky Hill,
860-721-9188
■ This bustling quartet has "comfortable and plain" "fish
house atmosphere", "very fresh" seafood and "wonderful"
large salads; reviewers especially like the fruit and nut
bowls for dessert; N.B. for an extra value try the $10.95
early-bird special.

Scoozzi Trattoria & Wine Bar   22 | 20 | 20 | $30 |
(New Haven) S
1104 Chapel St. (York St.), 203-776-8268
■ The "beautiful people" frequent this "wonderful"
contemporary Italian bistro in New Haven that's perfect
for pre- or post Yale Repertory performances; there's
"caring service", a large antipasti bar, an outdoor patio
and a cigar-friendly environment; what's more, it's "always
trying to better itself."

Scribner's (Milford) **S**   22 | 15 | 18 | $31
31 Village Rd. (King's Hwy.), 203-878-7019
☑ Despite a "depressing", "dim" atmosphere and "slow service", locals "can't get enough" of the "great" lobsters and steamers and "excellent" fish at this Milford seafooder; a few counter – "mediocre at best."

Seaman's Inne   15 | 18 | 15 | $29
Restaurant & Pub (Mystic) **S**
105 Greenmanville Ave. (I-95, exit 90), 860-536-9649
☑ "Convenient" for "tourists" visiting the Seaport, this American-seafooder serves "ok" chow; but, there's a "cool view", "interesting" decor and a staff in "period costumes"; try Sunday brunch or an off-season visit.

Seascape (Stratford) **S**   ▽ 13 | 15 | 17 | $23
14 Beach Dr. (Washington Pkwy.), 203-375-2149
■ The view from this Stratford seafooder is "great", but afishionados find the food "fair at best"; at least the prix fixe Sunday brunch is inexpensive.

Seasons (Avon) **S**   ▽ 23 | 22 | 21 | $33
Avon Old Farms Hotel, Rtes. 10 & 44, 860-677-1651
■ A restaurant for all seasons, this Avon Traditional American has "delicious" fare, a "lovely" and "surprisingly romantic" atmosphere and a staff that "tries hard to please"; it's recommended for a "very enjoyable" brunch.

Sesame Seed (Danbury) ⊅   20 | 15 | 16 | $21
68 W. Wooster St. (Division St.), 203-743-9850
■ The "dusty antiques" make you feel like you're "dining in grandmother's attic" at this "unassuming", "pleasantly quirky", "overcrowded" Middle Eastern in Danbury; it boasts a "healthy" veggie-friendly menu that's a "great value."

Sfizio Ristorante (Bridgeport)   ▽ 18 | 13 | 19 | $29
746 Madison Ave. (Wheeler Ave.), 203-367-4640
■ "Truly authentic" Italian "jewel" in Downtown Bridgeport that earns warm applause for "wonderful family" ambiance, "special" service and "reasonable" prices.

Shady Glen **S** ⊅   ▽ 23 | 17 | 21 | $10
360 W. Middle Tpke. (Rte. 84), Manchester, 860-643-0511
840 E. Middle Tpke. (Rte. 84), Manchester, 860-649-4245 ☽
■ The famed cheeseburgers, crispy cheese and milk shakes at these long-time Manchester Traditional Americans are "folklore" with locals and generations of UConn students; they're "booth-and-counter" settings that "keep improving."

Shell Station (Stratford) **S**   ▽ 19 | 16 | 18 | $25
Main St. (RR station), 203-377-1648
■ Don't let passing trains ("rattle your teeth") deter you from visiting this "creative", "high-quality" Japanese feeding locals at the Stratford train station for 20 years; there's "basic" decor but "lots of seafood" and a "friendly staff."

Shish Kebab House   – | – | – | **M**
of Afghanistan (Hartford)
360 Franklin Ave. (bet. Bushnell & Preston Sts.), 860-296-0301
Forget the trek to the Big Apple for Afghan; kebab-heads
say this Downtown Hartford eatery is "as good as NYC" and
a "great" value that's "always enjoyable" when you're in
the mood for spicy lamb, chicken and rice dishes.

Siam Rialto (South Norwalk) **S** ▽ 19 | 16 | 17 | $25
128 Washington St. (Maritime Ctr.), 203-855-7855
■ There's solid service and a "nice selection" of "better
than average" Thai at "reasonable" prices at this "plain"
South Norwalk locale.

Sidetracks (Fairfield) **S**   13 | 13 | 15 | $20
2070 Post Rd. (S. Pine Creek), 203-254-3606
◪ Supporters of this Traditional American in Fairfield call
it a "great family" spot – "wings are a must"; detractors
say don't get sidetracked 'cause they serve "ordinary"
pub food at what's basically a "pickup joint with nachos."

SILVERMINE TAVERN (Norwalk) **S** 16 | 24 | 18 | $33
194 Perry Ave. (Silvermine Ave.), 203-847-4558
◪ This "lovely" old Norwalk inn with fireplaces in winter
and a "beautiful", "peaceful" deck in summer has what
everyone agrees is an enviable location; but the "plain"
Traditional American is at best "satisfactory"; a few
defenders say the kitchen's "finally recovering" from a
"disastrous rep" and suggest you try the sticky buns.

SIMSBURY 1820 HOUSE   21 | 25 | 23 | $32
(Simsbury)
731 Hopmeadow St., 860-658-7658
■ Enter this Traditional American "time capsule" and
"return to a more gracious era" for a "fine", "comfortable"
"relaxing meal in front of a huge fireplace"; a few call it
"a letdown" but more say "first-rate in all respects."

64 Greenwich Avenue   21 | 22 | 19 | $39
(Greenwich) **S**
64 Greenwich Ave. (E. Putnam Ave.), 203-861-6400
◪ "Important business people" and "gorgeous" "yuppies"
head to this "noisy" and "trendy" Greenwich New American
with seasonal menus, "homemade breads and pastas"
and generally "excellent" "fussed-over" dishes; there's
"attentive" service from an "efficient" staff.

Sloppy Jose's (Milford) **S**   ▽ 17 | 14 | 17 | $19
186 Hillside Ave. (Merwin Ave.), 203-878-9847
◪ This Milford south-of-the-border has been around for
20 years, but patrons still can't agree if the food is
"outstanding" or a "poor excuse for Mexican"; they do
agree that the "noise is off the meter", the margaritas and
salsa are "musts", the service could be better, and the bill
will have you shouting olé!

Snowpea Restaurant (Fairfield) **S** ⁻|⁻|⁻| M
2480 Black Rock Tpke., 203-374-6868
Not too many of our reviewers have discovered this local
Chinese hidden in the corner of a Fairfield strip mall; those
who have find it pleasing on all counts due to a "light and
airy" interior, "large" portions of "good" multiregional
fare and "friendly" staff.

SOLE E LUNA RISTORANTE TUSCANO (Westport) **S** 21|21|19|$39
25 Powers Ct. (Post Rd.), 203-222-3837
■ A "noisy" celeb-packed "casual" Italian near the
Westport theater that's now under new management and
ownership; most praise their efforts: "has it all together",
"continues as a superior place", "talented new chef",
although a few worry that service has "slipped"; "expensive
but worth it" is the consensus.

Somers Inn Restaurant (Somers) **S** ⁻|⁻|⁻| M
585 Main St. (Rtes. 83 & 190), 860-749-2256
A 200-year-old rural historic inn serving Traditional
American comfort fare such as prime rib, chicken and to-
die-for cheesecake; bring along the kids because they
rate their own menu.

Sono Seaport Seafood, Inc. (South Norwalk) **S** 16|13|13|$22
100 Water St., 203-854-9483
■ "Say the name three times fast" then head to the "fun"
outdoor deck of this South Norwalk seafooder overlooking
the Sound; sip a brew and slowly take in the view because
there are long waits for "cheap" lobster eaten with
"paper and plastic."

Southport Brewing Co. (Southport) **S** ⁻|⁻|⁻| M
2600 Post Rd./Rte. 1 (Bronson Rd.), 203-256-2337
A casual, noisy Southport watering hole with the usual
pub food lineup of burgers, pizzas, and salads plus house
specialties such as pork loin and Maryland crab cakes;
some complain about terminally slow service.

Spazzi Trattoria (Fairfield) **S** 21|18|18|$32
1229 Post Rd. (bet. Beach & Unquowa Rds.), 203-256-1629
■ This "bustling" Fairfield Italian bistro is a "garlic lover's
Eden" that has an "open kitchen" so the "odors keep
coming"; boosters (the majority) say "they try harder" and
"everyone has a smile" when digging into the "wonderful
bread"; naysayers gripe its "reputation exceeds reality."

Spinell's Litchfield Food Company (Litchfield) S   – | – | – | M |
39 West St. (South & Meadow Sts.), 860-567-3113
A popular choice for "casual" eating overlooking the
Litchfield green, this American serves "delicious", "top-
quality" dishes that travel well as takeout; hard-core
followers can't get enough of the goods from the on-site
bakery, especially the wonderful breads.

Spinning Wheel Inn (Redding) S   18 | 23 | 20 | $32 |
107 Black Rock Tpke. (Giles Hill), 203-938-2511
◪ An increase in ratings supports those who say this
"lovely" country inn gets "better every time" and is a "good"
choice for traditional "Yankee" cooking; there's "attentive"
service and it's a "must" when the holiday decorations
are up; nonbelievers insist it's "unreliable" and suggest
you hold off "until you've been invited to a wedding."

Splash! A Spirited Bar & Grill   – | – | – | E |
(Southbury) S
Heritage Inn, Heritage Rd. (I-84, exit 15), 203-264-8200
If you can "tolerate" the noise at this bar and grill in
Southbury, there's typical American pub fare in an art deco
setting; it's truly casual, and cigar lovers can puff away.

Splash Pacific Rim Grill   22 | 21 | 18 | $36 |
(Westport) S
Inn at Longshore, 260 S. Compo Rd. (Greens Farms Rd.),
203-454-7798
◪ This "trendy" Pacific Rim sibling of Greenwich's Baang
has made a "splash" on the Westport restaurant scene
with "innovative" cuisine served family-style so groups
"share" the wealth; it's "loud and crowded" with a "great"
location on the water and decor that'll require you to "wear
shades"; "semirude" service draws the only boos.

Sprouts Café (Fairfield) S   – | – | – | M |
2057 Black Rock Tpke. (Stilson Rd.), 203-333-3571
This organic foods cafe sprouted up on busy Black Rock
Turnpike a year ago and has already moved to larger digs
across the street; part cafe/part store, the eclectic selection
of foods appeals to vegetarians and nonveggies alike who
view it as a wonderful stop "for lunch" or a take-home dinner.

Stagecoach Hill Inn   – | – | – | E |
(Sheffield, MA) S
Stagecoach Hill Inn, 854 Rte. 41 (Rte. 23 E.), 413-229-8585
Since 1829 this New England landmark inn, just over the
border, has been serving weary travelers "delicious"
American fare; loyalists "keep going back" because they're
"in love with its charm."

85

Steak Loft (Mystic) S 16 15 15 $26
Old Mystic Village, Rte. 27, 860-536-2661
☑ For "uncomplicated" beef and salad this "steakhouse mill" is a convenient rest stop when heading to the Cape; there are "reasonable" prices and "fast" service in a "busy", "noisy" and kid-friendly "barn" atmosphere; those "disappointed" are "hoping it gets better."

STEVE'S CENTERBROOK CAFÉ 25 20 23 $36
(Centerbrook) S
78 Main St., 860-767-1277
■ "A must if going to the Goodspeed Opera", this New American is another example of why chef-owner Steve Wilkinson's cooking "never misses"; it continues "going strong" with "excellent", "creative" fare, "delightful" atmosphere, a "friendly" staff and an "affordable" bill; P.S. check out the special 15-bottles-at-$15 wine list.

STONEHENGE (Ridgefield) S 25 27 25 $49
Stonehenge Inn, 35 Stonehenge Rd. (Rte. 7), 203-438-6511
■ Newcomers to Christian Bertrand's "classic" Ridgefield Continental–New French next to a pond consider it a culinary "discovery" akin to its namesake; there's "outstanding" classic dishes such as "excellent rack of lamb", more "up-to-date" selections and a "formal", "attentive" staff; it's certain to "impress your friends."

Su Casa Restaurant ∇ 17 15 15 $21
(Branford) S
400 E. Main St. (Featherbed Ln.), 203-481-5001
☑ A south-of-the-border veteran that always draws mixed reviews: loyalists praise "plain and simple" but "above-average" fare in an "exciting atmosphere with live music"; detractors bemoan "another overrated Mexican" with "not much to compare it to"; N.B. "the hot salsa is the best, but you have to ask for it."

Sunrise Pizza Cafe S 19 11 16 $17
211 Liberty Sq. (Seaside Ave.), Norwalk, 203-838-0166
299 Long Ridge Rd. (Merritt Pkwy., exit 34), Stamford, 203-348-3433
☑ "Lovable little places" for thin-crust, "designer", "mix-and-match" pizzas, salads, sandwiches and pasta; despite "nothing fancy" decor they're called "great places to relax" after work.

Sunset Grille (East Norwalk) S ∇ 18 20 18 $28
52 Calf Pasture Beach Rd. (Norwalk Cove Marina), 203-866-4177
☑ Visitors to this waterside East Norwalk Italian-seafooder say there's "nothing better" than trying it at sunset for al fresco dining; the limited menu is a "good value" that "sometimes has outstanding dishes" but also can be "ordinary"; N.B. it's "owned by NFL great Vince Promuto."

Taj Mahal (Riverside) **(CLOSED)** ▽ 23 20 21 $31
1114 E. Putnam Ave. (next to Howard Johnson's),
203-698-2952
☑ "Who would have thought the best Indian would be next door to a Howard Johnson's?"; take a "magic carpet into the realm of good Indian" at this Greenwich outpost that combines a "beautiful atmosphere" with a "$9.95 lunch special"; a few doubters say the food's only "so-so", but they're outvoted.

Tapas (West Hartford) **S**   ▽ 20 10 17 $18
1150 New Britain Ave. (Quaker Ln. & Mayflower St.),
860-521-4609
■ Don't let the "savage exterior" or "sardine-can space" of this "hard-to-describe" West Hartford Mediterranean–Middle Eastern stop you from discovering "very fresh" (no freezer), "very tasty" fare that's easy on the wallet.

Tartaglia's (Bridgeport) **S**   ▽ 21 16 20 $21
1439 Madison Ave. (Robin St.), 203-576-1281
Tartaglia's of Derby (Derby) **S**
285 Main St. (Rte. 34), 203-734-2462
■ "Good", basic "hearty" Italians serving nice-sized portions of "family-style food"; while they don't aim to be nouvelle a few still quibble that they "lack imagination"; the separately owned Derby location, in an old bank building complete with vaults, is "more attractive."

Tartufo (Southbury) **S**   ▽ 21 24 24 $38
900 Main St. S., 203-262-8001
■ "One of the most romantic" Italians in the state, this "quiet" Southbury locale with working fireplaces is known for "delicious", "nicely presented" dishes and a "pleasant" staff; it's perfect for "special occasions" or Sunday brunch; N.B. jackets, though not required, are preferred.

Tavern on Main (Westport) **S**   21 20 19 $33
146 Main St., 2nd fl. (Post Rd.), 203-221-7222
☑ "Lovely sloping wood floors" are part of the "warm and homey", "New England" atmosphere of this Traditional American "surprise" in Downtown Westport; most wonder "what's not to like?" citing "hearty portions" of "tasty" dishes such as "excellent pork loin"; a few grumblers respond that it's "cramped" and "noisy" at night.

Telluride (Stamford) **S**   – – – M
245 Bedford St. (Forest St.), 203-357-7679
We missed it, but our reviewers were quick to point out this "reasonably priced", "lovely" new addition to the Stamford restaurant scene; there's a seasonal "healthy", "innovative menu" of Contemporary American food with Southwest and Vegetarian influences.

Tequila Mockingbird   15 18 17 $25
(New Canaan) **S**
6 Forest St. (East Ave.), 203-966-2222
☑ While the atmosphere at this New Canaan haunt may always be "a Mexican party", appraisals of the kitchen are less upbeat; some insist it's still "good" but others say "stick with drinks" because the quality's "deteriorated"; a drop in the food rating supports the critics.

Terra Mar Grille (Old Saybrook) **S** – – – E
2 Bridge St. (Rte. 154), 860-395-3246
Critics warn that even though the food at this Italian-Continental in Saybrook is generally "good" the decibel level calls for "earplugs"; although a few locals say "it's not like the old days", most think the "charm will win you over."

Terra Ristorante Italiano   21 19 16 $36
(Greenwich) **S**
156 Greenwich Ave. (bet. Elm & Lewis Sts.), 203-629-5222
☑ Luckily, the "chic", "beautiful" crowd that frequents this "crowded" Greenwich Italian views it as a place "to be seen" because it's so "deafeningly noisy" that it's "too loud for conversation"; the "upscale pastas and pizzas" are reportedly "excellent", but some gripe that "you have to be well-known here to be taken care of properly."

Thai Orchid (New Haven) (CLOSED) 19 13 16 $21
1027 State St. (Lawrence St.), 203-624-7173
☑ Although it "doesn't look like much" from the street, this "adventurous" Thai in New Haven is known for "fresh", "flavorful" dishes; the "distracted" staff may account for the significant drop in the service rating since our last *Survey*.

Thataway Café (Greenwich) **S** 14 12 15 $23
10 High St. (Railroad Ave.), 203-622-0947
☑ "A basic burger joint with dreams of being a real restaurant", this "cheap eats" Greenwich Traditional American has a "choice location" ("eat outside") that makes it "good for a quick bite" before a movie or after a day of shopping on the Avenue.

That Little Italian Restaurant – – – M
(Greenwich) **S**
228-230 Mill St. (Henry St.), 203-531-7500
How we missed this little Italian gem in Greenwich we'll never know, but you sure filled us in; the menu is "huge", the dishes "tasty" and "delicious", the portions "perfect" and all at "reasonable" prices; and as the title suggests it's "small" and "cozy" with well-spaced tables; it's "not fancy at all" but that's part of its charm; N.B. be sure to try the bread and baked clams.

Three Bears Restaurant   17 | 20 | 18 | $33
(Westport) **S**
333 Wilton Rd. (Newtown Tpke.), 203-227-7219
☑ An "old low-ceilinged Westport inn" with a large menu of "ok" Traditional and Contemporary American fare; the real attraction is "wonderful", "homey" "Connecticut Yankee atmosphere" including "antique crystal" and "Tiffany lamps"; the unenthused say "undeservedly popular"

Three Brothers (Fairfield) **S**   ▽ 16 | 14 | 16 | $21
601 Kings Hwy. E. (I-95, exit 24), 203-367-5359
☑ A "local" Fairfield Italian labeled a "good value"; but those who want more wish they "would go back to their old menu" and wonder "why do people love this restaurant?"

Tiger Bowl (Westport) **S**   17 | 7 | 15 | $18
1872 Post Rd. E. (Buckley Ave.), 203-255-1799
☑ You won't find tablecloths at this "old time" Westport Chinese, but you will find "cheap", "solid" fare including the usual lineup of "very good" egg rolls and hot and sour soup; a few call it "run of the mill."

Tigin (Stamford) **S**   – | – | – | M
175 Bedford St. (Atlantic St.), 203-353-8444
Tigin means cottage in Gaelic and this new Downtown Stamford pub has Irish antiques, food, drinks and music; N.B. try the boxty – stuffed potato pancakes.

TOLLGATE HILL   21 | 26 | 22 | $36
INN & RESTAURANT (Litchfield) **S**
Rte. 202 & Tollgate Rd., 860-567-4545
■ There's been an improvement in ratings across the board at this Litchfield Traditional American in a "firelight and candlelight", "cozy" "landmark" inn; the atmosphere alone is enough to make it a "memorable and romantic" experience, but with a new chef the food is also deemed "exceptional"; it's becoming "everything a New England inn should be."

Tomiko Japanese Restaurant   ▽ 19 | 15 | 16 | $27
(Wilton) **S**
15 River Rd. (next to Wilton Ctr.), 203-761-6770
☑ "You have to go looking for this" "out-of-the-way" Wilton Japanese but it's worth finding for "beautifully presented", "surprisingly good" dishes that make it a "wonderful addition to the town"; just ignore the "tacky" atmosphere that "feels more like a Chinese restaurant."

Tommy's (Fairfield) **S**   14 | 13 | 16 | $24
1418 Post Rd. (Unquowa Rd.), 203-254-1478
☑ "Nothing special" sums it up for this "dark" Fairfield Center Italian that might be "nice" for "a nibble" but "seems to cater more to serious drinkers than diners."

Torrington Bagels   – – – I
(Torrington) S⊅
689 Main St., 860-482-1773
1758 E. Main St., 860-489-3200
Occasional lines out the door testify to the appeal of the
bagels and sandwiches served at this pleasant Torrington
spot, open daily for breakfast and lunch; soups and salads
round out the offerings; P.S. the east side location is new.

Tributary, The (Winsted) S   ▽ 20 | 15 | 20 | $29
19 Rowley St. (bet. Rte. 44 & Main St.), 860-379-7679
◪ You get a "real neighborhood experience" at this Winsted
local seafooder, but even if you're an out-of-towner "they
still care"; try it for the Thursday night "lobster bargain" or
the Tuesday–Saturday early-bird discount; N.B. the food
rating has improved since our last *Survey*.

Trout Brook Brewery House   – – – M
(Hartford) ◑S
4555 Bartholomew Ave. (Park St.), 860-951-1680
A "bustling" new microbrewery in Hartford on the site
of the old Spaghetti Warehouse; try it for the house
beer, Traditional American fare and live entertainment
on weekend nights.

Truc Orient Express (Hartford) S ▽ 19 | 13 | 17 | $24
735 Wethersfield Ave. (I-91 N., exit 27), 860-296-2818
◪ While once a "landmark" for "authentic" Vietnamese
fare, and still "worth a trip" for "the best duck salad" and
"outstanding crab and asparagus soup", reviewers feel
this Hartford spot has "gone downhill"; still some wish
"we had one in our neighborhood."

Tucson Cafe (Greenwich) S   15 | 16 | 16 | $26
130 E. Putnam Ave./Rte. 1 (Milbank Ave.), 203-661-2483
■ "Margaritaville" meets Greenwich at this Southwestern
where lots of young "willing men and women" gather at
the "noisy", "lively" bar; while it's "not a serious place to
go for food", it can be "decent" for fajitas.

Tuscan Oven Trattoria (Norwalk) S 17 | 18 | 16 | $27
544 Main Ave. (Rte. 7, next to DMV), 203-846-4600
◪ Respondents are mixed on this Norwalk Italian with an
"interesting", "upscale" menu; devotees say the "pizzas
and risotto keep luring me back" but a larger group
yawns – "just ok."

Two Steps Downtown Grill   – – – M
(Danbury) S
5 Ives St. (White St.), 203-794-0032
Set in a restored 1800s firehouse, this Danbury Cajun-
Southwestern serves fiery fare that always delivers; bring
the kids to check out the interesting items hanging from
the ceiling, including memorabilia from the Danbury Fair.

Uncle Dai's (Stamford) **S**   ▽ 18 | 11 | 17 | $20
109 Atlantic St. (Tresser Blvd.), 203-327-5757
▨ The Downtown Stamford lunch crowd call this Chinese "great for lunch" because they have "good food/good prices"; but the "horrible decor" leads some to take out.

Under Mountain Inn (Salisbury) ▽ 19 | 21 | 20 | $42
Under Mountain Inn, 482 Under Mountain Rd. (N. Beaver Dam Rd.), 860-435-0242
▮ When driving through rural Connecticut, head to the NW corner to discover this "small" but "very cozy" inn with good English pub food that's sure to "relax" any road warrior; the owner's Lancashire accent adds to the atmosphere.

UNION LEAGUE CAFE   22 | 24 | 21 | $36
(New Haven) **S**
1032 Chapel St. (bet. Crown & High Sts.), 203-562-4299
▨ An "urban", "clubby" "dowager classic" in Downtown New Haven "within walking distance of Yale"; the French bistro fare is usually "well-executed", there's a "superb wine list" and the "informative" waiters are "always trying hard"; those not in union find it "stuffy" and "overpriced."

USS Chowder Pot **S**   17 | 16 | 17 | $24
560 E. Main St. (I-95, exit 56), Branford, 203-481-2356
165 Brainard Rd. (I-91, exit 27), Hartford, 860-244-3311
▨ "If you're not looking for gourmet" then you might be tempted by the "large portions" of "fair-priced" seafood at this duo; however, despite their popularity ("long waits") many don't take the bait, saying the fish is "pedestrian" and the interior "gimmicky" and "overdecorated."

Valbella! (Riverside) **S**   23 | 20 | 21 | $45
1309 E. Putnam Ave./Rte. 1, 203-637-1155
▮ "Wow, what a place"; this "yuppie heaven" is a "noisy", "warm" and "friendly" Riverside Italian providing "excellent food and service in a room to match"; sure it's "expensive" but when you're sampling "the best shrimp you can find anywhere" you forget cost.

Valentino (Stamford) **S**   – | – | – | M
348 Hope St. (Church St., I-95, exit 9), 203-325-9600
An "excellent", "underrated" newcomer to Downtown Stamford "with a very different" Italian menu; service needs fine tuning, but picky eaters note: they "cook to please."

V – A Restaurant & Wine Bar   – | – | – | M
(Westport) **S**
(fka Pompano Oyster Bar and Seafood Grill)
1460 Post Rd. E. (bet. exits 18 & 19), 203-259-1160
Replacing the Pompano Oyster Bar, this new Westport entry features a large menu of Eclectic fare and a 25-dispenser cruvinet for wines by the glass; it attracts a cross-section of diners from young couples to seniors; while it's too early to claim 'V' for culinary victory it looks promising.

Vazzy's (Bridgeport)   – – – M
Beardsley Plaza, 513 Broadbridge Ave. (Huntington Tpke.),
203-371-8046
"Energetic" and "lively", this "friendly" and "inexpensive"
north Bridgeport Italian is a favorite with locals on the
weekend for "great" basic fare; the more subdued can't
deal with the fact that it's "very loud" and say it "needs
a better atmosphere."

Venetian Restaurant   ▽ 19 15 20 $27
(Torrington) **S**
52 E. Main St., 860-489-8592
☑ How do you like your Italian?; if you're a traditionalist
looking for "good gourmet meals", then this long-time
Torrington institution (over 75 years) with "authentic"
Northern and Central Italian dishes is "the place"; nouvelle
types shouldn't worry either because the kitchen is up-to-
date and they cook to order.

Versailles (Greenwich) **S**   22 14 17 $31
315 Greenwich Ave. (Arch St.), 203-661-6634
■ A "small", "quiet" "intimate" patisserie–French bistro
that's perfect for "afternoon tea" and "great" pastries to
make "calorie counters go ballistic"; highlights of the
bistro menu include "delicious quiche" and "onion soup
so good it'll make you cry"; the "plain" decor's not exactly
Versailles but still "pleasant."

Via Sforza Trattoria (Norwalk) **S**   22 18 18 $29
250 Westport Ave. (¼ mi. from Stew Leonard),
203-846-1116
■ "They need better PR" at this "little-known" strip mall
Norwalk Italian that would be right at home "on a street in
Italy"; with "excellent breads" baked on the premises, a
winning ravioli with vodka creme sauce and "efficient,
pleasant waiters", it's a "genuine delight."

Violets Dinner Club (Stamford)   – – – M
261 Main St. (bet. Summer & Clark Sts.), 203-316-0278
Noisy, Cajun-Southwestern in Stamford that's "the place
to be" when the live bands (Tuesday–Sunday) hit the floor.

Viva Zapata Mexican   15 16 15 $22
Restaurant (Westport) **S**
530 Riverside Ave., 203-227-8226
☑ This "popular", "cheap" Mexican in "close quarters"
has been holding down the fort in Westport for 30 years; it
has a busy "pickup" bar scene but reactions to the food
are unenthusiastic – "it shows how much we need good
Mexican when people say this is authentic."

WATER'S EDGE (Westbrook) **S**   22 25 20 $37
Water's Edge Inn, 1525 Post Rd. (I-95, exit 65), 860-399-5901
◪ A "sumptuous", "grand" Westbrook inn, this New
American has a "knockout" view, especially when you sit
next to the "double windows facing the ocean"; the vittles
"can be terrific", especially at lunch or for Sunday brunch;
however, a few quibblers say they "need to concentrate
more on the food prep."

Water Street Cafe   ▽ 23 18 21 $32
(Stonington) **S**
142 Water St. (bet. Grand & Pearl Sts.), 860-535-2122
■ For "imaginative" Contemporary American fare, including
lots of "fresh" fish, head to this Stonington eatery on the
water that's "crowded", "fun" and "surprisingly creative";
N.B. there's classical guitar on Thursday nights.

Wellington's Market   ▽ 23 16 22 $32
(Huntington)
51 Huntington Ctr. (Rte. 108), 203-929-0336
◪ This former Bridgeport Traditional American–Continental
has moved to nicer digs in a residential area in Huntington;
there's now a lounge and outdoor dining along with the same
"very good food" and "gracious and accommodating" staff
that regulars have come to expect.

West Main Cafe (Sharon) **S**   ▽ 23 17 21 $30
13 W. Main St. (Rtes. 4 & 41), 860-364-9888
■ Reviewers say Matthew Fahrner's cafe is "the only
place to eat well in Sharon" and "a destination" in itself
thanks to its "very interesting" menu of American cuisine
with an Asian influence; it's "intimate" with "pleasant"
service and a "good wine selection."

WEST STREET GRILL (Litchfield) **S** 24 21 22 $40
43 West St. (on the green), 860-567-3885
■ A "celebrity-filled" Litchfield locale that's like a "slice
of NYC in the country" or the "Upper East Side in tweed";
it's still "one of the champs" for "imaginative" Contemporary
American in a "charming", "very low-profile" setting with
what most say is a "friendly" staff (a few murmur "snooty");
N.B. reservations are a must on weekends.

White Hart Inn, The (Salisbury) **S** 21 23 22 $38
Village Green (Rtes. 41 & 44), 860-435-0030
■ You "get more than you expect" at both restaurants – the
American Grill and the Garden and Tap Room – housed in
this "lovely" 1867 landmark inn; the Grill has Traditional
American fare and the G and T has a lighter, more casual
and contemporary menu; both serve "original" and
"excellent" food and have "friendly" service.

Whitman, The (Farmington) **S**　　16 | 20 | 18 | $34
1125 Farmington Ave. (bet. Rte. 4 & Melrose Pl.), 860-678-9217
◪ A Contemporary American in Farmington for grown-ups
accompanying their mothers; it's especially popular for the
early-bird dinner, the Friday and Sunday night lobster
special and the Sunday brunch; reviewers say all the
discounts add up to "a good value."

Wine & Roses (Old Saybrook) **S** ▽　19 | 16 | 20 | $28
150 Main St. (I-95, exit 67), 860-388-9646
◼ A "pretty", "hidden jewel" in Old Saybrook that's a
"surprise find" for "creative" American that's always
"steady" and "very good."

Woodland, The (Lakeville) **S**　　19 | 16 | 15 | $29
192 Sharon Rd./Rte.41 (bet. Rtes. 44 & 112), 860-435-0578
◼ A "great variety" of "good" Traditional American fare at
"reasonable" prices means there's always a "long wait"
at this "charming" restaurant in Lakeville.

Yankee Pedlar (Torrington) **S**　　15 | 22 | 19 | $32
Yankee Pedlar Inn, 93 Main St. (Rte. 8, exit 44),
860-489-9226
◪ There's a new chef and new management at this "dark
paneled", "country, cozy" Litchfield inn dating from
1891; early reports are that the Traditional American
fare has improved considerably.

Yankee Silversmith Inn　　16 | 21 | 19 | $31
(Wallingford) **S**
1033 N. Colony Rd./Rte. 5 (Merritt Pkwy., exit 66), 203-269-5444
◪ Fans say this Wallingford landmark with "unique decor"
has a menu for all appetites from "light to heavy", covering
the landscape from popovers to prime rib; detractors say
it's a "ghost of its previous self" and warn "if you don't
use blue hair rinse this is not the place for you."

Indexes to Connecticut Restaurants

Special Features and Appeals

TYPES OF CUISINE

Afghan
Shish Kebab

American (New)
Amberjacks
Ann Howard's Apricots
Bee and Thistle
Bistro East
Black Goose
Boston Market
Boulders Inn
Breakaway
Bridge Café
Brookfield Bistro
Cafe Allègre
Cafe Lulu
Café Lafayette
Cannery
Capers
Carole Peck's
Citron
ClearWaters
County Seat
Dome
G.P. Cheffields
Inn/Chester
Inn/Lake Waramaug
Ivy Rest.
Kathleen's
Madd Hatter
Main & Hopewell
Max Downtown
Mayflower Inn
Metropolitan
Museum Cafe
Pantry
Paradise B&G
Pierpont's
Rest. at National Hall
Sadler's
64 Greenwich Ave.
Steve's
Telluride
Three Bears
Water St. Cafe
Water's Edge
West Main
West St. Grill
White Hart
Whitman
Wine & Roses
Yankee Silversmith

American (Regional)
Bistro Café
Mayflower Inn
Spinning Wheel
Stagecoach Hill

American (Traditional)
American Pie Co.
Archie Moore's
Ash Creek
Avon Old Farms
Backstreet
Bank St. Brewing
Barkie's
Bee and Thistle
Bobby Valentine's
Bogey's
Boston Market
Brannigan's
Brewhouse
Brookside Rest.
Center Grille
Chart House
Cherry St. East
Christopher's
Coach's Sports B&G
Cobb's Mill Inn
Colonial Tymes
Congress Rotisserie
Crab Shell
Curtis House
David's American
Eastside
Elizabeth's
Elms Rest.
Fiddler's
Flood Tide
Gathering
Golden Lamb
Greenwoods Mkt.
Griswold Inn
G.W. Tavern
Hawthorne Inn
Jimmy's
John Harvard's
Lily's
Little Mark's
Mackenzie's Grill
MacKenzie's Redding
Mansion Clam Hse.
Mario's Place

Italian

(N=Northern; S=Southern; N&S=Includes both)

Abruzzi Kitchen (N&S)
Adriana's (N&S)
Aleia's (N&S)
Alforno (N&S)
Alla Bettola (N&S)
Angelina's (S)
Applausi (N)
Aspen Gardens (N&S)
Bacco's (N&S)
Bella Italia (N)
Bentley's (N&S)
Bertucci's (N&S)
Biscotti (N&S)
Bluewater Café (N)
Boccaccio (N)
Brick Oven (N&S)
Bricks (N&S)
Brookside Rest. (N&S)
Buon Appetito (N)
Cafe Allègre (N)
Cafe Morelli (N&S)
Carbone's (N)
Carmela's (N&S)
Cavey's (N)
Centro (N&S)
Chef Eugene's (N&S)
Christopher Martin's (N&S)
Ciao! Cafe (N&S)
Cinzano's (N&S)
Clemente's (S)
Columbus Park (N&S)
Da Pietro's (N)
Da Vincenzo (N&S)
Da Vinci's (N)
DeRosa's Italian (N&S)
Diorio (N)
Doc's (N&S)
Dolce Vita (N)
Eclisse (N)
Elizabeth's (N)
Ettorucci's (N&S)
Fat Cat (N)
First & Last (N&S)
500 Blake St. Cafe (N&S)
Gaetano's (N&S)
Gennaro's (N&S)
Grappa (N&S)
Hot Tomato's (N&S)
Il Falco (N&S)
Il Mulino (N&S)
La Taverna (S)
La Trattoria (N)
La Villa (N&S)
Leon's (N&S)
Luigi's (N&S)
Luna Pizza (S)
Maria's Trattoria (N&S)
Mario's Place (N&S)
Mario the Baker (N&S)
Marisa's (S)
Max-A-Mia (N)
Max Amoré (N)
Mona Lisa (N&S)
Monica's (N&S)
Mumbo Jumbo (N)
Netto's (N&S)
Paci (N&S)
Pane Vino (N&S)
Pasta Garden (N&S)
Pasta Nostra (N&S)
Pasta Vera (N&S)
Pellicci's (S)
Peppercorn's (N&S)
Per Bacco! (N)
Piccolo Arancio (N&S)
Portofino (N)
Prezzo (N)
Quattro Pazzi (N&S)
Ralph 'n' Rich's (N&S)
Red Lion (N&S)
Rest. Bravo Bravo (N&S)
Roberto's (N&S)
Rocco's (N)
Rosy Tomatoes (N&S)
Scoozzi (N)
Sfizio (N&S)
Sole e Luna (N)
Spazzi (N&S)
Sunset Grille (N&S)
Tartaglia's (N&S)
Tartufo (N)
Terra Mar Grille (N)
Terra Ristorante (N)
That Little Italian (N&S)
Three Brothers (N&S)
Tommy's (N&S)
Tuscan Oven (N)
Valbella! (N)
Valentino (N&S)
Vazzy's (N&S)
Venetian (N)
Via Sforza (N&S)

Japanese

Abis
Japanica

Kotobuki
Kujaku
Mako of Japan
Murasaki
Osaka
Plum Tree
Sakura
Shell Station
Tomiko

Jewish
Rein's NY

Mediterranean
Barcelona Wine Bar
Bridge Café
Cafe Pika Tapas
Diana
G.P. Cheffields
Grist Mill
Madd Hatter
Mediterranean Grill
Mediterraneo
Meson Galicia
Post Corner
Rest. Bricco
Tapas

Mexican/Tex-Mex
Bobby Valentine's
Calexico
Cuckoo's Nest
Hogan's Miguels
La Hacienda
Margaritas
Miguel's
San Miguel
Sloppy Jose's
Su Casa
Tequila Mockingbird
Viva Zapata

Middle Eastern
Diana
Greenwoods Mkt.
Sesame Seed
Tapas

Noodle Shops
Char Koon

Pacific Rim
Splash Pacific Rim

Peruvian
El Inca

Pizza
Bertucci's
Brick Oven
Bricks
DeRosa's Firehse.
Doc's
First & Last
Frank Pepe Pizzeria
Frank Pepe's The Spot
Harry's Pizza
Luna Pizza
Mystic Pizza
Post Corner
Sally's Apizza
Sunrise Pizza

Portuguese
Chale Ipanema
Dolphins Cove

Scandinavian
Fjord Fisheries

Seafood
Abbott's Lobster
Allen's Clam Hse.
Amberjacks
Atlantis
Bennett's
Bloomfield Seafood
Carmen Anthony
ClearWaters
Crab Shell
Dakota
Dolphins Cove
Elm St. Oyster
Fiddler's
Fjord Fisheries
Flanders Fish Mkt.
Giovanni's Serious
G.P. Cheffields
Jimmy's
Lenny & Joe's
Manero's
Mansion Clam Hse.
Mooring
Oyster House
Peppermill
Rest. Bravo Bravo
Rusty Scupper
Saybrook Fish Hse.
Scribner's

Seaman's Inne
Seascape
Sono Seaport
Sunset Grille
Tributary
USS Chowder Pot

Southwestern

Arizona Flats
Arizona Grill
Boxcar Cantina
Boxing Cat Grill
Hogan's Miguels
Rattlesnake
Telluride
Tucson Cafe
Two Steps
Violets

Spanish

Barcelona Wine
Cafe Pika Tapas
Costa Del Sol
Meson Galicia

Steakhouses

Angus
Bennett's
Bugaboo Creek
Carmen Anthony
Cedar's Steak Hse.
Charley's Place
Chuck's
Dakota
Eric & Michael's
Giovanni's Serious
Manero's
Mario's Place

Max Steaks
Moody's B&G
Peppermill
Ruth's Chris
Steak Loft

Swiss

Ragamont Inn
Rudy's

Thai

Bangkok
Bangkok Gdns.
King and I
Lemon Grass
Mhai Thai
Siam Rialto
Thai Orchid

Vegetarian

(Most Chinese, Indian and
Thai restaurants)
Bloodroot
Claire's
It's Only Natural
Lime
Sprouts Café
Telluride

Viennese

Amadeus

Vietnamese

Bamboo Grill
La Maison
Lotus
Truc Orient

NEIGHBORHOOD LOCATIONS

500 Blake St. Cafe
Frank Pepe Pizzeria
Frank Pepe's The Spot
Gennaro's
Rusty Scupper
Sally's Apizza
Scoozzi
Thai Orchid
Union League

Newington
Bertucci's
Boston Market
Ruth's Chris

New London
Chuck's
Don Juan's

New Milford
Bistro Café
Carmela's
Rudy's

New Preston
Boulders Inn
Doc's
Hopkins Inn
Inn/Lake Waramaug
Le Bon Coin

Newtown
G.P. Cheffields

Noank
Abbott's Lobster

Norfolk
Greenwoods Mkt.
Pub and Rest.

North Haven
Amber Rest.
Boston Market

North Stonington
Mystic Pizza
Randall's Ordinary

Norwalk
Abruzzi Kitchen
Bobby Valentine's
Bricks
Chan's Choice
Côte d'Azur
La Taverna

Lime
Meson Galicia
Maria's Trattoria
Panda Pavilion
Pasta Nostra
Silvermine
Sunrise Pizza
Tuscan Oven
Via Sforza

Norwich
Prince of Wales

Old Greenwich
Applausi
Boston Market
Boxing Cat Grill

Old Lyme
Bee and Thistle
Old Lyme Inn

Old Saybrook
Aleia's
Alforno
Cuckoo's Nest
Luigi's
Pat's Kountry Kit.
Saybrook Fish Hse.
Terra Mar Grille
Wine & Roses

Orange
China Pavilion

Oxford
Oxford House

Redding
MacKenzie's Redding
Spinning Wheel

Ridgefield
Biscotti
Boston Market
Chez Noüe
Elms Rest.
Gail's Station Hse.
Inn/Ridgefield
Kismet
Red Lion
Stonehenge

Riverside
Taj Mahal
Valbella!

SPECIAL FEATURES AND APPEALS

Breakfast
(All hotels and the
following standouts)
American Pie Co.
Atlantis
Aux Delices
Bee and Thistle
Bistro on the Green
Bull's Head Diner
Claire's
Firehouse Deli
Gail's Station Hse.
Hearth Cafe
Hopkins Inn
Inn/Lake Waramaug
Little Mark's
Madd Hatter
Mayflower Inn
Métro bís
Mooring
Orem's Diner
Oscar's
Pantry
Pat's Kountry Kit.
Pierpont's
Playwright
Prince of Wales
Randall's Ordinary
Rein's NY
Roger Sherman
Sadler's
Seasons
Shady Glen
Spinell's
Water's Edge
White Hart
Yankee Pedlar

Brunch
(Best of many)
Abis
Altnaveigh Inn
Ann Howard's Apricots
Avon Old Farms
Bee and Thistle
Bellini
Bentley's
Biscotti
Black Goose
Black Rock
Bloodroot

Boxing Cat Grill
Bridge Café
Cafe Allègre
Cafe Christina
Cherry St. East
Christopher's
Cobb's Mill Inn
Colonial Tymes
Dakota
500 Blake St. Cafe
Flanders Fish Mkt.
Flood Tide
Gates
Griswold Inn
G.W. Tavern
Hearth Cafe
Homestead Inn
Inn/Chester
Inn/Ridgefield
Inn/Woodstock Hill
Inn/Lake Waramaug
L'Abbee
Lily's
Old Lyme Inn
Pierpont's
Roger Sherman
Rusty Scupper
Seasons
Silvermine
64 Greenwich Ave.
Spinning Wheel
Splash Pacific Rim
Stonehenge
Three Bears
Tollgate Hill
Water's Edge
Whitman
Yankee Silversmith

Buffet Served
(Check prices, days
and times)
Abis
Ambassador of India
Atlantis
Avon Old Farms
Bombay B&G
Bonani Indian
Buster's BBQ
Dakota
Diorio

500 Blake St. Cafe
Flanders Fish Mkt.
Flood Tide
Hawthorne Inn
Inn/Woodstock Hill
Kismet
MacKenzie's Redding
Meera Cuisine
Paradise B&G
Promis
Rusty Scupper
Sadler's
Seaman's Inne
Seascape
Seasons
Silvermine
Spinning Wheel
Terra Mar Grille
Tollgate Hill
Via Sforza
Water's Edge
Whitman
Yankee Silversmith

Business Dining

Copper Beech Inn
Golden Lamb
Homestead Inn
Inn/Lake Waramaug
Max Downtown
Mayflower Inn
Roger Sherman

BYO

Abbott's Lobster
Abis
Bamboo Grill
Buon Appetito
Cafe Allègre
Calexico
County Seat
Doc's
Don Juan's
Flanders Fish Mkt.
Greenwoods Mkt.
It's Only Natural
Lenny & Joe's
Rosy Tomatoes
Spinell's
Tiger Bowl

Caters

(Best of many)
Abis
Aleia's
Altnaveigh Inn
Applausi
Arizona Flats
Arizona Grill
Atlantis
Aux Delices
Avon Old Farms
Baang Café
Bali of Greenwich
Bamboo Grill
Beach House
Bella Italia
Bellini
Bistro East
Black-Eyed Sally's
Bluewater Café
Bombay B&G
Boxcar Cantina
Brannigan's
Bridge Café
Brookfield Bistro
Brookside Rest.
Buster's BBQ
Cafe Pika Tapas
Caffe Adulis
Capers
Carbone's
Carole Peck's
Cavey's
Center Grille
Centro
Cherry St. East
ClearWaters
Columbus Park
DeRosa's Italian
Diana
Doc's
Don Juan's
Eclisse
Elizabeth's
Elms Rest.
Elm St. Oyster
Eric & Michael's
Firehouse Deli
Gail's Station Hse.
Giovanni's Serious
Grappa
G.W. Tavern
Homestead Inn
Hot Tomato's

Cigar Friendly

Dancing/Entertainment

(Check days, times and performers for entertainment; D=dancing)

Aleia's (piano)
Altnaveigh Inn (guitar)
Amadeus (piano)
Ambassador of India (sitar)
Amberjacks (blues/jazz)
Ann Howard's Apricots (piano)
Arizona Grill (D/bands)
Atlantis (D/reggae)
Avon Old Farms (piano)
Bank St. Brewing (varies)
Beach House (blues/jazz)
Bee and Thistle (guitar/harp)
Bellini (opera)
Bistro East (D/varies)
Bistro on the Green
   (guitar/piano)
Black-Eyed Sally's (bands/blues)
Black Rock (bands)
Bobby Valentine's (karaoke)
Boccaccio (piano)
Bombay B&G (sitar/tabla)
Boxing Cat Grill (bands)
Brewhouse (D/varies)
Buster's BBQ (bands)
Butterfly Chinese (varies)
Café Lafayette (D/jazz/piano)
Cafe Lulu (r&b)
Caffe Adulis (jazz)
Carole Peck's (jazz)
Cavey's (jazz piano)
Chef Eugene's (piano/singers)
Christopher Martin's (varies)
Christopher's (jazz)
Cinzano's (D/DJ/bands)
Citron (D/varies)
Civic Cafe (jazz)
Claire's (guitar/singer)
Coach's Sports B&G (D/bands)
Colonial Tymes (jazz/piano)
County Seat (jazz/folk)
Crab Shell (bands)
Cuckoo's Nest (jazz)
Diorio (piano)
Dolphins Cove (bands)
Drawbridge Inne (varies)
500 Blake St. Cafe (piano)
Flood Tide (piano)
Gates (jazz)
Gathering (bands)
Gelston House (jazz)

Golden Lamb (guitar/singer)
Griswold Inn (varies)
Hawthorne Inn (D/bands)
Hearth Cafe (acoustic guitar)
Hogan's Miguels (bands)
Inn/Chester (harp/piano)
Inn/Ridgefield (piano)
Inn/Woodstock Hill (piano/violin)
Inn/Lake Waramaug (piano)
Japanica (karaoke)
Jimmy's (bands)
John Harvard's (band)
La Trattoria (jazz Sun. brunch)
Leon's (piano)
MacKenzie's Redding (varies)
Madd Hatter (jazz/Irish folk)
Main & Hopewell (jazz)
Margaritas (acoustic)
Mayflower Inn (piano)
Miguel's (comedy/music)
Mooring (piano)
Museum Cafe (varies)
North Cove (varies)
Oasis Diner (varies)
Old Lyme Inn (guitar/piano)
Onion Alley (bands)
Paradise B&G (piano)
Pasta Garden (accordionist)
Pearl of Budapest (piano/violin)
Playwright (D/bands)
Prince of Wales (piano)
Promis (piano)
Ralph 'n' Rich's (piano)
Randall's Ordinary (classical)
Rattlesnake
   (cartoonist/magician)
San Miguel (varies)
Saybrook Fish Hse. (harp)
Seasons (piano/varies)
Silvermine (jazz)
Southport Brewing
   (blues/magician)
Spinning Wheel (D/varies)
Steak Loft (varies)
Su Casa (guitar)
Tartaglia's (D/blues/jazz)
Tartufo (piano)
Thataway Café (acoustic
   guitar/jazz)
Tigin (bands)
Tollgate Hill (piano)
Tommy's (piano)
Tributary (piano/violinist)
Trout Brook (bands)

Tucson Cafe (jazz/r&b)
Vazzy's (music)
Violets (music)
Viva Zapata (varies)
Water St. Cafe (classical guitar)
White Hart (bands)
Whitman (jazz/piano)
Wine & Roses (piano)
Yankee Silversmith (piano)

Delivers*/Takeout

(Nearly all Asians, coffee shops, delis, diners and pasta/pizzerias deliver or do takeout; here are some interesting possibilities; D=delivery, T=takeout)

Abbott's Lobster (T)
Abis (T)
Adriana's (T)
Alla Bettola (T)
Amadeus (D,T)
Ambassador of India (T)
Amberjacks (T)
Amber Rest. (T)
American Pie Co. (T)
Archie Moore's (T)
Arizona Flats (T)
Arizona Grill (T)
Ash Creek (T)
Atlantis (T)
Aux Delices (T)
Avon Old Farms (T)
Bacco's (T)
Backstreet (T)
Bamboo Grill (D,T)
Barcelona Wine (T)
Barkie's (T)
Beach House (T)
Bennett's (T)
Bentley's (T)
Biscotti (T)
Bistro East (T)
Bistro on the Green (T)
Black-Eyed Sally's (T)
Black Goose (T)
Black Rock (T)
Bloomfield Seafood (T)
Bluewater Café (T)
Bogey's (D,T)
Bombay B&G (D,T)
Bombay's Authentic (T)
Bonani Indian (D,T)
Boston Market (T)

Boxcar Cantina (D,T)
Boxing Cat Grill (T)
Brannigan's (T)
Breakaway (D,T)
Brewhouse (D,T)
Bridge Café (T)
Brookfield Bistro (T)
Brookside Bistro (T)
Buster's BBQ (D,T)
Cafe Christina (T)
Cafe Lulu (T)
Cafe Morelli (T)
Cafe Pika Tapas (T)
Caffe Adulis (T)
Calexico (D,T)
Capers (T)
Carmela's (T)
Carmen Anthony (T)
Carole Peck's (T)
Cavey's (T)
Center Grille (T)
Centro (T)
Charley's Place (T)
Chart House (T)
Cherry St. East (T)
Chez Noüe (T)
Christopher Martin's (T)
Ciao! Cafe (D,T)
Citron (D,T)
Civic Cafe (T)
Claire's (T)
ClearWaters (D,T)
Columbus Park (T)
Congress Rotisserie (T)
Costa Del Sol (T)
County Seat (T)
Crab Shell (T)
Cuckoo's Nest (T)
Curtis House (T)
Dakota (T)
Da Pietro's (T)
David's American (D,T)
Da Vincenzo (T)
Da Vinci's (T)
Diana (T)
Doc's (T)
Dome (T)
Don Juan's (T)
Drawbridge Inne (T)
Eastside (T)
Eclisse (T)
El Inca (T)
Elm St. Oyster (T)
Eric & Michael's (T)

Steak Loft (T)
Taj Mahal (T)
Tapas (T)
Tavern on Main (T)
Telluride (D,T)
Tequila Mockingbird (T)
Terra Ristorante (T)
Thai Orchid (T)
Thataway Café (T)
That Little Italian (D,T)
Tigin (T)
Tommy's (T)
Torrington Bagels (D,T)
Tributary (T)
Trout Brook (T)
Tuscan Oven (D,T)
Uncle Dai's (D,T)
Venetian (T)
Via Sforza (T)
Water St. Cafe (T)
Whitman (D,T)
Wine & Roses (T)
Woodland (T)
Yankee Pedlar (T)
(* Call to check range and charges, if any)

Dessert/Ice Cream

Aleia's
Baang Café
Bee and Thistle
Copper Beech Inn
Splash Pacific Rim
Venetian
Whitman
Yankee Silversmith

Dining Alone

(Other than hotels, coffee shops, sushi bars and places with counter service)
Aux Delices
Bloomfield Seafood
Gennaro's
Golden Lamb

Fireplaces

Arizona Grill
Avon Old Farms
Bee and Thistle
Bistro East
Black Goose
Brookside Rest.
Chez Pierre

Cobb's Mill Inn
Colonial Tymes
Curtis House
Dolce Vita
Elms Rest.
First & Last
500 Blake St. Cafe
Flood Tide
Golden Lamb
Griswold Inn
G.W. Tavern
Hopkins Inn
Inn/Chester
Inn/Ridgefield
Inn/Woodstock Hill
Ivy Rest.
Maiden Lane
Margaritas
Marlborough
Miguel's
Old Lyme Inn
Oxford House
Paradise B&G
Pat's Kountry Kit.
Pellicci's
Promis
Ragamont Inn
Randall's Ordinary
Rudy's
Sadler's
Sakura
Saybrook Fish Hse.
Silvermine
Simsbury 1820 Hse.
64 Greenwich Ave.
Spinning Wheel
Splash Pacific Rim
Stagecoach Hill
Steve's
Su Casa
Sunset Grille
Tartufo
Tavern on Main
Three Bears
Tollgate Hill
Tuscan Oven
Union League
Valbella!
Whitman
Yankee Silversmith

Game In Season

Amadeus
Arizona Grill
Bee and Thistle

Bistro East
Black Goose
Bogey's
Brookfield Bistro
Buster's BBQ
Cafe Allègre
Cannery
Carole Peck's
Cavey's
Civic Cafe
Cobb's Mill Inn
Colonial Tymes
Copper Beech Inn
Da Vincenzo
Doc's
Dome
Elms Rest.
Flood Tide
G.P. Cheffields
Griswold Inn
G.W. Tavern
Hopkins Inn
Il Falco
Inn/Chester
Inn/Ridgefield
Ivy Rest.
Jean-Louis
John Harvard's
La Bretagne
La Colline Verte
La Hacienda
Le Bistro des Amis
Le Bon Coin
Leon's
Madd Hatter
Maiden Lane
Max Downtown
Max Steaks
Old Lyme Inn
Ondine
Paci
Peppercorn's
Randall's Ordinary
Rest. at National Hall
Rest. Bricco
Rest. du Village
Rudy's
Sadler's
Simsbury 1820 Hse.
Southport Brewing
Spinning Wheel
Sprouts Café
Telluride
Three Bears

Tigin
Tollgate Hill
Tuscan Oven

Health/Spa Menus

(Most places cook to order to
meet any dietary request; call
in advance to check; almost all
Chinese, Indian and other
ethnics have health-conscious
meals, as do the following)
Amadeus
Carole Peck's
Claire's
DeRosa's Italian
Mayflower Inn
Pantry
Spinell's
Sprouts Café
Sunset Grille
Telluride

Historic Interest

(Year Opened)
1685 Randall's Ordinary*
1736 Curtis House
1740 Marlborough*
1748 Spinning Wheel
1757 Avon Old Farms
1765 Stagecoach Hill*
1768 Somers Inn
1776 Griswold Inn
1867 White Hart
1875 Golden Lamb*
1880 Inn/Lake Waramaug*
(*Building)

Hotel Dining

Avon Old Farms Hotel
    Seasons
Bee & Thistle Inn
    Bee & Thistle
Boulders Inn
    Boulders Inn
Curtis House
    Curtis House
Drawbridge Inne
    Drawbridge Inne
Foxwoods Resort Casino
    Cedar's Steak Hse.
Goodwin Hotel
    Pierpont's
Greenwich Harbor Inn
    Atlantis

Griswold Inn
  Griswold Inn
Hawthorne Inn
  Hawthorne Inn
Heritage Inn
  Splash! B&G
Homestead Inn
  Homestead Inn
Inn at Café Lafayette
  Café Lafayette
Inn at Chester
  Inn/Chester
Inn at Longshore
  Splash Pacific Rim
Inn at Mystic
  Flood Tide
Inn at National Hall
  Rest. at National Hall
Litchfield Inn
  Bistro East
Mayflower Inn
  Mayflower Inn
Mystic Hilton Hotel
  Mooring
Norwich Inn & Spa
  Prince of Wales
Ragamont Inn
  Ragamont Inn
Roger Sherman Inn
  Roger Sherman
Saybrook Point Inn
  Terra Mar Grille
Simsbury 1820 House
  Simsbury 1820 Hse.
Stagecoach Hill Inn
  Stagecoach Hill
Stonehenge
  Stonehenge
Under Mountain Inn
  Under Mountain
Westport Inn
  Hearth Cafe
Whalers Inn
  Rest. Bravo Bravo
White Hart
  White Hart
Yankee Pedlar Inn
  Yankee Pedlar

"In" Places
Amberjacks
Baang Café
Bank St. Brewing
Boxing Cat Grill

Crab Shell
Dolphins Cove
Frank Pepe Pizzeria
Frank Pepe's The Spot
Le Figaro Bistro
Mackenzie's Grill
Mario's Place
Max-A-Mia
Max Amoré
Max Downtown
Meson Galicia
64 Greenwich Ave.
Tucson Cafe
West St. Grill

Jacket Required
Copper Beech Inn
Golden Lamb
Jean-Louis
Ondine

Late Late – After 12:30
(All hours are AM)
Bobby Valentine's (1)
Trout Brook (1)

Meet for a Drink
(Most top hotels and the
following standouts)
Amberjacks
Ann Howard's Apricots
Archie Moore's
Arizona Flats
Bank St. Brewing
Barcelona Wine
Bertucci's
Black Rock
Bobby Valentine's
Bogey's
Boxcar Cantina
Brewhouse
Chart House
Citron
Civic Cafe
Crab Shell
Dolphins Cove
Mackenzie's Grill
Mario's Place
Max-A-Mia
Max Amoré
Max Downtown
Tommy's
Tucson Cafe

Outstanding Views

Atlantis
Beach House
Boulders Inn
Chart House
Cobb's Mill Inn
Crab Shell
Flood Tide
Golden Lamb
Hopkins Inn
Inn/Lake Waramaug
Mayflower Inn
Paradise B&G
Silvermine
Splash Pacific Rim
Sunset Grille
Water's Edge

Parking/Valet

(L=parking lot;
V=valet parking;
*=validated parking)
Abbott's Lobster (L)
Adriana's (V)
Aleia's (L)
Alforno (L)
Alla Bettola (L)
Altnaveigh Inn (L)
Amadeus*
Ambassador of India (L)
Amberjacks (L)
Amber Rest. (L)
American Pie Co. (L)
Angelina's (L)
Ann Howard's Apricots (L)
Arizona Flats (L)
Arizona Grill (L)
Ash Creek (L)
Atlantis (L)
Aux Delices (L)
Avon Old Farms (L)
Bacco's (L)
Backstreet (L)
Bamboo Grill (L,V)
Bangkok (L)
Barcelona Wine (L)
Beach House (L,V)
Bee and Thistle (L)
Bella Italia (L)
Bertucci's (L)
Biscotti (L)
Bistro East (L)
Black Goose (L)
Bloodroot (L)
Bloomfield Seafood (L)

Bogey's (L)
Bombay B&G (L)
Bonani Indian (L)
Boston Market (L)
Boulders Inn (L)
Boxcar Cantina (L)
Boxing Cat Grill (L)
Brannigan's (L)
Breakaway (L)
Brewhouse (L)
Bricks (L)
Brookside Rest. (L)
Bugaboo Creek (L)
Bull's Head Diner (L)
Buon Appetito (L)
Buster's BBQ (L)
Butterfly Chinese (L)
Cafe Allègre (L)
Café Lafayette (L)
Cafe Lulu (L)
Cafe Morelli (L)
Caffe Adulis (L)
Capers (L)
Carbone's (L)
Carmela's (L)
Carmen Anthony (L)
Carole Peck's (L)
Cavey's (L)
Cedar's Steak Hse. (L)
Centro (L)
Chan's Choice (L)
Char Koon (L)
Charley's Place (L)
Chart House (L)
Chef Eugene's (L)
Cheng Du (L)
Cherry St. East (L)
Chez Noüe (L)
Chez Pierre (L)
China Pavilion (L)
Christopher Martin's (V)
Christopher's (L)
Chuck's (L)
Cinzano's (L)
Citron (L)
Civic Cafe (V)
Clemente's (L)
Coach's Sports B&G (L)
Cobb's Mill Inn (V)
Colonial Tymes (L)
Columbus Park (L)
Congress Rotisserie (L)
Copper Beech Inn (L)
Costa Del Sol (L)

White Hart (L)
Whitman (L)
Woodland (L)
Yankee Pedlar (L)
Yankee Silversmith (L)

Parties & Private Rooms
(Any nightclub or restaurant
charges less at off-times;
* indicates private rooms
available; best of many)
Abis*
Altnaveigh Inn*
Amadeus*
Applausi
Arizona Grill
Atlantis*
Avon Old Farms*
Bali of Greenwich*
Bamboo Grill
Bank St. Brewing*
Barkie's*
Beach House
Bee and Thistle*
Bellini
Bennett's*
Bistro East*
Black-Eyed Sally's*
Black Goose*
Bloomfield Seafood
Boccaccio*
Bombay B&G*
Boulders Inn*
Boxing Cat Grill*
Brannigan's*
Brewhouse*
Brookside Rest.
Cafe Allègre
Cafe Christina*
Café Lafayette*
Capers*
Carbone's*
Carmela's*
Carmen Anthony*
Carole Peck's*
Cavey's*
Cedar's Steak Hse.*
Center Grille
Charley's Place*
Chart House*
Chez Pierre*
China Pavilion*
Christopher Martin's*
Christopher's*

Chuck's*
Ciao! Cafe
Cinzano's*
Civic Cafe*
Cobb's Mill Inn*
Colonial Tymes*
Columbus Park
Copper Beech Inn*
Costa Del Sol
County Seat
Crab Shell*
Cuckoo's Nest*
Curtis House*
Dakota*
Da Pietro's
David's American
Da Vinci's*
Diana
Doc's*
Dome*
Elizabeth's
Elms Rest.*
Fat Cat*
First & Last*
500 Blake St. Cafe*
Gaetano's*
Gail's Station Hse.*
Gathering*
Gelston House*
Gennaro's*
Giovanni's Serious*
Golden Lamb*
G.P. Cheffields*
Grappa*
Great Taste*
Greenwoods Mkt.
Griswold Inn*
G.W. Tavern*
Hawthorne Inn*
Hearth Cafe*
Homestead Inn*
Hot Tomato's*
Il Falco*
Inn/Chester*
Inn/Ridgefield*
Inn/Woodstock Hill*
Inn/Lake Waramaug*
Ivy Rest.*
Japanica*
Jimmy's*
Kathleen's*
L'Abbee*
La Bretagne*
La Colline Verte*

People-Watching

Power Scenes

Pre-Theater/Early Bird Menus

(Call to check prices, days and times)

Amadeus
Amberjacks
Bellini
Bloomfield Seafood
Cafe Lulu
Chez Noüe
Cobb's Mill Inn
Copper Beech Inn
Maiden Lane
Marlborough
Max-A-Mia
Miguel's
Playwright
Quattro Pazzi
San Miguel
Saybrook Fish Hse.
Sono Seaport
Spinning Wheel
Venetian
Whitman

Prix Fixe Menus

(Call to check prices, days and times)

Abruzzi Kitchen
Amadeus
Avon Old Farms
Beach House
Bonani Indian
Butterfly Chinese
Cafe Christina
Cavey's
Colonial Tymes
Copper Beech Inn
Dakota
Da Pietro's
Dolce Vita
Fiddler's
Flanders Fish Mkt.
Flood Tide
Homestead Inn
Inn/Ridgefield
Kismet
La Trattoria
Le Petit Café
MacKenzie's Redding
Maiden Lane
Meera Cuisine
North Cove
Ondine

Peppercorn's
Peppermill
Randall's Ordinary
Rest. at National Hall
Roger Sherman
Rusty Scupper
Saybrook Fish Hse.
Seaman's Inne
Seascape
Seasons
Silvermine
Tartufo
Terra Mar Grille
Three Bears
Union League
Water's Edge

Pubs/Bars/Sports TV

Ann Howard's Apricots
Bank St. Brewing
Black Rock
Bobby Valentine's
Brewhouse
John Harvard's
Southport Brewing
Tigin
Trout Brook
White Hart

Quiet Conversation

Bee and Thistle
Bloomfield Seafood
Boulders Inn
Cobb's Mill Inn
Copper Beech Inn
Golden Lamb
Homestead Inn
Inn/Lake Waramaug
Jean-Louis
Silvermine
Tavern on Main
Tollgate Hill

Reservations Essential

Bacco's
Boulders Inn
Cafe Allègre
Cavey's
Cedar's Steak Hse.
Center Grille
Centro
Christopher Martin's
Cobb's Mill Inn
Copper Beech Inn

Fiddler's
500 Blake St. Cafe
Flood Tide
Gennaro's
Golden Lamb
Kotobuki
La Bretagne
La Colline Verte
Lotus
Mediterranean Grill
Meson Galicia
Mhai Thai
Miguel's
Mona Lisa
North Cove
Ondine
Ralph 'n' Rich's
Randall's Ordinary
Rest. Bravo Bravo
Scoozzi
Tuscan Oven
Under Mountain
Venetian
West St. Grill

Romantic Spots
Amadeus
Ann Howard's Apricots
Bee and Thistle
Boulders Inn
Christopher's
Cobb's Mill Inn
Copper Beech Inn
Golden Lamb
Homestead Inn
Inn/Chester
Inn/Lake Waramaug
Jean-Louis
Mayflower Inn
Randall's Ordinary
Rest. at National Hall
Rest. du Village
Roger Sherman
Silvermine
Stonehenge
Tavern on Main
Tollgate Hill

Saturday – Best Bets
(B=brunch; L=lunch;
best of many)
Abis (L)
Allen's Clam Hse. (L)
Amberjacks (L)

Ann Howard's Apricots (L)
Archie Moore's (L)
Arizona Flats (L)
Ash Creek (L)
Aspen Gardens (L)
Aux Delices (L)
Avon Old Farms (L)
Backstreet (B,L)
Bali of Greenwich (L)
Bank St. Brewing (L)
Beach House (B,L)
Bee and Thistle (L)
Bistro Café (L)
Bistro East (L)
Bistro on the Green (L)
Black Rock (L)
Bloomfield Seafood (L)
Bluewater Café (L)
Boccaccio (L)
Breakaway (L)
Brewhouse (L)
Bridge Café (L)
Brookfield Bistro (L)
Brookside Bistro (L)
Brookside Rest. (L)
Cafe Allègre (L)
Cafe Christina (L)
Café Lafayette (L)
Cafe Pika Tapas (L)
Calexico (L)
Capers (L)
Carmela's (L)
Carole Peck's (L)
Cavey's (L)
Centro (L)
Charley's Place (L)
Cherry St. East (L)
Christopher Martin's (L)
Ciao! Cafe (L)
Claire's (L)
Colonial Tymes (L)
Côte d'Azur (L)
Crab Shell (L)
Cuckoo's Nest (L)
Curtis House (L)
Diana (L)
Dolce Vita (L)
Drawbridge Inne (L)
Eastside (L)
El Inca (L)
Elms Rest. (L)
Elm St. Oyster (L)
Firehouse Deli (L)
First & Last (L)

Sunday – Best Bets

(B=brunch; L=lunch; D=dinner; plus most hotels and Asians)

Abis (B,L,D)
Aleia's (D)
Amadeus (D)
Ambassador of India (L,D)
Amberjacks (L,D)
Ann Howard's Apricots (B,L,D)
Archie Moore's (L,D)
Arizona Flats (D)
Arizona Grill (D)
Ash Creek (L,D)
Aspen Gardens (L,D)
Avon Old Farms (B,D)
Baang Café (D)
Bacco's (L,D)
Backstreet (L,D)
Bali of Greenwich (L,D)
Bank St. Brewing (B,L,D)
Barcelona Wine (D)
Beach House (L,D)
Bee and Thistle (B,D)
Bella Italia (L,D)
Bellini (B,D)
Bennett's (D)
Bentley's (B,D)
Biscotti (B,D)
Bistro Café (L,D)
Bistro East (L,D)
Bistro on the Green (L,D)
Black Goose (B,L,D)
Black Rock (B,L,D)
Bloodroot (B)
Bluewater Café (B,L,D)
Bobby Valentine's (L,D)
Boccaccio (L,D)
Bogey's (B,L,D)
Boulders Inn (D)
Boxcar Cantina (D)
Boxing Cat Grill (B,L,D)
Brannigan's (L,D)
Breakaway (B,L,D)
Brewhouse (L,D)
Bridge Café (B,D)
Brookfield Bistro (D)
Brookside Bistro (L,D)
Brookside Rest. (L,D)
Buon Appetito (D)
Cafe Allègre (B,D)
Cafe Christina (B,L,D)
Café Lafayette (L,D)
Calexico (L,D)

Cannery (B,D)
Capers (L,D)
Carmela's (L,D)
Carmen Anthony (D)
Carole Peck's (L,D)
Cedar's Steak Hse. (L,D)
Charley's Place (B)
Cherry St. East (B,L,D)
Chez Noüe (B,D)
Christopher Martin's (L,D)
Christopher's (B,D)
Ciao! Cafe (B,L,D)
Claire's (L,D)
Cobb's Mill Inn (B,D)
Colonial Tymes (B,D)
Congress Rotisserie (L,D)
Copper Beech Inn (L,D)
Crab Shell (L,D)
Cuckoo's Nest (B,D)
Dakota (B,D)
DeRosa's Italian (L,D)
Dolce Vita (L,D)
Drawbridge Inne (L,D)
Eastside (L,D)
El Inca (L,D)
Elms Rest. (L,D)
Firehouse Deli (L)
First & Last (D,L)
500 Blake St. Cafe (L,D)
Flanders Fish Mkt. (B,L,D)
Flood Tide (B,L,D)
Gail's Station Hse. (L,D)
Gates (B,L,D)
Gelston House (L,D)
Great Taste (L,D)
Greenwoods Mkt. (L)
Grist Mill (B,D)
Griswold Inn (B,D)
Hearth Cafe (B,D)
Hogan's Miguels (L,D)
Homestead Inn (B,D)
Hopkins Inn (L,D)
Hot Tomato's (L,D)
Inn/Chester (B,D)
Inn/Ridgefield (B,D)
Inn/Woodstock Hill (B,L,D)
Inn/Lake Waramaug (B,D)
It's Only Natural (B,D)
Ivy Rest. (D)
John Harvard's (L,D)
Kismet (B,D)
L'Abbee (B,L,D)
La Colline Verte (L,D)
La Maison (L,D)

La Trattoria (B,D)
Lemon Grass (L,D)
Lenny & Joe's (L,D)
Leon's (L,D)
Lily's (B,L,D)
Little Kitchen (L,D)
Little Mark's (L,D)
Luigi's (L,D)
Luna Pizza (L,D)
Mackenzie's Grill (B,L,D)
Madd Hatter (L)
Magic Wok (L,D)
Manero's (L,D)
Margaritas (L,D)
Mario's Place (L,D)
Mario the Baker (L,D)
Marlborough (B,L,D)
Max-A-Mia (L,D)
Max Steaks (D)
Mayflower Inn (L,D)
Métro bís (B,L,D)
Mill Pond Café (L,D)
Mystic Pizza (L,D)
Netto's (L,D)
Old Lyme Inn (B,L,D)
Oliver's Taverne (L,D)
Ondine (D)
One Way Fare (B,L,D)
Onion Alley (L,D)
Oxford House (L,D)
Paci (D)
Panda Pavilion (L,D)
Paradise B&G (B,L,D)
Pasta Garden (L,D)
Pasta Vera (L,D)
Peppercorn's (D)
Peppermill (B,L,D)
Pequot Grill (L,D)
Pierpont's (B,D)
Playwright (B,L,D)
Portofino (L,D)
Post Corner (L,D)
Prince of Wales (L,D)
Pub and Rest. (L,D)
Ragamont Inn (B,D)
Rattlesnake (L,D)
Rest. at National Hall (D)
Rest. Bravo Bravo (D)
Rest. Bricco (D)
Rest. du Village (D)
Roger Sherman (B,D)
Rosy Tomatoes (L,D)
Rudy's (B,D)
Russell's Ribs (L,D)

Rusty Scupper (B,D)
Sadler's (L,D)
Savannah (L)
Saybrook Fish Hse. (D,L)
Scoozzi (D)
Seaman's Inne (B,D)
Seascape (B,D)
Seasons (B,L)
Shady Glen (L,D)
Siam Rialto (L,D)
Sidetracks (L,D)
Silvermine (B,D)
64 Greenwich Ave. (B,L,D)
Snowpea (L,D)
Somers Inn (L,D)
Sono Seaport (L,D)
Southport Brewing (L,D)
Spazzi (L,D)
Spinning Wheel (B,D)
Splash Pacific Rim (B,D)
Steak Loft (L,D)
Stonehenge (B,D)
Sunrise Pizza (L,D)
Sunset Grille (L,D)
Taj Mahal (L,D)
Tartufo (B,D)
Tavern on Main (L,D)
Terra Mar Grille (B,D)
Terra Ristorante (D)
Thataway Café (B,L,D)
Three Bears (B,D)
Tigin (B,L,D)
Tollgate Hill (B,D)
Tributary (L,D)
Trout Brook (L,D)
Truc Orient (L,D)
Tuscan Oven (B,L,D)
Two Steps (B,L,D)
Uncle Dai's (L,D)
V - A Rest. (D)
Valbella! (D)
Valentino (L,D)
Venetian (L,D)
Versailles (B,D)
Via Sforza (L,D)
Water's Edge (B,D)
Water St. Cafe (D)
West Main (L,D)
West St. Grill (L,D)
Whitman (B,D)
Wine & Roses (L,D)
Woodland (D)
Yankee Pedlar (L,D)
Yankee Silversmith (B,D)

Senior Appeal
Bloomfield Seafood
Cafe Lulu
Hawthorne Inn
Hearth Cafe
La Bretagne
Panda Pavilion
Saybrook Fish Hse.
Silvermine
Three Bears
Three Brothers
Whitman

Singles Scenes
Amberjacks
Ann Howard's Apricots
Archie Moore's
Arizona Flats
Bank St. Brewing
Boxing Cat Grill
Centro
Chart House
Coach's Sports B&G
Frank Pepe Pizzeria
Frank Pepe's The Spot
La Hacienda
Mackenzie's Grill
Paradise B&G
Playwright
Rattlesnake
64 Greenwich Ave.

Sleepers
(Good to excellent food, but
little known)
Adriana's
Aleia's
Altnaveigh Inn
Ambassador of India
Ash Creek
Bacco's
Barcelona Wine
Bellini
Bennett's
Bentley's
Biscotti
Bistro Café
Bistro East
Brookfield Bistro
Brookside Bistro
Brookside Rest.
Buon Appetito
Cafe Allègre
Cafe Pika Tapas

Cannery
Carmen Anthony
Cavey's
Cedar's Steak Hse.
Cheng Du
Chez Pierre
China Pavilion
ClearWaters
Clemente's
Colonial Tymes
Costa Del Sol
Côte d'Azur
Dakota
Diana
Diorio
Drawbridge Inne
El Inca
Fiddler's
First & Last
Flanders Fish Mkt.
Flood Tide
Fortune Village
Gaetano's
Gennaro's
Golden Lamb
Golden Pagoda
G.P. Cheffields
Great Taste
Greenwoods Mkt.
Grist Mill
G.W. Tavern
Harry's Pizza
Hawthorne Inn
Hogan's Miguels
Il Mulino
It's Only Natural
King and I
Kotobuki
La Taverna
La Trattoria
Le Bon Coin
Lemon Grass
Lenny & Joe's
Leon's
Lily's
Little Mark's
Lotus
Luigi's
Luna Pizza
Main & Hopewell
Mako of Japan
Marisa's
Métro bís
Metropolitan

Murasaki
Netto's
North Cove
Olive Tree
Ondine
Paci
Pane Vino
Pantry
Pearl of Budapest
Peppercorn's
Per Bacco!
Piccolo Arancio
Pierpont's
Plum Tree
Prince of Wales
Ragamont Inn
Ralph 'n' Rich's
Randall's Ordinary
Rest. Bravo Bravo
Rib House
Sadler's
Scribner's
Seasons
Sesame Seed
Shady Glen
Shish Kebab
Simsbury 1820 Hse.
Snowpea
Somers Inn
Spinell's
Splash! B&G
Sprouts Café
Stagecoach Hill
Steve's
Taj Mahal
Tapas
Tartaglia's
Tartufo
Tollgate Hill
Tributary
Valentino
Water St. Cafe
West Main

Teflons

(Get lots of business, despite
so-so food, i.e. they have
other attractions that prevent
criticism from sticking)
Bertucci's
Boston Market
Onion Alley
Rattlesnake
Rusty Scupper

Smoking Prohibited

(May be permissible at bar or
outdoors)
American Pie Co.
Arizona Flats
Arizona Grill
Aspen Gardens
Bamboo Grill
Bangkok Gdns.
Beach House
Bee and Thistle
Bella Italia
Bellini
Bentley's
Biscotti
Bistro on the Green
Bloodroot
Bloomfield Seafood
Bombay's Authentic
Boston Market
Boulders Inn
Bridge Café
Brookfield Bistro
Brookside Bistro
Buon Appetito
Cafe Allègre
Calexico
Cannery
Center Grille
Char Koon
Cheng Du
Claire's
Clemente's
Copper Beech Inn
County Seat
Cuckoo's Nest
Curtis House
DeRosa's Firehse.
Doc's
Elms Rest.
Fiddler's
Flanders Fish Mkt.
Frank Pepe's The Spot
Golden Lamb
Grappa
Greenwoods Mkt.
Grist Mill
Griswold Inn
Hearth Cafe
Hopkins Inn
Inn/Lake Waramaug
It's Only Natural
King and I
La Colline Verte

Sloppy Jose's
Steak Loft
Sunrise Pizza
Tartaglia's
Three Brothers
Tommy's
Wine & Roses
Yankee Pedlar

Visitors on Expense Accounts

Amadeus
Baang Café
Cavey's
Da Pietro's
Elms Rest.
Homestead Inn
Inn/Ridgefield
Jean-Louis
L'Abbee
La Colline Verte
Max Downtown
Mayflower Inn
Meson Galicia
Rest. at National Hall
Rest. du Village
Spazzi
Splash Pacific Rim
Stonehenge
West St. Grill

Wheelchair Access
(Most places now have wheelchair access; call in advance to check)

Wine/Beer Only
Abruzzi Kitchen
Ambassador of India
American Pie Co.
Angelina's
Aspen Gardens
Bangkok
Bentley's
Bloodroot
Bloomfield Seafood
Bombay's Authentic
Brick Oven
Brookfield Bistro
Center Grille
Chan's Choice
Char Koon
Costa Del Sol
DeRosa's Firehse.

Dolce Vita
Elm St. Oyster
First & Last
Frank Pepe Pizzeria
Frank Pepe's The Spot
Gail's Station Hse.
Harry's Pizza
King and I
Kotobuki
Lemon Grass
Lime
Little Mark's
Luna Pizza
Madd Hatter
Mako of Japan
Maria's Trattoria
Mario the Baker
Mona Lisa
Monica's
Mumbo Jumbo
Murasaki
Museum Cafe
Mystic Pizza
North Cove
Orem's Diner
Pantry
Pasta Nostra
Pasta Vera
Plum Tree
Post Corner
Russell's Ribs
Sadler's
Sally's Apizza
Sesame Seed
Snowpea
Sunrise Pizza
Tapas
Terra Ristorante
Thai Orchid
Truc Orient

Winning Wine Lists
Amadeus
Barcelona Wine
Biscotti
Boulders Inn
Cavey's
Copper Beech Inn
Maiden Lane
Rest. at National Hall
Rest. du Village
Stonehenge

Young Children
(Besides the normal fast food places; * indicates children's menu available)

Archie Moore's
Barkie's*
Bertucci's*
Biscotti*
Boston Market*
Boxcar Cantina*
Breakaway
Brick Oven
Bricks*
Brookside Rest.*
Bugaboo Creek
Bull's Head Diner
Buster's BBQ*
Center Grille*
Chuck's*
County Seat*
Curtis House*
DeRosa's Firehse.
Dome*
Elizabeth's*
Firehouse Deli
Frank Pepe Pizzeria
Frank Pepe's The Spot
Gail's Station Hse.*
John Harvard's*
Lily's*
Luna Pizza
Mackenzie's Grill
Manero's
Marlborough*
Max Steaks*
Miguel's*
Mill Pond Café*
Moody's B&G*
Mooring*
Museum Cafe*
Mystic Pizza

Oasis Diner*
Orem's Diner*
Oxford House*
Panda Pavilion
Pasta Garden*
Pat's Kountry Kit.*
Pellicci's*
Peppermill*
Post Corner*
Rattlesnake
Red Lion*
Rein's NY*
Roberto's*
Rudy's*
Russell's Ribs*
Sadler's*
Sakura
Sally's Apizza
San Miguel*
Saybrook Fish Hse.*
Seascape*
Shady Glen*
Sidetracks*
Sloppy Jose's*
Sono Seaport*
Southport Brewing*
Steak Loft*
Su Casa*
Sunrise Pizza*
Sunset Grille*
Tartaglia's
Three Brothers
Trout Brook*
Two Steps*
Vazzy's*
Viva Zapata*

Southern New York State

Southern NY's Favorites

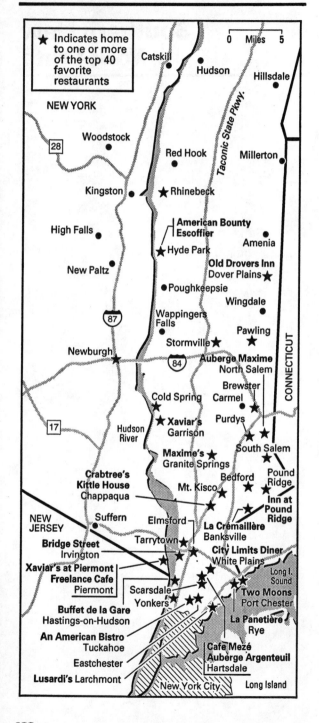

★ Indicates home to one or more of the top 40 favorite restaurants

0   Miles   5

NEW YORK

NEW JERSEY

CONNECTICUT

Taconic State Pkwy.

Catskill

Hudson

Hillsdale

Woodstock

28

Red Hook

Millerton

Kingston

★ Rhinebeck

High Falls

American Bounty Escoffier

Amenia

★ Hyde Park

New Paltz

Old Drovers Inn
Dover Plains ★

87

Poughkeepsie

Wingdale

Wappingers Falls

Pawling

Stormville ★

Newburgh

84

Auberge Maxime
North Salem

Cold Spring

Brewster

Carmel

17

Hudson River

★ **Xaviar's**
Garrison

Purdys

South Salem

Maxime's ★
Granite Springs

Bedford

Pound Ridge

Crabtree's Kittle House
Chappaqua

Mt. Kisco

Inn at Pound Ridge

Suffern

Elmsford

La Crémaillère
Banksville

Bridge Street
Irvington

Tarrytown

City Limits Diner
White Plains

Xaviar's at Piermont
Freelance Cafe
Piermont

Long I. Sound

Scarsdale

Yonkers

Two Moons
Port Chester

Buffet de la Gare
Hastings-on-Hudson

La Panetière
Rye

An American Bistro
Tuckahoe

Eastchester

Cafe Mezé
Auberge Argenteuil
Hartsdale

Lusardi's Larchmont

New York City

Long Island

Southern New York's Favorite Restaurants

Each of our reviewers has been asked to name his or her five favorite restaurants. The 40 spots most frequently named, in order of their popularity, are:

1. La Panetière
2. Xaviar's at Piermont
3. Crabtree's Kittle House
4. Freelance Cafe
5. La Crémaillère
6. Xaviar's
7. Two Moons
8. American Bounty
9. Escoffier
10. Lusardi's
11. Maxime's
12. An American Bistro
13. Inn at Pound Ridge
14. Buffet de la Gare
15. Auberge Maxime
16. Auberge Argenteuil
17. City Limits Diner
18. Cafe Mezé
19. Bridge Street
20. Old Drovers Inn
21. Le Chateau
22. Beekman 1766 Tavern
23. Harralds
24. Bistro Twenty-Two
25. Plumbush
26. Lexington Square Cafe
27. Bengal Tiger
28. Arch
29. Box Tree
30. Il Cenàcolo
31. Bird & Bottle Inn
32. Hunan Village
33. McKinney & Doyle
34. Pinocchio
35. Azuma Sushi
36. La Camelia
37. Ruth's Chris
38. Luna
39. Ichi Riki
40. Il Cigno

It's obvious that many of the restaurants on the above list are among the most expensive, but Connecticut/Southern New York diners also love a bargain. Were popularity calibrated to price, we suspect that a number of other restaurants would join the above ranks. Thus, we have listed over 75 Best Buys on pages 144–145.

Top Ratings*

Top 40 Food Ranking

28 Xaviar's at Piermont
   Xaviar's
   Il Cenàcolo
   Maxime's
   Freelance Cafe
   La Panetière
27 Harralds
   Buffet de la Gare
   La Crémaillère
   Azuma Sushi
   American Bounty
   Le Pavillon
26 Escoffier
   Auberge Maxime
   Aubergine
   Caterina de Medici
   España
25 Zephs'
   Marcello's
   Le Chateau

   McKinney & Doyle
   Box Tree
   Cafe Tamayo
   Arch
   Bois d'Arc
   Citrus Grille
   Calico
24 DePuy Canal House
   L'Europe
   Le Chambord
   Crabtree's Kittle House
   Bistro Twenty-Two
   An American Bistro
   Pinocchio
   Marichu
   Il Cigno
   Le Petit Bistro
   Il Portico
   Inn at Pound Ridge
   Hunan Village

Top Spots by Cuisine

Top Additiona
   Dolcigno Tuscan Grill
   Down by the Bay
   Laudau Grill
   Restaurant X
   Scarsdale Cafe

Top American (New)
28 Xaviar's at Piermont
   Xaviar's
   Freelance Cafe
25 McKinney & Doyle
   Cafe Tamayo

Top American (Traditional)
23 Troutbeck
22 Bird & Bottle Inn
20 Carl's
18 Red Hook Inn
   Hudson House

Top Brunch
28 Xaviar's at Piermont
   Xaviar's
   Maxime's
25 Marcello's
   McKinney & Doyle

Top Chinese
24 Hunan Village
23 Ray's Cafe
22 K. Fung's
21 China Rose
20 Jade Palace

Top Continental
24 L'Europe
23 Inn at Osborne Hill
   Plumbush
22 Satsuma-Ya
21 Locust Tree Inn

---

* Excluding restaurants with low voting.

Top Eclectic
27 Harralds
25 Arch
   Citrus Grille
24 Bistro Twenty-Two
23 Bridge Street

Top French
28 Maxime's
   La Panetière
27 Buffet de la Gare
   La Crémaillère
   Le Pavillon

Top Hotel Dining
25 Box Tree
24 Crabtree's Kittle Hse.
23 Old Drovers Inn
   Troutbeck
   Inn at Osborne Hill

Top Indian
23 Jaipore
22 Malabar Hill
   India House
   Bengal Tiger
   Dawat

Top Italian (Northern)
28 Il Cenácolo
26 Caterina de Medici
24 Il Cigno
   Il Portico
23 Lusardi's

Top Italian (North & South)
25 Marcello's
24 Pinocchio
23 Rustico
   Pane E Vino
22 Guida's

Top Japanese
27 Azuma Sushi
23 Ajiyoshi
   Gyosai
22 Ichi Riki
   Sushi Raku

Top Mexican/Tex Mex/SW
21 Santa Fe Tivoli
   El Coyote Flaco
19 Casa Miguel
   Armadillo
18 Santa Fe

Top Seafood
24 Il Portico
22 Conte's Fishmarket
   Eastchester Fish Gourmet
20 Caravela
   Aquario

Top Steakhouses
23 Ruth's Chris
22 Willett House
19 Tony's
18 Mitty's
17 Westchester Brewing Co.

Top Worth a Drive
28 Xaviar's/Piermont
   Xaviar's/Garrison
   Il Cenàcolo/Newburgh
   Freelance Cafe/Piermont
   Maxime's/Granite Springs

Top Yearlings/Rated
25 Bois d'Arc
23 Rustico
   Bridge Street
21 El Coyote Flaco
20 Cafe Antico

Top Yearlings/Unrated
L'Air de Paris
Blue Heron
Equus
Loft
Mountain Brook

Top 40 Decor Ranking

27 Le Chateau
Troutbeck
La Crémaillère
Box Tree
Maxime's
26 Escoffier
La Panetière
Aubergine
Harralds
Xaviar's
DePuy Canal House
Old Drovers Inn
25 Xaviar's at Piermont
Plumbush
Le Chambord
Locust Tree Inn
Auberge Maxime
Inn at Pound Ridge
American Bounty
24 Arch

Bird & Bottle Inn
Mount Fuji
Two Moons
Crabtree's Kittle House
Bistro Twenty-Two
23 Beekman 1766 Tavern
Pane E Vino
Old '76 House
St. Andrew's Cafe
Capriccio
22 Buffet de la Gare
Chart House
Mulino's
Monteverde
Il Cenàcolo
Giulio's
Il Portico
Gasho of Japan
Travelers Rest
Ruth's Chris

Top Outdoor

Arch
Auberge Maxime
Bois d'Arc
Cafe Tamayo

Crabtree's
Le Pavillon
Maxime's
Xaviar's

Top Romantic

Arch
Bird & Bottle Inn
Bistro Twenty-Two
Buffet de la Gare
Giulio's

La Duchesse Anne
Le Chambord
Maxime's
Plumbush
Xaviar's

Top Rooms

Harralds
Inn at Pound Ridge
Jaipore
La Crémaillère
La Panetière

Locust Tree Inn
Maxime's
Troutbeck
Two Moons
Xaviar's

Top Views

Bear Mountain Inn
Belvedere Inn
Brass Anchor
Breakneck Lodge
Capriccio

Crystal Bay
Goldie's
Locust Tree Inn
Monteverde
Northgate

Top 40 Service Ranking

27 Xaviar's
Xaviar's at Piermont
Maxime's
26 Harralds
La Panetière
Escoffier
25 American Bounty
Auberge Maxime
La Crémaillère
Troutbeck
Il Cenàcolo
DePuy Canal House
Arch
24 Freelance Cafe
Le Pavilion
Box Tree
Aubergine
Le Chateau
Buffet de la Gare
Plumbush

Le Petit Bistro
Calico
Bistro Twenty-Two
Marcello's
23 Piemonte
Caterina de Medici
Le Chambord
Crabtree's Kittle House
Zephs'
Il Portico
L'Europe
St. Andrew's Cafe
Capriccio
22 Citrus Grille
Bird & Bottle Inn
Old Drovers Inn
Mulino's
Inn at Pound Ridge
Auberge Argenteuil
McKinney & Doyle

Best Buys

Top 50 Bangs For The Buck

This list reflects the best dining values in our *Survey*. It is produced by dividing the cost of a meal into the combined ratings for food, decor and service.

1. Red Rooster Drive-In
2. Boston Market
3. Blazer Pub
4. Pizza Pizzazz
5. Grandma's of Yorktown
6. Candlelight Inn
7. Hunan 100
8. Taconic Diner
9. Imperial Wok
10. Golden Wok
11. India House
12. Cafe Mozart
13. El Coyote Flaco
14. Hartsdale Garden
15. Uno Chicago Bar & Grill
16. China Rose
17. David Chen
18. Temptations Cafe
19. Horsefeathers
20. K. Fung's
21. Hunan Village
22. Westchester Brewing Co.
23. Tarrytown Diner
24. Isabel's Cafe
25. City Limits Diner
26. Bear Cafe
27. Bengal Tiger
28. Rolling Rock Cafe
29. Ajiyoshi
30. Foster's Coach House
31. Calico
32. Nanuet Hotel
33. La Manda's
34. Armadillo
35. Pizza & Brew
36. St. Andrew's Cafe
37. Pizza Beat
38. Jade Palace
39. T.G.I. Friday's
40. Schneller's Restaurant
41. Sam's
42. Doubleday's
43. Epstein's Kosher Deli
44. Santa Fe Tivoli
45. Malabar Hill
46. Santa Fe
47. Pas-Tina
48. Casa Miguel
49. Rustico
50. Khan's Mongolian

Additional Good Values
(A bit more expensive, but worth every penny)

Amalfi
Blue Dolphin
Cafe Tamayo
Cascade Mountain
Freelance Cafe
Golden Duck
Gyosai
Ichi Riki
Jaipore
La Duchesse Anne
Latin American Cafe
Le Canard Enchainé
Le Provençal
Lexington Square Cafe
Marcel's
McKinney & Doyle
Mill House Panda
New World
Noda's
Osaka
Osteria Xe Sogni
Painter's
Pantanal
Pasta Cucina
Priya Indian Cuisine
Ray's Cafe
Scarborough Fair
Spiga
Susan's
Swaddee House

Southern NY State
1999 Additions

```
    R  = Recommendation Ratings
 ††††  = Don't Miss
  †††  = Very Good Bet
   ††  = Worth a Try, Not a Detour
    †  = Interesting, But No Big Deal
```

R | C

Beech Tree Grill ⬤Ⓢ   †† | I
1-3 Collegeview Ave. (opp. Vassar College), Poughkeepsie,
914-471-7279
Not a college kid hangout, this Poughkeepsie New American
caters to a loyal clientele that appreciates the easygoing
tavern ambiance, creative salads, sandwiches and the more
adventurous specials; beer hounds lap up the interesting
selection of brews on tap.

Bench & Bar, The   †† | M
44 Grand St. (Broadway), Newburgh, 914-562-4444
The name reflects this new, casual Contemporary
American's location close to the offices of the Orange
County D.A.; chef-owner John Grossi's weekly-changing
menu makes the most of seafood; there's live Chicago-
style blues on Thursday, jazz on Saturday and the bar, if not
the bench, is jumpin' till the wee small hours on weekends.

Cafe Segale   ††† | E
92 Purchase St. (Purdy Ave.), Rye, 914-967-2098
Like its siblings, Mount Kisco's Cafe Antico and NYC's Cafe
Nosidam, this Rye Italian has a casual bistro-style; where it
differs from its kin is in the menu's emphasis on game and
the quieter ambiance; downstairs, there's a glossy, apple red
space with windows that open to the sidewalk in summer,
while the intimate upstairs room is a more subdued shade.

Catamount Cafe Ⓢ   †† | M
Rte. 28, Mount Tremper, 914-688-7900
This Mount Tremper American flaunts its Catskill location by
proudly featuring foods from local purveyors on its seasonal
menu; the haute heartland cooking is complemented by
rustic log cabin decor and views of the Esopus Creek;
there's live music on weekends and at Sunday brunch.

Cinema Ristorante Ⓢ   ††† | M
468 Ashford Ave. (west of Rte. 9A), Ardsley, 914-693-9200
There's a marquee over the bar but no popcorn on the menu
at this Ardsley Italian; the movie posters and film music
provide an apropos backdrop for classic cooking, and
seafood is a particular strength; set in a cul-de-sac off
Route 9A, Cinema can be hard to find and parking is limited –
ask about valet service when making a reservation.

Dolcigno Tuscan Grill S ††† M
91 Main St., Cold Spring, 914-265-5582
A welcome addition to Cold Spring, this stylish Northern
Italian take on the trattoria emphasizes simply prepared
seasonal foods; it's apt that the wooden walls are lined
with bottles as there's a frequently changing wine list
chosen by co-owner/manager Cathryn Fadde, whose
partner is Sali Hadzibrahimi, owner of the highly rated Il
Cenàcolo in Newburgh.

Down by the Bay S †††† M
410 W. Boston Post Rd., Mamaroneck, 914-381-6939
Set smack across the street from the water, this superb
Mamaroneck seafood house was once home to James
Fenimore Cooper; today under the ownership of brothers
Scott and Ken Jagr it's regained the glory it once enjoyed as
a tavern/restaurant; Ken runs the pleasant, accommodating
front of the house, which includes a busy bar, while
Scott's behind the stove preparing precisely cooked and
deftly seasoned seafood.

Fireworks Brewery S †† M
25 S. Broadway, White Plains, 914-448-BEER
Every night is the Fourth of July at this red-white-and-blue-
bedecked microbrewery in Downtown White Plains; the
menu ranges from New American to upscale renditions
of traditional pub fare, all designed to complement the
handcrafted brews stored in enormous beer tanks.

Gadaleto's Seafood Market & Restaurant †† M
1 Cherry Hill Ctr. (Main St.), New Paltz, 914-255-1717
Regulars had been forever asking Steven Gadaleto to add a
restaurant to his family's long-standing New Paltz seafood
market because they gobbled up its grilled and fried takeout fare; so he created an aquatic-hued dining room
featuring the best of what NY, Boston and Maine have to
offer; a 'fresh fish wish list' allows diners to sample some
of the more unusual species available in the market, but
there are also some meat and vegetarian options.

Grill F/X S ††† M
112 N. Main St. (Willett St.), Port Chester, 914-939-4745
Billing itself as the northeast's only South African restaurant,
this Port Chester newcomer reflects that nation's diverse
population, offering dishes that combine the sweet and
spicy flavors of Indian and Malay cuisines with more
straightforward European-influenced grilled meat, fish
and fowl (yes, ostrich is on the menu); the culinary safari
is supplemented by a wide selection of South African wines
and beers, and the imported African arts and crafts on
display in the airy, high-ceilinged space are for sale.

Hunan Garden ⑤   ttt | I

Southside Plaza, 134 North Ave., New Rochelle,
914-633-3232
The bright pink walls are matched by the vibrant food and
sunny service at this refreshing New Rochelle Chinese;
the lengthy menu includes all the typical offerings, but
also features casseroles and other entrees not found at
every fried rice palace; since the kitchen uses very fresh
ingredients and makes its own noodles, you can distinctly
taste a difference in even the most basic dishes.

Ipanema Grill ⑤   tt | M

7 Pondfield Rd. (Sagamore Rd.), Bronxville, 914-395-3411
Bronxville native Alfredo Pedro comes home with this new
Brazilian sibling of his NYC restaurant; unlike its older
namesake, it's a *rodizio* where, for a reasonable set price,
diners can partake of a never-ending supply of rotisserie-
cooked meats and fish, plus side dishes, as well as an
ever-changing array of hot and cold fare from a handsome
tiled buffet table; as in Brazil, the famed black bean stew,
feijoada, is served only on Saturday, while *bossa nova*
music is performed Thursdays – Saturdays.

John's Harvest Inn ⑤   t | M

633 Rte. 17M, Middletown, 914-343-6630
Time marches on and also stands still at this stalwart
Middletown Continental where chef-owner John Botti
displays his collection of over 100 clocks in two Victorian-
style dining rooms; not all of the timepieces are ticking,
so diners are treated to a symphony, not a cacophony, of
chimes and can enjoy the and hearty cooking.

Landau Grill, The ⑤   tttt | M

17 Mill Hill Rd. (Rte. 212), Woodstock, 914-679-8937
Making Woodstock feel and look a little like South Beach,
this hip New American with its large sidewalk patio and
huge wrap-around bar is a big scene, but it's also well worth
a visit for co-owner Niels Nilson's creative cooking, which
emphasizes seafood; best of all, despite being trendy this
newcomer values service and food over fashion.

Le Mas ⑤   ttt | E

325 Bedford Rd. (Rte. 117), Bedford Hills, 914-242-3417
Michel Mastantuono owned several much-lauded
restaurants in California; now with his son Eric he's brought
his sunny take on French cuisine to a 150-year-old colonial
whose cozy interior is reminiscent of a typical Provençal
farmhouse or *mas*; the post-performance prix fixe that's
available in summer during Caramoor's classical music
concerts is a good value.

Loretta Charles' S   ††† │ M │
7159 Rte. 28 (4 mi. west of Phoenicia), Shandaken, 914-688-2550
Named for co-owner Loretta Jones who manages the front
of house and her husband Charles who mans the stoves,
this Shandaken New American is a snug, hospitable spot
with gracious service and a grill menu; chef Jones cooks
over a natural wood fire, changing his menu almost daily
to make the best use of the freshest available ingredients;
N.B. the restaurant does not accept reservations and the
dining room is small.

Marco Restaurant   ††† │ E │
612 Rte. 6 (Main St.), Lake Mahopac, 914-621-1648
Self-taught chef-owner Marco Donelli has been honing his
culinary and front-of-house skills over the last six years
and steadily building up a band of diners dedicated to his
Mahopac Contemporary American; the seasonally-changing
menu features unusual game, and the wine list focuses
on small boutique producers; while the dining room is
nonsmoking, the lounge lures cigar smokers with a humidor;
N.B. open Sundays in summer.

Mariner, The S   †† │ M │
701 Piermont Ave., Piermont, 914-365-1360
River views abound at this slick new Piermont seafooder
with an extensive selection of fresh oysters as well as a
variety of cooked fish and shellfish; the twinkling lights of
the Tappan Zee Bridge are visible from the tiered dining
room, which has a subtle nautical motif; there's an outdoor
deck in summer, while in the colder months three fireplaces
provide a cozy indoor focus.

Nino's S   †† │ M │
355 Rte. 123, South Salem, 914-533-2671
This South Salem colonial has been a restaurant for
over 100 years and its new owner is also a veteran of the
restaurant scene: this is Nino Camaj's 17th eatery and it's
a much fancier establishment than his identically named
NYC pizzeria; good pies are available for takeout, while
more extensive Italian fare is served in comfortable,
expansive dining rooms with huge windows that look out
to the woods beyond.

Oliver's of Goshen S   † │ M │
40 Park Pl. (near racetrack), Goshen, 914-294-5077
Blimey, we overlooked this Goshen landmark serving
Traditional American and British fare; Oliver Twist would
be right at home in the dark, Victorian-style rooms (one has
views of the neighboring historic racecourse) and he'd
probably quaff an English ale or two from the extensive
selection available here.

Oriental House, The S   tt | M
36 Main St. (Rte. 52), Pine Bush, 914-744-8663
The links between Korean and Japanese cuisine are
apparent at this family-run Pine Bush Asian; there's an
admirable sushi bar, but the menu's real strength lies with
Korean specialties such as *chul pan gooyi* or cooking on
the grill, which is similar to Japanese hibachi; the room is
small, tables are close together and the decor is somewhat
utilitarian, but service is friendly and the Korean owners
love introducing novices to their native cuisine.

Pillars Carriage House, The S   t | M
Rte. 20 (1 mi. west of Rte. 22), New Lebanon, 518-794-8007
Old-fashioned excess rules at this New Lebanon American-
Continental where co-owner Patti Bock welcomes guests
to what was a popular roadhouse during prohibition and
the carriage house of a grand estate long before that; Bock,
with her chef/husband Peter, have created an elegant
interior where each meal begins with light, fluffy popovers,
and entrees come with complimentary soup and salad.

Restaurant X and Bully Boy Bar S   tttt | M
117 Rte. 303 (NY Twy., exit 12), Congers, 914-268-6555
Peter Kelly, chef-owner of Xaviar's at Piermont and Xaviar's,
the top two rated restaurants for food in the *SoNYS Survey,*
expands his empire with this more casual and less pricey,
yet still top-notch, Congers New American where the menu
combines the old world (an updated Beef Wellington) with
the new (red snapper with fennel and star anise broth);
the largest of Kelly's enterprises, it seats 250 in a roomy
bar replete with roaring fire and several dining areas, each
with a different character.

Rocky's Broadway Cafe S   tt | M
*90 Broadway (bet. Grand & Liberty Sts.), Newburgh,
914-561-8466*
This spacious Newburgh Continental with an Italian accent
has a wrap-around balcony, tin ceilings and chandeliers
that evoke turn-of-the-century NYC; upstairs there's an
up-to-the-moment cigar bar complete with pool table.

Rosendale Cafe S⊄   tt | I
435 Main St. (Rte. 213), Rosendale, 914-658-9048
Changing exhibits by mostly local artists decorate the walls
of this homey Ulster County Vegetarian; in what was once
the Astoria Hotel, self-taught cooks and partners Susan
Morganstern and Susan Foss have created a casual place
to hang out and on Friday and Saturday nights the cafe
showcases live music.

Scarsdale Cafe, The 🅂   ⊞ M |
874 Scarsdale Ave. (Garth Rd.), Scarsdale, 914-472-2424
The name might lead you to expect casual fare, but chef-owner Connie Crupi creates intricate, architectural-looking cuisine at her classy New American located just around the corner from the local landmark, Zachy's wine store; she's built up a loyal following who feels the weeknight prix fixe is an especially good deal.

Tandoori 🅂   ⊞ M |
163 N. Main St. (I-95, exit 2), Port Chester, 914-937-2727
30 Division St., New Rochelle, 914-235-8390
These new Westchester Indians not only serve food cooked in the intense heat of the brick-and-clay tandoor oven, but also many of the dishes, including excellent vegetarian options, found at their popular older sibling, Elmsford's Malabar Hill; try bringing the kids to these friendly spots where service is brisk and dishes can be hot, or not.

Tramonto 🅂   ⊞ M |
27 Saw Mill River Rd., Hawthorne, 914-347-8220
Classic Italian cooking at moderate prices is the draw at this Hawthorne Italian run by three sisters; a long cherrywood bar sets the scene for a casual dining room where corporate types predominate at lunch, families and couples in the evenings.

Turquoise 🅂   ⊞ M |
236 Mamaroneck Ave., Mamaroneck, 914-381-3693
With a name like Turquoise you'd expect brilliant blue-green walls and you get them, along with a Turkish take on Middle Eastern cuisine; presentation is kept to a minimum, but the dips, salads and simple char-grilled meats are inviting; there's no liquor license and this popular place, across the street from a movie theater, can be very busy on weekends.

Alphabetical
Directory of
Southern NY State
Restaurants

Abatino's (N. White Plains) **S**   ▽ 17 | 9 | 14 | $17 |
N. White Plains Shopping Ctr., 670 N. Broadway (I-287),
914-686-0380
■ "The best marinara sauce" and "above-average pizza
and pasta" keep a coterie of faithful fans returning to
this veteran North White Plains Italian; there are also
"surprisingly good entree specials", but "no ambiance"
and "tight squeeze" seating lead some to suggest "takeout."

Abhilash India Cuisine   17 | 12 | 16 | $21 |
(New Rochelle) **S**
30 Division St. (bet. Main & Huguenot Sts.), 914-235-8390
☑ Perhaps "not what it used to be", this New Rochelle
Indian is still valued for "good breads", "interesting"
vegetarian choices and overall "inexpensive" pricing;
however, phobes complain about "service without a
smile", "tired" decor, a need for better housekeeping and
the "dumpy" neighborhood.

Abis (Mamaroneck) **S**   19 | 16 | 17 | $26 |
406 Mamaroneck Ave. (RR station), 914-698-8777
■ "A lively, fun introduction to Japanese cuisine", this
"handsome" Mamaroneck fixture (with a younger sibling
in Greenwich, CT) provides "learners' chopsticks" to help
novices manage the "crisp tempura"; devotees of "fresh"
sushi say the "Sunday brunch is a must, if you can handle
raw fish in the morning"; the main quibble is over "erratic
service" that can be "friendly" but "hopelessly slow."

Ajiyoshi (White Plains) **S**   23 | 16 | 21 | $26 |
291 Central Ave. (Rte. 119), 914-948-6651
■ "Like a trip to Japan" say admirers of this "bare-bones"
White Plains Japanese where "quality cuts of fish" are
transformed into sushi that's "as good as it gets"; "hot food"
is also "first class", and the staff is "kid friendly" too, so it's
easy to overlook the frequent "din" in the "small", busy room.

Albanese's (Scarsdale) **S**   13 | 8 | 15 | $19 |
807 Post Rd. (Brook St.), 914-472-0556
☑ Really a "pizza joint at heart", this "no-frills", "tavern"-
like Scarsdale Italian dishes out "thin-crusted" pies that are
"good", but "that's all"; while old-timers say the "typical
red sauce food has declined", devotees still keep coming
and the place is "often a madhouse."

Alba's (Port Chester) **S**   18 | 14 | 16 | $34 |
400 N. Main St. (Rectory St.), 914-937-2236
☑ "Informal, bustling" Northern Italian that attracts Port
Chester locals with "good-buy midweek specials" and
"excellent fish and pasta"; but critics carp that it's "nothing
to write home about" and even some fans bemoan the
"obtrusive" waiters; nevertheless, the majority considers
this a "very dependable" choice.

Alex & Henry's Roman Gardens   14   16   17 $31
(Scarsdale) **S**
Vernon Hills Shopping Ctr., 680 White Plains Rd. (bet. California & Wilmot Rds.), 914-725-4433
■ This "somewhat glitzy" Scarsdale Continental "catering hall" has a rep as "a wedding factory" with "mass-produced" fare, and many caution that it's better for parties than "a regular meal"; so "go for the dancing, not the food."

Allie's American Grille   ▽ 15   15   16 $23
(Tarrytown) **S**
Westchester Marriott Hotel, 670 White Plains Rd. (Rte. 87, exit 9), 914-631-2200
◪ There's no disguising the fact that the kitchen turns out somewhat "rushed hotel food", yet Tarrytowners who frequent this Marriott American explain it may be "plain vanilla" but it's "dependable."

Allyn's (Millbrook) **S**   19   19   18 $36
Rte. 44 (4 mi. east of Millbrook Village), 914-677-5888
◪ A haunt of "the horsey set", this "always crowded" Dutchess County farmhouse lures patrons with its "charming atmosphere" and "bucolic setting"; the "pricey" New American cooking "can be very good" but also "erratic", and some visitors detect a certain "attitude" from staff; try the "country" Sunday brunch on the "lovely porch."

Amalfi Restaurant   19   16   20 $29
(Briarcliff Manor) **S**
1112 Pleasantville Rd. (North State Rd.), 914-762-9200
◪ "Innovative" with "tasty, fresh pastas" say partisans of this "friendly" but "noisy" Italian; "twas better before they enlarged" and "lost their Arthur Avenue roots" lament naysayers who point out that "locals patronize it, but that's probably because there's not much else in the area."

Amendola's (Elmsford) **S** (CLOSED) – – – M
12 W. Main St. (Rte. 119), 914-592-6799
Few respondents have navigated Elmsford waters to the site of the former Westchester Trawler where the same ownership now provides seafood with an Italian slant.

AMERICAN BOUNTY   27   25   25 $40
RESTAURANT (Hyde Park)
Culinary Institute of American, 433 Albany Post Rd./Rte. 9 (across from W. Dorsey Ln.), 914-471-6608
■ "A joy for foodies", this "very special" CIA Regional American in Hyde Park generally provides "imaginative" food and "excellent" service that make it "worth the drive from anywhere"; the student cooks and waiters "really try hard" ("it helps when you're being graded"), and it's "fun to tour the kitchens"; N.B. "plan ahead" for a reservation and note that there's "nowhere to sleep nearby."

Amity Bakery   ▽ 24 | 11 | 20 | $24
(Warwick) **(CLOSED)**
110 Newport Bridge Rd./Amity Rd. (County Rte. 1), 914-258-3500
■ The few respondents who've made their way to this
Orange County bakery/cafe say "if you can find it" you'll
enjoy the "unusual" New American food, particularly the
array of "imaginative salads" offered "at reasonable prices"
in a "dressed-down, relaxed atmosphere."

AN AMERICAN BISTRO   24 | 17 | 21 | $32
(Tuckahoe) **S**
174 Marbledale Rd. (bet. Fisher Ave. & Main St.), 914-793-0807
■ Don't let the "out of the way" "industrial location" in
Tuckahoe deter you from trying the "creative, wholesome"
New American food at this "adorable dollhouse"; the
"presentation is wonderful" and fans sigh that it's "the
closest you will get to Union Square Cafe in the suburbs",
but the no reserving policy and "tight quarters" would
make "even Lilliputians feel crowded."

Angelina's Italian (Tuckahoe) **S**   20 | 14 | 18 | $25
97 Lake Ave. (Tuckahoe Rd.), 914-779-7976
◪ "It looks just like a typical pizza joint", but this Tuckahoe
entry has built a following for its "good, affordable"
"homemade Italian" dishes and "friendly" atmosphere;
while some sniff that it's "unremarkable" with "macho
waiters", most regard it as a "pleasant neighborhood place."

Antonio's (White Plains)   – | – | – | M
(fka La Bella Napoli)
105 Mamaroneck Ave. (Post Rd.), 914-946-2411
White Plains residents find this storefront Italian
reassuringly familiar: owner Antonio took over La Bella
Napoli, where he was manager, and left the decor and
much of the reasonably priced menu unchanged, which
attracts a business lunch crowd and families at dinner.

Aquario (West Harrison) **S**   20 | 16 | 19 | $34
141 E. Lake St. (on Silver Lake), 914-287-0220
■ "Generous portions" of "hearty" Portuguese-Brazilian
seafood, the "best lobster and grilled shrimp" and
"hospitable" treatment make this chef-owned West Harrison
spot "a welcome change" and "a fun place to try new
dishes"; while fans find the service "cheerful", a number of
others fault it as "unbelievably slow" and "overbearing."

ARCH RESTAURANT (Brewster) **S**   25 | 24 | 25 | $52
Rte. 22N (end of I-684), 914-279-5011
■ For a "special occasion" this "fixed-price, formal but
excellent" countryside Eclectic-French gets high marks;
inevitably a few find it "pretentious" and "pricey", but
they're outvoted by the many who adore the "wonderful
food, lovely service" and "romantic garden."

Ardsley Ale House (Ardsley) 🇸 ▽ 12 | 12 | 13 | $19
*660 Saw Mill River Rd./Rte. 9A (Ashford Ave.),
914-674-0000*
◪ If you're hungry this Ardsley "bar with food" will suffice, but most consider it a better place for sipping a brew from the "large selection of beers"; weather permitting, the patio makes for "good outside dining."

Aria (Yonkers) 🇸   19 | 15 | 17 | $26
2375 Central Park Ave. (Jackson Ave.), 914-779-9888
■ "Good, straightforward" "tabletop Korean barbecue" hits high notes with fans of this popular Yonkers eatery; some find it "pricey" for the "small portions", but "kids love" the "grill-your-own" approach and families are advised to "go early" because it can get "crowded and smoky."

Armadillo Bar & Grill   ▽ 19 | 16 | 18 | $24
(Kingston) 🇸
97 Abeel St. (Wurts & Dock Sts.), 914-339-1550
◪ "Funky and good" with service that can either be "friendly" or "in your face", this Kingston Tex-Mex has a "deafening margarita scene" best appreciated by those who like to come out of their shell; though some write off the food as strictly "standard", others enthuse it's "surprisingly good" and "sometimes brilliant."

Armonk Crossings   14 | 15 | 15 | $26
(Armonk) 🇸 (CLOSED)
465 Main St./Rte. 128, 914-273-5700
◪ It's the "lively bar scene" more than the "very ordinary" menu that draws many to this Armonk American; critics snipe it's just a "smoky", "crowded pickup joint" serving up "strange flavors", but fans say "some jammin' music" on weekend nights, along with "nice outdoor tables" and "friendly, informal service", make it worth crossing over the threshold.

Armonk Grill (Armonk) 🇸   13 | 11 | 14 | $24
1 Kent Pl. (Rte. 128), 914-273-6444
◪ "A hamburger joint pretending to be a restaurant" is one way to look at this Westchester casual American; a few supporters say it's "good" if "a little overpriced", but the consensus is that the food is "no big deal" and it's best to "go to socialize, have a beer and sit on the outside patio."

Ashley's (White Plains) ◖🇸   13 | 13 | 14 | $21
51 Mamaroneck Ave. (Martine Ave.), 914-683-5999
◪ An "action-packed bar" and a "convenient" Downtown location are what bring many diners to this "unexceptional" White Plains Traditional American; though a few feel it's "good for lunch" or a "quick snack", most say it's "seen better days."

Atrium (Rye Brook) **S** | – | – | – | E |
*Doral Arrowwood, Anderson Hill Rd. (east of SUNY
Purchase), 914-935-6600*
Set in a "big, big room with several levels", this Rye Brook
hotel American has a "soothing, peaceful" ambiance and
excellent views of the "Westchester County airport traffic at
sunset"; while some find the food "nothing original", others
praise the "exquisite buffet" and "fabulous brunch", calling
it a good choice for "special occasions."

At the Reef (Cortlandt Manor) | – | – | – | M |
(fka Reef 'N Beef)
*Rte. 9/Annsville Circle (3 mi. east of Bear Mtn. Bridge),
914-737-4959*
They took the beef out of the reef, but left it on the menu
at this Cortlandt Manor seafooder-steakhouse; loyalists
say "it's one of the few good values in Westchester for
fair food", but sophisticates sigh it's "commercial" and
"tired" – "that they have a salad bar says it all."

AUBERGE ARGENTEUIL | 22 | 20 | 22 | $44 |
(Hartsdale)
42 N. Healy Ave. (Central Park Ave.), 914-948-0597
■ "Almost as good as when it was new", this "romantic old
house high on a hill" in Hartsdale offers "old-fashioned
Classic French" fare in a "warm and friendly" atmosphere;
on the downside, some find it "snobby" and "hard to
find", particularly at night.

AUBERGE MAXIME | 26 | 25 | 25 | $53 |
(North Salem) **S**
721 Titicus Rd. (Rtes. 116 & 121), 914-669-5450
■ This "quintessential French inn" in Northern Westchester
is "the place to go for that special evening", especially if you
fancy "excellent duck" or "the best soufflé in the world";
respondents' sighs are almost audible as they recall "haute
cuisine and service at its finest" in a "wonderful room"; the
only quibble is that it's expensive and the "extra charges
on the prix fixe menu are obnoxious."

AUBERGINE (Hillsdale) **S** | 26 | 26 | 24 | $49 |
(fka L'Hostellerie Bressane)
Rtes. 22 & 23, 518-325-3412
■ Word is that the owners are "doing an excellent job" at
this "charming" antiques-filled Columbia County 1783 inn
offering overnight accomodation; chef David Lawson's
French-inspired American cooking is much appreciated as
are "great desserts", an extensive wine list and "friendly
service"; it's "as good as it gets in our area" and for those
en route to Tanglewood, it's well worth a visit.

AZUMA SUSHI RESTAURANT   27 | 16 | 19 | $33 |
(Hartsdale) **S**
219 E. Hartsdale Ave. (Central Park Ave.), 914-725-0660
■ Its numerous fans agree "it's the best sushi on the
planet" – perhaps that's why "it's almost impossible to get
a table" at this small Hartsdale Japanese that serves no
cooked dishes; but few mind waiting for such "swimmingly
delicious" fare, and insiders suggest "reserving a seat at
the sushi bar" to watch the chefs and "get tips on what to
order"; however, even enthusiasts cite service that can
be "sour" and "escalating prices."

Baci (Larchmont)   – | – | – | M |
154 Larchmont Ave. (1 block south of Boston Post Rd.),
914-833-3399
A Northern Italian newcomer with a strong Mediterranean
influence and an extensive wine list, this Larchmont
spot is a partnership between chef Joseph Vuli and
John Nickach, who were previously at Giardino's in
Briarcliff; expansive windows make the large storefront
setting light and airy.

Backwater Grill (Canaan) **S**   – | – | – | M |
(fka Hagan's Queechy Lake Inn)
Queechy Lake Dr. (Rtes. 295 & 22), 518-781-4933
Off the beaten track, this Columbia County newcomer has
lake views to enhance its plain American fare; reasonable
prices help make it particularly popular with families.

Bamboo Garden   ▽ 14 | 12 | 15 | $18 |
(White Plains) **S** (CLOSED)
Cross Road Shopping Ctr., 425 Tarrytown Rd., 914-683-7906
☑ While some say this White Plains "shopping center"
Chinese is a "reliable" choice that offers "excellent lunch
specials" and "good soup noodles", others dismiss it as
"average" and "nothing special"; "fast service" pleases
eat-and-run types.

Banta's Steak & Stein   12 | 13 | 15 | $22 |
935 Union Ave. (south of Rte.17K), New Windsor,
914-564-7678
Nine Mall Plaza, 859 South Rd. (Rte. 9), Wappingers Falls,
914-297-6770 **S**
☑ Many respondents "can't understand the popularity" of
these veteran "steakhouses with tough steaks" and warn
"don't try to impress a date here"; still, supporters say
they're "dependable" and "good for a quick meal" adding
that "the patio is great" in summer.

Bear Cafe (Bearsville) S
22 | 21 | 20 | $29

295A Tinker St. (Rte. 212), 914-679-5555

■ Chef and co-owner Eric Mann's "imaginative" New American food is served in a suitably "lovely setting" beside a stream in a hamlet of the town of Woodstock; no hidden gem, this "trendy" place is a "big local scene" with frequent "celebrity sightings", so it's often "too crowded on weekends."

Bear Cafe Catering at The Petersen House (Bearsville) S
– | – | – | M

295 Tinker St. (Rte. 212 & Whittenburg Rd.), 914-679-8990

Just west of Woodstock in a stunning streamside setting, this New American with an International Mix is from the "earnest" owners of the neighboring Bear Cafe; N.B. open only for Sunday brunch.

Bear Mountain Inn (Bear Mountain) S
12 | 19 | 14 | $27

Bear Mtn. State Park, Rte. 9W South (Palisades Pkwy.), 914-786-2731

■ The consensus is that the Traditional American fare "won't match the setting" at this "tourist trap" "park inn with poor food"; but the "unique", "very rustic" decor gets higher marks and there's nothing but praise for the "outstanding views of the lake and hills."

Beechmont Restaurant (New Rochelle) S
▽ 15 | 12 | 14 | $18

750 North Ave. (Eastchester Rd. & Beechmont Dr.), 914-636-9533

◪ "Excellent for a roadhouse" is the verdict on the "BBQ ribs", "burgers and pub food" served up at this New Rochelle "college hangout"; a few Iona alumni report that it "seemed better long ago", but that may be nostalgia talking; then as now, amidst the smoke and camaraderie few notice the "delightful country setting."

Beekman 1766 Tavern, The (Rhinebeck) S
22 | 23 | 21 | $38

The Beekman Arms, 4 Mill St. (Market St.), 914-871-1766

◪ The "wood-paneled dining rooms" of "the oldest [continually operating] inn in America" are so authentic you "expect George Washington to enter", but while fans pity George for having "missed out" on the "sophisticated" American Regional fare at Larry Forgione's Rhinebeck outpost, critics find it "highly overrated" and feel "Forgione should pay more attention"; still, it's a "good choice" for a "wonderful Sunday brunch."

Belvedere Inn   ▽ 21 | 27 | 18 | $42 |
(Staatsburg On Hudson) **S**
10 Albany Post Rd. (Rte. 9 & County Rte. 84), 914-889-8000
■ The owners of Manhattan's Panarella's have created a "sophisticated menu and surroundings" at their new restaurant and inn on a 10-acre Dutchess County estate; the French-Tuscan cuisine is "creative", if "pricey", but service can be "ditzy"; there are amazing mountain and river views from the dining room or one of the three terraces.

Bengal Tiger (White Plains) **S**   22 | 18 | 19 | $25 |
140 E. Post Rd. (bet. Mamaroneck Ave. & Court St.), 914-948-5191
■ "If you want Indian, this is the place" roar the many Westchester devotees who consider this "exotically decorated" White Plains veteran "still the best"; several surveyors agree the cooking "has improved over the last year" and are prepared to endure a "long wait" to enjoy the "seductive Indian food with plenty of variety"; a few dissenters cite "smaller portions and slightly higher prices", but all consider "the bountiful buffet lunch" "a bargain."

Benny's Landmark   16 | 9 | 14 | $26 |
(Irvington) **S** (CLOSED)
6 S. Broadway (Rte. 9 & Main St.), 914-591-2033
◪ Critics say this "real '60s seafood place" is "living off its past reputation", which keeps it "noisy, crowded and smoky" with regulars who appreciate the "$5 lunch specials"; loyalists also value this Irvington institution for a "quick, tasty meal" and "cheerful service", managing to overlook the "American Legion decor."

Bird & Bottle Inn, The (Garrison) **S** 22 | 24 | 22 | $44 |
Bird & Bottle Inn, Rte. 9/Old Albany Post Rd., 914-424-3000
◪ "Tucked away in Northern Westchester", this pre-Revolutionary inn is "a classic that still delivers", albeit at a "high price"; a few faultfinders believe the cooking is not as memorable as the colonial ambiance, but as the ratings show, most consider the American food "superb"; with its "huge fireplaces", this "cozy, charming and comfortable" place is an ideal "romantic hideaway."

Bistro Maxime (Chappaqua)   22 | 20 | 22 | $41 |
136 N. Greeley Ave. (King St.), 914-238-0362
◪ "Hard to find but excellent" is the word on this Chappaqua bistro, the baby of the Maxime clan; with "fresh ingredients and straightforward preparation", Francophiles say the food is "pretty authentic", if "a bit overpriced"; the "intimate and refined" ambiance makes for "classy dining", though many find it "noisy beyond belief"; for those watching their wallet "lunch is a better buy."

Bistro Twenty-Two (Bedford) S   24 24 24 $48
391 Old Post Rd. (east of Rte. 684), 914-234-7333
■ Compliments abound for Bedford's Eclectic-French favorite, which actually turns 21 this year; though it "looks like a joint outside", inside all is "understated elegance", with "professional waiters", "perfect presentation" and "wonderful food"; while a few critics carp that it's "overpriced", many call this all-round winner "about the best in Westchester."

Black Bass Grille (Rye) S   19 18 18 $30
2 Central Ave. (Post Rd. S.), 914-967-6700
☑ With its "roaring fire" and "cozy cabin atmosphere", this popular Rye yuppie hangout makes "a wonderful snowy winter retreat"; but foes gripe that it's "bustling and noisy", there's often "too long a wait" for a table and, once seated, "portions are small and prices are rich"; however, loyalists note the "attentive service" adds to the charm of the creative American bistro menu, which features "good fish dishes" that often include bass.

Blazer Pub, The (Purdys) S⌿   20 10 16 $15
Rte. 22 (5 mi. north of Katonah), 914-277-4424
■ "Still the best burgers in Westchester" rave aficionados of this "loud, cheerful", "totally unpretentious" pub with "great music" and a "convivial crowd"; though the "ramshackle ambiance" reminds one reviewer of a "badly decorated basement", the "great value" beers and burgers are the draw.

Blue Dolphin (Katonah)   18 10 17 $21
175 Katonah Ave. (bet. Rtes. 117 & 35), 914-232-4791
■ There's often "long lines of locals" queued up for the "good, honest pasta" served up at this "glorified Italian diner" in Katonah; less of an attraction are the "rude owners", but there are no complaints about the hard-working staff and the "cheap prices."

Blue Heron, The (Montgomery) S – – – M
631 Rte. 17K (I-84), 914-567-0111
The Contemporary American cooking with Cajun-Creole and Californian accents is "brave" and interesting say the few surveyors who have dined at chef-owner Bill Guilfoyle's Orange County restaurant; service is suitably professional, only the "dismal" decor fails to come up to par.

Blue Mountain Bistro   ▽ 15 14 14 $27
(Woodstock) S
1633 Glasco Tpke. (Rte. 212), 914-679-8519
■ Newly relocated, this Woodstock eatery now has a zinc-topped bar where antipasti and tapas are served; the regular bistro menu earns compliments for its "fresh Mediterranean food", but even fans agree "the kitchen is as slow as molasses" and service can be "amateurish."

BOIS D'ARC RESTAURANT   25 | 18 | 22 | $38
(Red Hook) **S**
29 W. Market St. (Rte. 9), 914-758-5992
◪ Chef-owner Jim Jennings named his Red Hook restaurant after a small Texas town and he cooks updated East Texas fare with a CIA-trained flair; while a few find the food "hit or miss", most agree the "fresh local ingredients" are "imaginatively" prepared and "well presented"; opinions also differ as to whether the atmosphere is "intimate" or "chilly" – you choose.

Boston Market **S**   14 | 8 | 12 | $11
667 W. Boston Post Rd. (across from Mamaroneck High School), Mamaroneck, 914-777-1017
130 N. Bedford Rd. (next to Outlet Mall), Mount Kisco, 914-241-8800
32 N. Main St. (New Hempstead Rd.), New City, 914-638-3847
77 Quaker Ridge Road (North Ave.), New Rochelle, 914-235-0550
650 Central Park Ave. (next to A&P), Scarsdale, 914-472-5038
Cross County Mall, 32 Xavier Dr., Yonkers, 914-963-1305
◪ This "McDonald's of the '90s" is a "quick and easy" option that's "great in a pinch" and the "kids like it"; while fans crow that the chain's takeout "chicken and fixings" are "excellent", foes sniff "mediocre" and criticize "portions getting smaller" and the food that's "not really as healthy as people think", citing "high-fat side dishes" and "loading with salt" as problems.

BOX TREE, THE (Purdys) **S**   25 | 27 | 24 | $55
Box Tree Inn, Rte. 22 (Rte. 116), 914-277-3677
◪ "A combination of warmth and old-world elegance" along with "very fine" Classic French food give this Purdy's "jewel box" with "gem-like decor" a top-notch reputation; while a few dissenters carp it's "shamelessly expensive" and "not worth it", the majority says it's "just lovely for a special occasion or a romantic night"; you can even prolong the experience by staying over in one of the well-appointed rooms; N.B. as we go to press the Box Tree is temporarily closed for renovations and is expected to reopen in late May.

Brass Anchor (Poughkeepsie) **S**   16 | 19 | 18 | $28
31 River Point Rd. (Rte. 9), 914-452-3232
■ The "lovely view overlooking the Hudson" is what brings surveyors back to this "picturesque" Poughkeepsie American; while there's a "wide variety of seafood" to choose from, most say the "consistently mediocre" fare just can't compare with the "outdoor dining" on two expansive decks; but nautical types might want to cast their own anchors here since you can "boat right up" to the door.

Brasserie Swiss (Ossining) **S**   16 | 13 | 18 | $31 |
118 Croton Ave./Rte. 133 (bet. Rtes. 9 & 9A),
914-941-0319
■ As reliable as a cuckoo clock, Westchester's only Swiss is
worth a visit "for the fondue and other authentic dishes"·
however, in these weight-watching times the food is
considered "different and good but heavy on the fat";
critics add "the menu hasn't changed in 20 years", and
considering the less than stellar decor rating, it looks like
neither have the surroundings.

Breakneck Lodge Restaurant   17 | 19 | 16 | $30 |
(Cold Spring) **S**
Rte. 9D (bet. Bear Mt. & Newburgh-Beacon Bridges),
914-265-9669
☑ Overlooking the Hudson and Breakneck Mountain
means this veteran American-Continental offers "great
views" and has a decidedly "romantic setting"; some say
the food is just "average roadside fare", but loyalists insist
it's "enjoyable", particularly the "great sauerbraten"; they
also appreciate the "old-style charm" of this "leisurely,
pleasant" dining room.

Brezza (Armonk) **S**   17 | 15 | 16 | $24 |
A&P Shopping Ctr., 454 Main St. (Rte. 128),
914-273-8811
■ Though "it's no Carmine's", there's "fun and plenty of
food" (some say "too much") to be found at this "noisy"
Armonk Northern Italian, which provides "good value" and
"great family dining" with "wonderful pasta and salads";
but some consider its sister restaurants, Eclisse and
Miraggio, "more pleasant."

Brickhouse, The (Marlboro) **S**   – | – | – | M |
1 King St. (Rte. 9W), 914-236-3765
The few respondents that have found their way to this
Marlboro American-Eclectic with a vegetarian emphasis
enthuse its "a relaxed country bar with food that shows
NYC imagination", adding "one trip and you'll love this
place", but it can be "noisy on weekends."

BRIDGE STREET (Irvington) **S**   23 | 20 | 20 | $35 |
1 Bridge St. (RR station ¼ mile west of Rte. 9),
914-591-2233
☑ "SoHo comes to Westchester" is the word on this
stylish Irvington newcomer; the "spare" post-industrial
decor provides a backdrop for "creative", "interesting
and different" American-Eclectic fare that fans call "a
real find"; several detractors fault the "bad acoustics"
and sometimes "flaky waiters", but generally the place
"tries hard to please."

Broadway Bar & Grill   ▽ 18 | 11 | 19 | $27
(Irvington) S
8 S. Broadway (Main St.), 914-591-9861
■ Some favor the burgers, others prefer the "delicious seafood" or the "nice lunches", but all agree that behind the "unassuming exterior" of this Irvington American lies a "good pub" where you'll find "fairly priced food" and "friendly service", but not much in the way of decor.

Broadway Pizza S   ▽ 15 | 7 | 11 | $13
393 Main St. (Rte. 684), Armonk, 914-273-2231
Katonah Shopping Ctr., 280 Katonah Ave., Katonah, 914-232-8027
616 N. Broadway (Virginia Rd.), N. White Plains, 914-428-1802
☑ There are two distinct schools of thought about this pizzeria chainlet; for some they're only "slightly better than ordinary" places for "basic" pies; however, loyal fans insist "the slices are huge and the toppings so fresh", adding this is where to go for "the best pizza in Westchester."

Broadway Pizza & Diamante's   ▽ 13 | 8 | 14 | $17
Restaurant (Millerton) S
Main St. (Maple Ave.), 518-789-4000
■ No relation to the aforementioned pizzerias, this "typical and reliable" "hometown Italian" dishes up big portions of basic pastas but no decor; the handy location makes it a "good afternoon shopping stop" and Northern Dutchess County locals call it ok if you're "in a pinch."

Brodie's North Pub (Mahopac) S   – | – | – | M
Old Rte. 6, 914-621-1208
No longer associated with the southerly Brodie's, this Mahopac "nice, friendly Irish pub" offers an American menu with British specialties; surveyors recommend its "good brunch" and "great wine list."

Brodie's Pub (Mohegan Lake) S▽ 15 | 12 | 16 | $17
Rte. 6/3262 E. Main St. (Lexington Ave.), 914-528-1614
■ The "food is an after-thought" say those who advise it's best to stick to the "good burgers" and beer at this Traditional American Mohegan Lake pub that features live bands and dancing on weekends.

BUFFET DE LA GARE   27 | 22 | 24 | $49
(Hastings-on-Hudson)
155 Southside Ave. (Spring St.), 914-478-1671
☑ "The ultimate dining experience" and "as close to France as you get in the suburbs", this highly rated but "pricey" Westchester favorite continues to win praise for its "absolutely superb and consistently so" French food; while a few find it "cold" and sniff it has the "haughtiest service on the Hudson", the majority finds it "comfortable" and "romantic" with a "friendly and unpretentious" staff.

167

Cafe Antico (Mount Kisco) **S**　　20　20　20　$36
251 Lexington Ave. (Moore Ave.), 914-242-7490

■ A "slightly upscale" addition to the Mount Kisco scene, this "attractive" Northern Italian is a suburban spin-off of NYC's Cafe Nosidam; it's the "best" newcomer in the area, offering "delicious pastas", "accommodating service" and a "nice ambiance"; but critics counter "it's promising but too expensive", adding "it's a horror on Saturday night" – "be prepared to wait for a table, even with reservations."

CAFE MEZÉ (Hartsdale) **S**　　23　21　21　$36
20 N. Central Ave. (Hartsdale Ave.), 914-428-2400

☑ From the Livanos family, who owns Scarsdale's City Limits Diner and NYC's notable Oceana and Molyvos, comes a "stylish" and "interesting, well-prepared Mediterranean" that has quickly become a Hartsdale hot spot; however, some quibble it's "overpriced" and find the "menu tries hard but the food misses"; even fans warn this "trendy" "gem is jammed" and "can be noisy", especially on weekends, but confess it's "fun to watch the crowd."

Cafe Morelli (Yonkers) **S**　　▽ 18　15　15　$29
2150 Central Park Ave. (Altavista Dr.), 914-961-1330

■ It's a case of "hit or miss" at this "typical" Yonkers Northern Italian; it's considered an "ok family place" and there are some good dishes on the casual menu, but you'd expect the service to be better at a long-standing family-run establishment.

Cafe Mozart (Mamaroneck) **S**　　16　14　14　$17
308 Mamaroneck Ave., 914-698-4166

☑ Fans of this Mamaroneck "relaxed coffeehouse" favor the light fare served in a "funky", "cool atmosphere" that's "better than Starbucks"; it's popular for pre- or post-movie snacks and "heavenly desserts"; but critics carp it's just "ok in a pinch" – "claustrophobic", "often crowded", "noisy" and the "service is slow."

Cafe Pongo (Tivoli) **S**　　▽ 20　15　19　$20
69 Broadway, 914-757-4403

■ A "laid-back setting", "friendly staff" and "interesting" cooking are the attractions of this Tivoli Eclectic serving lunch and dinner along with "delicious breakfasts" (Friday – Sunday only) starring "yummy baked goods" that reflect its bakery origins; the fireplace and porch are pluses.

Cafe Portofino (Piermont) **S**　　19　17　19　$30
587 Piermont Ave. (2 blocks north of Ash St.), 914-359-7300

☑ Supporters praise this "warm and friendly" Piermont Italian serving "inventive dishes", saying if it weren't for the spectacular views of the Hudson River and the classical guitarist, you "could be in Little Italy"; others counter it "used to be much better" and "now is nothing special."

CAFE TAMAYO (Saugerties) S   25   20   21 $34
89 Partition St. (Main St.), 914-246-9371

■ The "impeccable", "inventive and fresh food" never fails, chorus the many admirers of chef-owner James Tamayo's New American, calling it "a culinary bright star in the Hudson Valley"; adding to the experience is a professional and friendly front-of-house run by his wife, Rickie; their careful restoration of an 1864 tavern, replete with original ceiling fans and enormous walnut bar, also delights; if you're driving a distance to dine, note the Tamayos offer equally charming guestrooms.

Café 32 (Plattekill)   –   –   –   M
Rte. 32 (exit 17 off NY State Twy.), 914-566-1223

Pictures of matadors on the walls, paella on the menu and a wine list that features a wide selection of sherries clue you into the fact that this Plattekill favorite has a strong Spanish accent; but while the reasonably priced fare includes dishes from several regions of Spain, Mediterranean favorites are also on the culinary map here.

Caffe Strega (Pleasantville) S   21   17   20 $29
2 Broadway /Rte.117 (Bedford Rd./Rte. 141), 914-769-4040

■ This "top-quality" Westchester Italian is regarded as a "food find"; the pastas on the "limited" menu that changes daily are "the most creative around" and there's an "ever-changing selection" of microbrew beers on tap; though the space is "small" and frequently "crowded and noisy", service is friendly and the fare is a "good value."

CALICO RESTAURANT &   25   17   24 $29
PATISSERIE (Rhinebeck) S
9 Mill St./Rte. 9 (opposite Beekman Arms), 914-876-2749

■ "The best patisserie north of Manhattan" has fans swooning and declaring they would "die for" the "authentic French" desserts at this tiny, "charming" Rhinebeck cafe; in fact, most diners are so busy indulging their sweet tooths that they miss sampling the limited menu of Contemporary American food with a Gallic flair; the only complaint is that "the wine list is bigger than the dining room."

Camino Real (Pleasantville) S   16   15   17 $24
160 Marble Ave. (bet. Irvington St. & Stanley Ave.), 914-769-6207

■ Though the decor is "tacky", the food is "fresh and well-prepared" and the salsa is supposedly the "best" in Westchester at this Pleasantville Mexican; portions are large and it's "never busy", making it a fun family option; depending on your taste, weekend karaoke is either an added attraction or a reason to stay away.

169

Candlelight Inn (Scarsdale) ◐⑤⊄ | 17 | 10 | 14 | $14 |
519 Central Park Ave. (1 mi. south of Four Corners.),
914-472-9706
■ Don't be misled by the elegant name – this Scarsdale
"dive" is "a cross between a biker bar and college hangout";
while some come for the "great, cheap hamburgers and
fries, onion rings from heaven and hot, hot wings", others
savor the "raucous roadhouse setting" – "I never knew
bikers ate so well."

Capriccio Restaurant (Brewster) ⑤ | 21 | 23 | 23 | $43 |
Rte. 22N (north of Rte. 684), 914-279-2873
☑ Fans find "the food is as good as the scenery" at this
"expensive and elegant" Brewster Italian, which boasts a
"magnificent reservoir view" and a "warm" tuxedo-clad
staff; but foes find the fare "ordinary" and the decor "tired",
concluding it's "not worth the dollars."

Caputo's Ristorante　　　　▽ | 17 | 10 | 13 | $24 |
(Mount Kisco) ⑤ **(CLOSED)**
454 E. Main St. (Rte. 172), 914-666-3448
■ According to regulars, it's best to "stick to the pizza" at
this Mount Kisco "storefront Italian" where the food
"tries very hard but just misses"; it's a good value, but
there's no atmosphere and there are a few reports of
"unaccommodating" service.

Caravela (Tarrytown) ⑤　　 | 20 | 15 | 18 | $32 |
53 N. Broadway (bet. Central Ave. & Dixon St.),
914-631-1863
☑ Evoking "a little bit of the old country", this Tarrytown
Portuguese-Brazilian with "a flair for seafood" serves up
"good hearty food and friendly service"; some find the
cooking "salty" and gripe it's "too pricey for a restaurant in
this category", but most "still like it after all these years."

Carl's (Larchmont) ⑤　　 | 20 | 15 | 18 | $35 |
121 Myrtle Blvd. (bet. Chatsworth Ave. & Weaver St.),
914-834-1244
■ Its many fans tell us this Larchmont "neighborhood
standout" Traditional American offers "wonderful pub food
in a cozy setting" with "friendly service"; less pleasing is
the limited reservations policy, which means "always very
long waits"; though it's "enjoyable for family dinners",
regulars warn "go early."

Casa Mia (Highland) ⑤　　▽ | 17 | 14 | 18 | $22 |
515 Rte. 9W (Merrit Ave.), 914-691-2923
☑ Opinions about this Ulster County Italian are mixed; some
say the seafood menu is "surprisingly delicious", others
argue they're capable of "ruining pasta"; overall it's agreed
that the staff at the Highland veteran "tries very hard"
and it's "ok for the area"; early-bird specials offer good
value and the new farm market is an added attraction.

Casa Miguel (Mount Kisco) S   19 | 15 | 18 | $25 |
222 E. Main St. (Rte. 117), 914-666-7588
■ "A great Friday night place" in Mount Kisco with not much decor, but "good margaritas" and "great fajitas" and homemade chips; this "overcrowded" Mexican also gets kudos for "creativity" and is touted as "the best in Westchester" by ardent fans; as for supposed habitué Imus, we'd been told it's his "favorite", but doubting diners say he's never been spotted there.

Cascade Mountain Winery &   22 | 18 | 19 | $30 |
Restaurant (Amenia) S
Flint Hill Rd. (Cascade Mtn. Rd.), 914-373-9021
■ The food is a match for the vine at this Hudson River Valley winery; the new chef garners high praise for his "innovative" Regional American cooking, which is a "great value"; "lunch in the summer" is the best time to enjoy the "beautiful, rustic location" in Dutchess County; N.B. lunch is served daily, dinner on Saturdays – "reservations are often necessary."

CATERINA DE MEDICI (Hyde Park)   26 | 21 | 23 | $36 |
Culinary Institute of America, 433 Albany Post Rd./Rte. 9, 914-471-6608
☑ Whether this Hyde Park Northern Italian is "the best of the CIA's offerings" or "the least successful" is your call: fans find the food just "fabulous" and praise the prix fixe, which is "done with great flair", the "super service" and the "wonderful decor"; but critics call the cooking "imitation" Italian and snipe that the student "service has a *Fawlty Towers* quality" to it.

Central Square Cafe   16 | 17 | 16 | $24 |
(Scarsdale) ◖ S
870 Central Park Ave. (Central Ave. & Ardsley Rd.), 914-472-7828
☑ Catering to a diverse clientele, this "always crowded" "SoHo in Scarsdale" "upscale diner" is "very child friendly" and has a "happening singles scene"; admirers appreciate the "glitzy decor" and consider it a "fun place", even though the New American cooking rates as "standard", with "decent pizzas and pastas"; while it's "better at lunch" and "best at brunch", "service is erratic" and the limited reservations policy brings "outrageous" weekend waits.

Charleston (Hudson) S   – | – | – | E |
517 Warren St. (5th St.), 518-828-4990
Few surveyors have tried this Columbia County Regional American, but to those in the know it's a "favorite" for taking a break after antiquing on Warren Street; the menu features the foods of the Hudson Valley, but each Thursday Tex-Mex fare is the focus; in addition to being housed in a 1926 vintage setting, changing art exhibitions and occasional live performances add to the aesthetics here.

Charlie Brown's Steakhouse ◑ S   14 14 15 $22
181 E. Boston Post Rd. (Mamaroneck Ave.), Mamaroneck,
914-698-6610
1820 Central Park Ave. (Tuckahoe Rd.), Yonkers,
914-779-7227
▧ This "dark and crowded steak and chop chain" has
its devotees who say they "do a good job" for the price,
praising the "large portions" and "good salad bars" at these
"old, reliable" Westchester branches; others counter that
the "mediocre" food and "unimaginative decor" make it
obvious this is a chain, Charlie.

Chart House (Dobbs Ferry) S   18 22 17 $34
High St. (opposite RR station), 914-693-4130
▧ "The fantastic Hudson river setting" is the most popular
feature of the Westchester branch of this popular steak
and seafood chain; many patrons prefer to chart a course of
cocktails and appetizers on the patio while watching the
"summer sunset" and then "flee before dinner", with its
"huge portions" of "pedestrian food"; others complain that
the tab is "too expensive" for a place where "candlelight
and carpet can't hide the franchise taste."

Chef Antonio Restaurant   17 13 19 $27
(Mamaroneck) S
551 Halstead Ave. (Beach Ave.), 914-698-8610
▪ "Crowds of regulars" come to enjoy the "typical"
"home cooking" at this neighborhood Southern Italian,
which is good for "family and casual meals"; the "so-so"
"upscale diner decor" can't compare with the ultra-
accommodating chef-owner's "you name it, he'll make it"
food and "friendly" service.

Cherry Blossom (Fishkill)   – – – M
150 Main St. (exit 12 off Rte. 84), 914-897-9691
Those in the know say whether you want sushi, noodles,
tempura or teriyaki, this is the place for the best Japanese in
the northwestern reaches of Westchester; though the decor
is spare, friendly staffers make for a warm atmosphere;
tatami rooms provide private dining and parties of six or
more can reserve for a hibachi dinner.

China Rose (Rhinecliff) S   21 17 17 $24
100 Shatzell Ave. (2 mi. west of Rte. 9), 914-876-7442
▪ An unusual combination of "exotic and pleasing" Chinese
food, a non-Chinese CIA grad owner and romantic Victorian
decor produce what some call Dutchess County's "best"
Asian; surveyors suggest "sitting outside on a summer
evening" to enjoy the "beautiful views" of the Hudson River;
such popularity, together with a no reservations policy, can
result in "a long wait", especially on weekends.

172

Christopher's
16 | 17 | 16 | $31
(White Plains) **(CLOSED)**
*Westchester Residence Inn, 5 Barker Ave. (2 blocks north
of the Galleria), 914-288-9656*
■ You get "plenty and then some" at this attractively
decorated White Plains Contemporary American; but while
surveyors report there's good value for quantity, the overall
quality of the food is labeled just "so-so"; still even critics
believe it has "potential" and "will try it again."

Christy's (Woodstock)
– | – | – | M
85 Mill Hill Rd. (Rte. 212 at intersection of Rte. 375), 914-679-5300
The Irish brogue of the staff at this Woodstock veteran hints
at chef-owner Chistopher Lynch's Celtic origins, but his
menu is a solid International Mix, with lots of fresh fish,
pastas and an acclaimed roast duck; a crackling fire in
winter adds to the warm, unpretentious atmosphere.

Church Street Cafe, The
– | – | – | M
(Pine Plains) S **(CLOSED)**
Church St. (bet. Rtes. 82 & 199), 518-398-6755
Now in their own Northern Dutchess place, the former chefs
of the Cascade Mountain Winery continue their emphasis
on local produce; the limited menu at this small storefront
Contemporary American changes regularly to make use
of seasonal foods; fish preparations are particularly good.

Ciao! (Eastchester) S
16 | 13 | 15 | $23
5-7 John Albanese Pl. (Main St.), 914-779-4646
◪ For family dinner theater, take the kids to this Eastchester
Italian where they'll enjoy a "great show" watching chefs
in the "glass-enclosed pizza kitchen" creating thin-crust,
brick-oven pies; critics counter that the menu descriptions
"are better than the taste" and the "service is erratic",
simply saying "ciao" to the "pasta and noise."

CITRUS GRILLE (Airmont) S
25 | 21 | 22 | $39
430 Saddle River Rd. (Lake St. & Rte. 59), 914-352-5533
■ "Innovative food" makes this "tiny", "pretty" California-
influenced Eclectic "one of Rockland's best"; it's "noisy", not
intimate, so those in the know advise "eat downstairs if
you can"; some find you get "small portions for the price"
but the pre-theater "early-bird specials offer good value."

CITY LIMITS DINER S
17 | 17 | 16 | $21
*200 Central Ave. (Tarrytown Rd.), White Plains, 914-686-9000 ◗
The Westchester, 125 Westchester Ave. (Bloomingdale Rd.),
White Plains, 914-761-1111*
◪ "Not your typical diners", these White Plains twins have
bright "funky" neon decor, big booths ("great for families")
and a "something-for-everyone" menu, even if it's with
"mixed" results; boosters maintain the food is "five-star at
diner prices"; while considered "fun places", they can
also be "a madhouse" with long lines.

Claire's Mahopac Beach   18 19 17 $33
(Mahopac) **S**
(fka Clare's Cucina Rustica)
825 South Lake Blvd./Rte. 6N (Taconic Pkwy.,
Mahopac-Shrub Oak exit), 914-628-2702
◪ Perched right on the docks of Lake Mahopac, offering vistas of the water and distant hills, this is a "nice place" to enjoy International cuisine with an Italian focus; some say the "food doesn't measure up" to the view and is "overpriced for what it is", but the majority enjoys it.

Clarksville Inn (West Nyack) **S**   15 18 18 $29
1 Strawtown Rd. (W. Nyack Rd.), 914-358-8899
◼ Once upon a time this West Nyack 1840 inn was "much better"; now its "charming", "homey" setting is of more interest than the "solid" Continental fare, which is called "nothing creative"; service is good if "extremely slow" and there's poor ventilation in the nonsmoking room.

Clermont, The   ∇ 16 18 19 $25
(Woodstock) **(CLOSED)**
109 Mill Hill Rd. (Rtes. 212 & 375), 914-679-2221
◼ This newcomer housed in a large Civil War–era building offers several dining options: Traditional American food with an Italian accent is served in a soothingly decorated main dining room and on a glass-enclosed porch, and there's also a lounge that features live music and a wide selection of microbrews; however, dissidents say it's all "passable" but "nondescript."

Clove Valley Trading Co.   – – – E
(High Falls)
Rte. 213 (Mohonk Rd.), 914-687-7911
A diverse crowd – large groups, romantic couples, locals and weekenders – frequents this casual High Falls American-Continental whose constantly changing menu specializes in fresh fish, pasta and other light fare; beer connoisseurs will appreciate the microbrew menu with over 100 offerings and there's a cigar-friendly bar.

Cobble Creek Cafe (Purchase) **S**   19 19 19 $34
Anderson Hill Rd. (Purchase St. & Lincoln Ave.), 914-761-0050
◪ This "well-run" New American, convenient to plays and concerts at SUNY-Purchase, offers "fine food at high prices" and the wine bar has a good selection wines by the glass; the staff is "accommodating" (though "not to kids").

Cobble Stone (Purchase) ◑**S**   14 14 16 $22
Anderson Hill Rd. (New St.), 914-253-9678
◼ A "noisy and lively" "hangout" for the SUNY-Purchase crowd and Pepsi executives ("don't drink Coke" here), this Traditional American is altogether more basic than its Cobble Creek sibling; the "dimly lit" "roadside pub" is the venue for "basic beer and burgers."

Conca D'Oro (New Paltz) S   – – – M
125 Main St. (Prospect St.), 914-255-6002
"The same old menu brings the same mixed results"
say the few respondents who know this New Paltz
Southern Italian; there are kudos for the "great garlic
bread" and low prices, but some say it's a "nice place
with lousy food."

Conte's Fishmarket   22 10 20 $29
(Mount Kisco) ⊄
448 Main St. (St. Mark's Pl.), 914-666-6929
■ A Cinderella-like transformation occurs at this Mount
Kisco retail fish store every Friday and Saturday – it
becomes a restaurant serving "the best quality" seafood
in simple but "well-prepared" ways; hearty portions and
BYO are a plus, a sometimes "surly attitude" a minus; N.B.
meat eaters hunt elsewhere.

Coppola's (Poughkeepsie) S   15 13 17 $25
825 Main St. (Raymond Ave.), 914-452-3040
■ "Food your grandmother would make", meaning "lots
of red sauce and cheese", is the staple at this "basic"
Poughkeepsie veteran; the Continental-Italian fare is fine
if you're "nearby", but not worth going out of your way for.

Cornetta's Seafood   ∇ 17 14 17 $31
(Piermont) S
641 Piermont Ave. (Rte. 9W), 914-359-9852
◪ Its location, "right on the Hudson", means "great views"
at this old-style Piermont seafood house; and if the
"ambiance is missing", the seafood is "always reliable"
and for "soft-shell crabs in season" it can't be beat.

Cornucopia, The (Port Jervis) S   – – – M
176 Rte. 209 (2 mi. north of village), 914-856-5361
Don your lederhosen and head to Port Jervis for an
abundance of authentic, old-style German cooking, as
well as Continental favorites, served up in "huge portions"
that'll keep you full till Oktoberfest.

Corridos Mexican Grill &   16 14 16 $25
Cantina (Yonkers) S
(fka Corridos Mexicanos)
High Ridge Shopping Ctr., 1771 Central Park Ave. (¼ mi.
north of Tuckahoe Rd.), 914-779-0990
◪ Like the name, the menu has been Americanized at this
Yonkers Mexican, causing former devotees to lament "now
it's gone downhill" and "it's no better than any other";
slipping *Survey* results support that opinion, but fans still
maintain the food is "authentic" and served in a "warm
and friendly atmosphere."

175

Cosimo's on Union   ▽ 21 | 19 | 18 | $20
(Newburgh) S
2 Orr Ave. (Union Ave.), 914-567-1556
Cosimo's (Middletown)
620 Rte. 211 E. (Hwy. 17), 914-692-3242
☑ "Good designer pizzas", pastas and lunchtime panini
are staples at this crisply styled Newburgh trattoria; the
menu's mainstays are the wood-burning-oven pies that
range from the traditional to the inventive, but some
complain that the dining room bustle is "very loud"; the
Middletown branch is new and unrated.

Country Manor, The   ▽ 16 | 21 | 17 | $30
(Poughkeepsie) S
*221 Dutchess Tpke. Rd. (bet. Burnett & DeGarmo Rds.),
914-471-1246*
☑ The "cozy country" "rooms with fireplaces" are the
attraction at this pretty colonial mansion in Poughkeepsie
and not the "pedestrian" Continental food, leading one wag
to conclude "this is where the ladies who lunch draw the
line"; but the Sunday brunch is rated "excellent."

Crab Shanty Restaurant   15 | 14 | 15 | $28
(Mamaroneck) S
1521 E. Boston Post Rd. (Greenhaven Rd.), 914-698-1352
☑ Opinion is divided – fans of this Mamaroneck "Red
Lobster wanna-be" comment it's "always crowded"
because its "heaping portions " of "fresh" seafood are
"good for families"; but foes crab it's a "grim", "run of
the mill", "way over priced" experience; however, even
critics appreciate the "great views of the harbor."

CRABTREE'S KITTLE HOUSE   24 | 24 | 23 | $43
(Chappaqua) S
*Crabtree's Kittle House Country Inn, 11 Kittle Rd. (Rte. 117),
914-666-8044*
■ This "beautiful old inn", which boasts a "world-class wine
list", a "superb view" and "fresh, delicious" New American
fare, is "hard to find but worth the effort"; it's a place for
those who appreciate "old-fashioned elegance", albeit at
a price; those who find the Chappaqua location a little off
their beaten track can overnight in one of the inn's 12 rooms.

Cripple Creek Cafe   ▽ 20 | 20 | 20 | $37
(Rhinebeck) S
18 Garden St. (Market St.), 914-876-4355
■ Rhinebeck surveyors savor the "stylish", "inventive"
American-Eclectic cooking, frequently changing menus
and "accommodating" service in this "strip-mall, shoe-box
space"; less enticing are the "NY prices."

176

Crossroads (Kingston) S   – | – | – | M |
38 Broadway (Abeel St.), 914-340-0151
This Kingston newcomer offers Contemporary American cuisine in a sophisticated yet casual setting; jazz piano on the weekends adds to the ambiance; nocturnal diners take note, there's a special late-evening menu.

Crumpets (Pine Plains) S   – | – | – | M |
3800 W. Church St. (Rte. 199), 518-398-1600
As the name suggests, this Pine Plains spot has a veddy English accent; in addition to crumpets, there are "great pancakes" and this may be the place for "the best breakfast in Dutchess County"; "service is slow", so cozy up to the pot belly stove and bury yourself in a book borrowed from the cafe's library corner.

Crystal Bay Dining & Catering   16 | 20 | 18 | $31 |
(Peekskill) S
5 John Walsh Blvd. (Bertoline Way), 914-737-8332
☑ With "wonderful views of the Hudson" and a great outdoor deck, it's not surprising that the "scene surpasses the food" at this Peekskill American-Eclectic; the fish is a "pretty good" choice if you "stick to simple" preparations; less expected is that this romantic spot is "child friendly."

Daily Planet (Lagrangeville) S ▽ 16 | 19 | 18 | $18 |
284 Rte. 55 (Taconic Pkwy., exit 55W), 914-452-0110
☑ Americana abounds at this "very busy" Lagrangeville theme diner; different rooms are decorated with objects from each decade from the '40s–'70s and with so much to look at, it's a "great place for kids"; families also appreciate the "large portions", but critics carp that it's just "ok diner food"; N.B. there's a also a retail bakery.

Daniel's Restaurant (Tuckahoe) S 17 | 16 | 17 | $27 |
296 Columbus Ave. (Fisher Ave.), 914-337-1883
■ The Continental fare and the decor at this Tuckahoe eatery are "standard", but it's a "safe bet" for a "quiet and relaxing" evening in an "unpretentious" atmosphere; some find it "a little expensive" for what it is, suggesting for true value try the "great early-bird specials."

David Chen Chinese Restaurant   20 | 17 | 20 | $23 |
(Armonk)
85 Old Mount Kisco Rd., 914-273-6767
■ They serve the "best regular Chinese food outside of NYC" at this "always reliable" Armonk Asian and the staff is the "nicest around"; if the "typical setting" doesn't appeal, takeout will – it's "positively speedy."

Dawat (White Plains) S   22 | 18 | 19 | $29 |
230 E. Post Rd. (near the new Westchester Mall), 914-428-4411
■ This "upscale Indian" is so authentic respondents tell us
their "Indian friends love it", savoring the array of "different
dishes" you won't find "elsewhere"; Indian food authority
Madhur Jaffrey serves as culinary consultant here as she
does at its notable NYC sister; while service is "gracious"
but "slow", it's still the "best of the White Plains Indians."

Defemio Restaurant (Yonkers) ◗ S   13 | 10 | 14 | $23 |
600 Tuckahoe Rd. (Central Park Ave.), 914-337-2617
■ "Go for the jazz" and "eat before you go" advise regulars
of this old-time Yonkers Italian where they "haven't changed
the menu or the decor since 1965."

DEPUY CANAL HOUSE (High Falls) S   24 | 26 | 25 | $48 |
Rte. 213 (Lucas Ave.), 914-687-7700
■ To his many admirers, chef-owner John Novi's New
American food "gets better and better"; while a few say
the "very complicated menu" is "too far out", most find his
innovations "unfailingly excellent"; this "charming" 1797
Ulster County stone house offers "semi-private dining" and
colonial decor; though "very expensive", it's "wonderful for
celebrations" and overnight accommodations are available.

DiNardo's (Pound Ridge) S   17 | 12 | 16 | $30 |
76 Westchester Ave. (Scott's Corners), 914-764-4024
◪ The older sibling of Irvington's Il Sorriso Ristorante, this
"reliable" Pound Ridge Italian offers "good" cooking and
"nice service" in "simple surroundings"; but to foes the
menu is "caught in a '60s time warp and so are the waiters."

Dominick's (New Paltz) S   ▽ 12 | 11 | 15 | $25 |
30 N. Chestnut St./Rte. 32N, 914-255-0120
■ Still "trying hard" after all these years, this New Paltz
veteran serving up a mix of Regional American, French,
Italian and Mediterranean fare still has a "long way to go."

Doubleday's (Dobbs Ferry) S   14 | 13 | 14 | $19 |
83 Main St. (Chestnut St.), 914-693-9793
■ A "decent neighborhood place" where you'll always
find a crowd at the bar, this "noisy" Dobbs Ferry pub is
good for "gossip and burgers" "at a price you can't beat."

Dudley's Restaurant (Ossining) S   22 | 20 | 21 | $37 |
6 Rockledge Ave. (Rte. 9), 914-941-8674
◪ As befits its previous incarnation as a speakeasy, this
Ossining New American is difficult to find "but worth the
effort" for its "sophisticated", "interesting dishes" and
"solicitous service" in a "beautiful", "dark and romantic"
setting; but a few foes complain that "portion control is
practiced here" and overall it's "overpriced and overrated."

Dynasty Chinese Restaurant   ▽ 21 | 19 | 18 | $25 |
(Wappingers Falls) **S**
144A Old Post Rd. (Rte. 9), 914-298-0023
■ With little competition, this Wappingers Falls restaurant
easily garners the title "best Chinese food around here"
and some even say it could "compete with NYC"; the
Cantonese, Mandarin and Hunan dishes are "tasty" and
service is "very good."

Eastchester Fish Gourmet   22 | 11 | 17 | $29 |
(Scarsdale) **S**
837 White Plains Rd. (Summerfield St.), 914-725-3450
■ "To get any fresher fish you would have to catch it
yourself" supporters say of this Scarsdale seafooder;
though preparations are "plain" and the "unpretentious"
atmosphere is "strictly no frills", "the food more than
compensates"; the only sinking feeling you might get is
from the sight of the long lines that result from the
limited reservations policy.

Eclisse (Rye Brook) **S**   18 | 17 | 17 | $25 |
*Washington Park Plaza, 275 S. Ridge St. (Westchester Ave.),
914-937-5770*
■ Considered by some surveyors to be "the best of the
chain" (Brezza and Miraggio are siblings), this Rye Brook
Northern Italian has "large noisy rooms", leading one
reviewer to suggest it's "like eating at Grand Central"; there's
a big audience for its "usually good" pastas, "ample
portions" served family-style and a "casual" atmosphere
that's fun for "a group of kids."

Eduardo's (Mount Kisco) **S**   19 | 12 | 16 | $26 |
*77 S. Moger Ave. (1 block from RR station),
914-666-7005*
■ "Honest, good food" and "great homemade bread",
as well as pastries and ravioli, are what attracts Mount
Kisco locals to this "better than average" "neighborhood"
Italian veteran; seating is tight and there's "zero decor",
but service is "friendly" and the food is a "good value."

Egg's Nest, The (High Falls)   – | – | – | M |
Rte. 213 (Bruceville Rd.), 914-687-7255
Wildly decorated with antique hub caps on the walls and
toasters that serve as light fixtures, this High Falls Eclectic is
a local institution renowned for its constantly evolving
decor; it's a fun place with reasonably priced hearty fare
that's often as inventive as the embellishments.

El Coyote Flaco (Port Chester) **S**   21   9   15 $17
115 Midland Ave., 914-937-6969
■ "Too bad they don't have more than eight tables" howl fans of this "small, homey", "authentic" Port Chester Mexican that still resembles the hamburger stand it once was; the healthy fare relies on corn oil and olive oil not lard, but there are reports that it "doesn't take out very well" so grab one of the tables if you can and try this "great food for the price."

Emilio Restaurant (Harrison) **S**   21   19   20 $38
1 Colonial Pl. (bet. Harrison Ave. & Purdy St.),
914-835-3100
■ Surveyors cite the "uncompromising quality" of this Harrison Northern Italian offering a "fantastic" antipasti table, homemade pastas and an extensive wine list; "the elegant, very romantic" setting and "terrific service" make it a choice spot "for a special evening."

Enzo's Restaurant   18   14   18 $35
(Mamaroneck) **S**
451 Mamaroneck Ave. (RR station), 914-698-2911
◪ For Italian food in "a country club atmosphere" regulars head to this Mamaroneck favorite for "good portions" of "solid, reliable" fare and a "friendly atmosphere"; but critics carp it's "overrated and overpriced", adding the service can be "erratic" as "they favor those they know."

Epstein's Kosher Deli (Hartsdale) **S** 16   9   13 $17
Dalewood Shopping Ctr., 387 N. Central Ave. (Hartsdale Ave.),
914-428-5320
◪ With "good kosher food", "soup like mother makes" and "great overstuffed sandwiches", this deli is deemed "first-rate" by devotees; but dissenters counter "it's lucky it has a monopoly in Westchester" because it's "not the Carnegie"; all concur the decor is "lousy" and "needs a face-lift" and the service, while "surly", is "not as rude as the average NY deli."

Equus (Tarrytown)   -   -   -   E
Castle at Tarrytown, 400 Benedict Ave., 914-631-3646
This "relatively expensive newcomer" is a "hot" spot say those who wrote in to tell us it's a "romantic" castle with "elegant, clublike", "superb decor"; chef Phillip McGrath's sophisticated Contemporary American cooking is "excellent"; while still working out some early service problems, it's worth a visit since it "rivals Xaviar's."

ESCOFFIER RESTAURANT, THE   26 | 26 | 26 | $48 |
(Hyde Park)
Culinary Institute of America, 433 Albany Post Rd./Rte. 9
(across from W. Dorsey Ln.), 914-471-6608
■ Pricey and "absolutely perfect" for formal elegant
dining, this student-run Classic French is judged by some
surveyors as "the best of the CIA"; while the outcome
varies with the students, the commitment to excellence is
a constant and "it's fun to watch them cook behind the
glassed-in wall"; there are also "good tasting menus" and
a "sparkling, deluxe setting" so it's always "worth the
long drive from anywhere."

ESPAÑA RESTAURANT & GRILL   26 | 19 | 22 | $36 |
(White Plains) S
135 E. Post Rd. (Court St.), 914-428-8445
■ "A find" for "fabulous Spanish food" – both traditional
and modern – that "few seem to know about", this White
Plains newcomer is "expensive but worth it", particularly
for the "terrific and unusual ingredients" and "great fish";
there's "European ambiance", which in this case means
"attentive service" in a "low-key atmosphere."

Eveready Diner (Hyde Park) ●S ▽ 15 | 18 | 15 | $16 |
540 Albany Post Rd./Rte. 9, 914-229-8100
◪ On Fridays and Saturdays this shiny stainless-steel
Hyde Park diner charges up its batteries and lives up to
its name by staying open round-the-clock; fans call this
'50s eatery offering the likes of sandwiches and breakfast,
which is served all day long, "reliable and fun"; but
foes say the retro theme doesn't ring true – it's just an
"ok modern diner."

Farm Country (Millerton) S   ▽ 18 | 18 | 19 | $29 |
Railroad Plaza, Main St. (Rte. 22), 518-789-4143
◪ This "darling" Dutchess County place is an "appealingly"
renovated "former smokehouse" where the "imaginative"
Contemporary American cooking relies on farm-fresh
foods; besides serving unusually good dinners and
weekend lunches, there's super takeout available.

Fernwood (Palenville) S⇄   – | – | – | M |
Malden Ave. (Rte. 32A), 518-678-9332
There's always a warm welcome at this family-owned and
run Continental located on a quiet Greene County side
street; in addition to the restaurant, the former rooming
house boasts a bistro for light fare.

Foster's Coach House | 13 | 15 | 17 | $20 |
(Rhinebeck) **S**
22 Montgomery St. (E. Market St.), 914-876-8052
⬛ "Stick to the basics" – like the burgers and London broil – at this Traditional American "Northern Dutchess standby" offering "modestly priced food with quick service"; fans suggest bringing the family since they're "good with kids" and there are big booths, but others sniff "it's only a step up from McDonald's."

Foundry Cafe (Cold Spring) **S** ▽ | 16 | 15 | 15 | $24 |
55 Main St. (Fair St.), 914-265-4504
⬛ "A good brunch place", this casual Cold Spring Contemporary American emphasizes health food and offers a range of vegetarian choices; it's also "good for breakfast and lunch" and has a wide selection of specialty beers; for people-watching there's a sidewalk cafe.

FREELANCE CAFE & WINE BAR | 28 | 21 | 24 | $36 |
(Piermont) **S**⊅
506 Piermont Ave. (Ash St.), 914-365-3250
⬛ "The food is exceptional at this culinary delight" declare fans of Peter Kelly's "less haute cuisine version of Xaviar's, with whom it shares a kitchen"; the "tiny, inviting" Piermont Contemporary American cafe offers "wonderful wine", "accommodating service" and "the price is right"; there are "no reservations", but this one is certainly "worth the wait."

Fujinoya ▽ | 24 | 15 | 21 | $24 |
(White Plains) **S** (CLOSED)
522 Mamaroneck Ave. (Bloomingdale Rd.), 914-686-8854
⬛ "A touch of Tokyo" in a "tiny space", this White Plains Japanese is still something of a hidden treasure; there is a "good selection" of "authentic" food and the beautifully presented sushi wins special praise, but a few naysayers comment they're "trying hard" but they're "overrated."

Gager's Diner (Monticello) **S** | – | – | – | M |
345 Broadway (Pelton St.), 914-794-8450
A Downtown Monticello gem, this is a true, old-style diner where the staff still orders items "whiskey down", meaning pop the rye bread into the toaster; regulars believe it's "a cut above the average"; for oldies aficionados the only let down is the unfortunate refurbishment of the 1934 exterior.

Gasho of Japan **S** | 18 | 22 | 20 | $29 |
Rte. 32 (NY Twy., exit 16), Central Valley, 914-928-2277
2 Saw Mill River Rd. (Rte. 9A), Hawthorne, 914-592-5900
⬛ These hibachi-style steakhouse siblings are set in rebuilt 400-year-old Samurai farmhouses replete with tranquil gardens; boosters say cooking "great food right on your table" means a "fun time for the family", but critics consider them "a show more than a meal", adding they're good "if you've got guests from Iowa."

Gedney Grille (White Plains) **S**   18   17   18 $29
68 Gedney Way (Mamaroneck Ave.), 914-428-1264
☑ "Pleasant, well-prepared" food is the attraction at this
"inventive" White Plains Contemporary American; if some
say it's "nothing out of the ordinary" and the "menu needs
revamping", others like the "family orientation" and consider
it "a winner for the neighborhood" with "good value" and
a "very hospitable staff."

Gentleman Jim's   ▽ 20   16   19 $20
Bistro-Brewery (Poughkeepsie) **S**
522 Dutchess Tpke. (Rochdale Rd.), 914-485-5467
■ The menu at this Poughkeepsie American is wide-ranging,
offering everything from steaks to pot pies and pastas; as
for the early-bird special, we hear "they do it well; the bistro
has its own brewmaster who produces seven different styles
of beer and there's also a large selection of single-malts.

Giorgio's (Port Chester)   23   17   22 $40
11 Pearl St. (Westchester Ave.), 914-937-4906
■ "One of the best hideaways in Westchester", this
comfortable, family-run Northern Italian may be in a "lousy"
Port Chester location, but its "small menu" delivers "superb"
food and draws an "older regular crowd"; while some find
the service "gracious", others find the "waiters snobby."

Giulio's of Tappan (Tappan) **S**   22   22   21 $37
154 Washington St. (Conklin & Main St.), 914-359-3657
■ With its Victorian setting, fireplaces and candlelight, this
Rockland County Northern Italian is a "cozy and romantic"
jewel; old-timers say "it used to be the best" and is still
"very good all around"; a few find its traditional formality
"intimidating" but report the "staff is anxious to please."

Golden Duck (Scarsdale) **S**⊅   ▽ 14   5   12 $15
102 Garth Rd. (Great Rock Rd.), 914-723-1886
■ At this Scarsdale Chinese "hole-in-the-wall" there are
a few tables, but as ratings suggest the duck lays some
eggs when it comes to decor so you might want to stick
with the "good takeout"; however, be advised you "may
need an interpreter to get your order right."

Golden Ginza (Kingston)   – – – M
2428 Broadway (exit 19, NY State Twy.), 914-339-8132
Two large decorative fish hanging outside mark the
entry to Kingston's favorite Japanese; although they
offer tempura, teriyaki and sushi, it's actually the hibachi
cooking, which is done at special tables with set-in grills,
that this spot is known for.

Golden Wok (Yonkers) S | 18 | 13 | 17 | $19 |
2250 Central Park Ave. (Christopher St.), 914-779-8438
Golden Wok II (Ardsley) S
Ardsley Mall, 875 Saw Mill River Rd., 914-693-2110
■ These "better than average", "old-fashioned Chinese" Westchester siblings attract a loyal local crowd; while the decor is hardly golden and the space somewhat "cramped", service is "good" if sometimes "rushed"; the "nothing fancy but solid cooking" at reasonable prices are reasons to go Golden.

Goldie's by the Bridge | 21 | 17 | 20 | $35 |
(North Tarrytown) S
226 Beekman Ave. (Hudson St.), 914-631-9794
☑ Close by the Tappan Zee Bridge, Deborah Goldstein's New American with "terrific" river views is "a real find"; her "creative menu" is "prepared with care and some flair" and served by "a most pleasant staff"; some consider this a "slightly overpriced" "gourmet wanna-be", but they're outweighed by those who appreciate the emphasis on fresh market produce.

Grande Centrale Restaurant   ▽ | 24 | 18 | 21 | $33 |
(Congers) S
17 N. Rockland Ave. (Lake Rd.), 914-267-3442
☑ Chef-owner and CIA grad C. H. Michael Finelli adds international accents to his Contemporary American cooking and comes up with "very imaginative fare"; the menu changes seasonally, though "excellent presentations" are a constant; while touted as "one of the better newcomers", one fan worries that this Congers restaurant is "held back" by its location, which isn't exactly Grand Central.

Grandma's of Yorktown | 16 | 14 | 18 | $16 |
(Yorktown) S⊅
Rte. 202 (1 mi. west of Taconic Pkwy.), 914-739-7770
■ "Good breakfasts", burgers and "oh, those pies" entice Westchester families to this "cute, quick" and "inexpensive" American; while Grandma's "great desserts" draw "long lines", sweet-toothed surveyors swear it's "worth waiting" any time of day to sample the "best pies in the universe."

Greenbaum & Gilhooley's   ▽ | 16 | 13 | 16 | $29 |
(Wappingers Falls) S
1400 Rte. 9 (bet. Myers Corners & Old Hopewell Rds.), 914-297-9700
☑ Huge steaks, lobsters and "great prime ribs" are staples at this Wappingers Falls American-Continental that supporters swear "never disappoints"; but detractors say it's only "so-so", adding there's "no atmosphere" and "service can be spotty."

Gregory's (White Plains) S | 21 | 18 | 20 | $35 |
324 Central Ave. (Aqueduct Rd. & Cross St.), 914-684-8855
☑ At this "old-fashioned" Italian you'll find "ladies who lunch" and White Plains politicians ensconced in the cozy corner tables enjoying the "good home cooking" and the attention of a staff who "treats you like royalty"; a few claim it "doesn't live up to its reputation", but the majority asserts it's "always very good."

Guida's (Ossining) S | 22 | 18 | 20 | $37 |
199 Main St. (Rte. 9), 914-941-2662
☑ Fans of this "classy", "old-style" Ossining Italian praise the "imaginative preparation" of "really fine food", "lovely setting" and waiters who "cannot do enough for you"; a minority of critics complain that it's "overdecorated, overpriced and overdone."

Guidetti's (Wingdale) S ▽ | 21 | 23 | 22 | $37 |
Pleasant Ridge Rd. (2½ mi. west of Hwy. 22), 914-832-6721
☑ An "old politicians hangout", this "family-owned" Northern Italian in Dutchess County "has its ups and downs", but most maintain the food is "consistently good"; housed in a former '30s lodge, the "castle"-like stone house has working fireplaces and a romantic air about it and those in the know say "Jack's martinis are the best."

Gus's Franklin Park (Harrison) S | 17 | 10 | 15 | $29 |
126 Halstead Ave. (1st St.), 914-835-9804
☑ "Like an old shoe – comfortable but worn", this 1931 "neighborhood saloon" is a Harrison "landmark" ("everyone goes there because everyone goes there"); the simple pub fare emphasizes fish (the owners also own the seafood market next door) and if you "stick to lobster and beer" you won't notice it's "riding on its reputation and longevity."

Gyosai (Scarsdale) S | 23 | 14 | 19 | $29 |
30 Garth Rd. (Freightway Rd.), 914-725-3730
"Scarsdale's answer to Azuma", this "centrally located" "crowded" Japanese has "fresh fish and friendly" service; regulars are willing to overlook the lack of "atmosphere" to dine on "tasty" sushi and cooked food; there's also a "nice weekend lunch deal."

Happiness Is… (Cross River) | – | – | – | I |
Yellow Monkey Village, Rte. 35 (off Rte. 684), 914-763-2533
This brand-new Cross River cafe serves breakfast and lunchtime soups, sandwiches, salads and pastries in a small space that doubles in good weather with outdoor dining; once a month in summer it stays open on Saturday evening to offer tasty themes like lobster or clam bakes.

HARRALDS (Stormville) ♥   27 26 26 $61
3110 Rte. 52 (bet. Durrschmidt & Mountain Rds.),
914-878-6595
☑ "I don't care what it costs, it's simply the best!" declare
those who herald Harrald and Eve Boerger's "top-notch"
International cuisine; Harrald "strives for perfection" and
dining at his English Tudor cottage deep in the Dutchess
County countryside, "you really feel pampered"; for "special
occasions", "old-world charm" and "breathtaking mountain
views", it can't be beat.

Hartsdale Garden (Hartsdale) S   19 14 18 $21
Westchester Sq., 285 N. Central Ave. (Chatterlon Pkwy.),
914-683-1611
☑ "Trying hard to be better than ordinary", this mid-
Westchester Chinese serves "tasty" "food from many
provinces" and is considered a "good standby"; supporters
say there's "service with a smile" as well as "great dim
sum" on weekends.

Heidi's Brauhaus (Mahopac) S♥ ▽   16 16 17 $24
241 Rte. 6N (2 mi. east of Taconic Pkwy.), 914-628-9795
☑ For "good German food", this veteran Mahopac
Continental is the place to go; the Zimmerman "family does a
good job" turning out "lots of food" and their "Sunday buffet
can't be beat" because "prices are more than reasonable."

Hilltop Restaurant (Nyack) ◗S   17 11 15 $25
312 Main St./Rte. 59 (Rte. 9W), 914-358-2728
☑ They "haven't changed the decor since 1947 when they
opened" this family-style Italian seafooder in Nyack; while
foes rate it "mediocre", fans praise the "generous portions"
and "good bang for the buck."

Hope and Anchor Dining Room   17 15 19 $30
& Bar (Larchmont) S
141 Chatsworth Ave. (Palmer Ave.), 914-833-0340
☑ This Larchmont storefront restaurant is "ok if you're
near the train station"; the "friendly help" will serve
you an interesting International mix of "fair to good food"
in "rather dowdy surroundings."

Hoppfield's (Bedford) S   18 21 16 $42
954 Old Post Rd./Rte. 121 (bet. Rtes. 22 & 35), 914-234-3374
☑ The "beautiful rooms" at this Bedford "country inn"
provide a backdrop for American-Eclectic cooking that some
reviewers report is "sabotaged by inadequate service"; to
many it's "a nice place", if "a bit overpriced", and optimists
maintain there's still "great potential."

Horsefeathers (Tarrytown) **S**   16 | 14 | 16 | $20
94 N. Broadway (Wildey St.), 914-631-6606
☑ "Now this is comfort food" say devotees of the "large menu" with "burgers", all "the basics and a good beer selection" found at this "loud but fun" Tarrytown tavern with a "funky atmosphere"; others are simply "underwhelmed" by the "standard fare" at this "crowded" pub.

Hudson Cafe (Irvington) **S**   18 | 17 | 18 | $26
63 Main St., 914-591-2631
■ Regulars recommend "stay with the simple stuff" at this "good neighborhood spot for a relaxed dinner"; the "satisfying" Irvington American-Continental is set in a "charming old space" with a "warm, friendly atmosphere."

Hudson House, A Country Inn   18 | 20 | 17 | $31
(Cold Spring) **S**
2 Main St. (West St.), 914-265-9355
■ This "charming" Cold Spring B&B's "beautiful setting" with a "great view" of the Hudson is the backdrop for "pleasant" and "interesting" Americana; surveyors say it's "best for an occasion."

Hudson House of Nyack (Nyack) **S** 20 | 19 | 19 | $31
134 Main St. (bet. B'way & Franklin St.), 914-353-1355
☑ While there are no river views (the restaurant is named for co-owner Matt Hudson), this American-Eclectic has an unusual setting in Nyack's "lovely" Old Village Hall where former jail cells serve as the wine cellar; most find the "contemporary", "creative" and "interesting" menu a "great value", but a few criticize the "hit or miss" meals and "inconsistent service."

Hudson's Ribs & Fish   ▽ 20 | 16 | 19 | $27
(Fishkill) **S**
2014 Rte. 9 (½ mile from I-84), 914-297-5002
■ As you'd expect, this Fishkill steak and seafood house features fish and ribs; less expected are the signature fresh-baked popovers with strawberry butter and the hordes of hungry children; it's always busy and "very loud", but regulars advise if you "eat early" and "stick to the standbys", you'll enjoy "good food at a fair price."

Huff House, The (Roscoe) **S**   _ | _ | _ | E
100 Lake Anawanda Rd. (bet. Rtes. 17 & 97), 607-498-9953
■ Trout fishermen frequent this Catskill inn, which has been in the hands of the Forness family for over a hundred years; since reports indicate the restaurant is "well-run" and "friendly" with an appealingly "lazy wood fire" by which you can dine on old-time American food there's nothing to get 'n a huff about here.

Hunan 100 (Hartsdale) S　　18　13　18　$19
415 N. Central Ave. (Independence St.), 914-684-6505
■ The staff is "eager to please" at this popular new Hartsdale Chinese where the "consistently good food" includes "non-Americanized" options that are a "pleasant departure"; but keep your eyes on your plate as there's "not much ambiance."

Hunan Ritz (Thornwood) S　▽　18　12　16　$21
Rose Hill Shopping Ctr., 3-11 Columbus Ave. (Nannyhagen Rd.), 914-747-0701
■ All right, so it's not the Ritz, but for "good neighborhood Chinese", this eatery is a "better than average" choice; supporters say that there are "some unusual dishes" and "Peking duck from heaven."

Hunan Village (Yonkers) S　　24　18　21　$26
1828 Central Park Ave. (Slater Ave.), 914-779-2272
☑ "Delicious, unusual, gourmet Chinese" is served at what's "probably Westchester's best"; some "don't understand the fuss" over this "pricey" Yonkers veteran, but they're in a minority; for most this is the place for "excellent, creative food" and "great value and service"; P.S. their Chinese "New Year's dinner is a treat."

Ichi Riki S　　22　18　20　$28
Elmsford Plaza, 1 E. Main St. (Rtes. 119 & 9A), Elmsford, 914-592-2220
110 Main St. (bet. Franklin St. & Broadway), Nyack, 914-358-7977
■ For "fabulous fresh sushi" and other cooked Japanese dishes, these Southern New York siblings are "always satisfying" and "always crowded"; one partisan reports that "Elmsford is much better than Nyack", yet both "treat you nice"; dining in one of the private tatami rooms is recommended, but watch your wallet as "sushi can add up quickly."

IL CENÀCOLO (Newburgh) S　　28　22　25　$42
152 Rte. 52 (Rte. 300), 914-564-4494
■ "The best Northern Italian food in the area" makes it "absolutely worth the drive to Newburgh" to experience "serious" cooking, including "incredible sauces" and an outstanding antipasti table; of course it's "expensive", but in addition to the "fabulous food", there's "lovely decor", an "excellent staff" and a "fine wine list."

Il Cigno (Scarsdale) S　　24　18　20　$41
Colonial Village, 1505 Weaver St., 914-472-8484
■ "Don't be fooled by its shopping center location" advise the many loyal patrons of this "delicious and surprisingly novel" Scarsdale Northern Italian; even if "they favor regulars" and "it's pricey", "this is the standard by which Italian restaurants are measured."

Ile de France (Goshen)   – | – | – | M
6 N. Church St. (Main St.), 914-294-8373
Francophiles and gourmets are discovering this small French "island" in Orange County; chef-owner Christian Pierrel serves authentic bistro fare at lunch and takes a more classic Gallic turn at night; the prix fixe menu is a steal and the BYO policy makes any meal an even better value.

Il Portico Ristorante (Tappan) S   24 | 22 | 23 | $37
89 Main St. (Oak Tree Rd.), 914-365-2100
■ "First-class food" is served at this Tappan Northern Italian gem renowned for its seafood and fresh interpretations of classic dishes; while portions can be "small", service is "pleasant" in a "lovely", "no-fuss" setting.

Il Sorriso Ristorante Italiano   21 | 20 | 19 | $35
(Irvington) S
5 N. Buckhout St. (Main St.), 914-591-2525
■ For "very good pasta dishes" and brick-oven pizza you'll pay "NYC prices", but "the food is worth it" at this Irvington Italian with a seafood slant; while service is "pleasant", they "need more waiters on weekends" when it's "crowded and noisy"; try the "superb outdoor garden in the summer."

Imperial Wok S   19 | 17 | 18 | $20
736 N. Broadway (I-287), N. White Plains, 914-686-2700
13 Heritage Hills Dr. (Rte. 202), Somers, 914-277-8900
851 Franklin Ave. (Commerce St.), Thornwood,
914-747-3111
1940 Commerce St. (Rte. 35), Yorktown Heights,
914-245-3840 **(CLOSED)**
◪ "Reliable", "old-fashioned" Chinese chainlet that provides locals with an "economical way to eat good food"; while they may "lack originality", their "very consistent" kitchens make them a "good standby"; N.B. the Somers location has "great lake views."

India House (Montrose) S   22 | 19 | 20 | $24
199 Albany Post Rd. (Rte. 9A), 914-736-0005
■ "The smells are fabulous" at this Montrose Indian, which we hear is "friendlier" than its Bengal Tiger sibling; its "convenient" location, "great fish dishes" and "lunch specials" lead some loyalists to label it the "best Indian in northern Westchester."

Inn at Osborne Hill, The (Fishkill)   23 | 17 | 20 | $40
150 Osborne Hill Rd. (Rte. 9), 914-897-3055
◪ There's "imaginative cuisine and great presentation" at this "out of the way" Fishkill Continental–New American; with an award-winning wine list and monthly wine dinners, it's an oenophile's delight, but fans sigh "if only they could gussy up the dining room."

INN AT POUND RIDGE   24 25 22 $46
(Pound Ridge) S
258 Westchester Ave./Rte. 137 (Rte. 172), 914-764-5779
■ The "most beautiful restaurant in Westchester" is
"elegant, dignified and charming" and altogether
"wonderful" for special occasions; "it's nice to visit in
the spring with the beautiful flowers in the garden" or
at Christmas when the 18th-century inn is "especially
pretty"; all-year-round there's "creative" French-influenced
Contemporary American cuisine and "scrumptious
desserts"; the sole criticism is that "service can be spotty."

Isabel's Cafe (Tarrytown) ◑ S   15 14 15 $22
61 Main St. (Washington St.), 914-631-9819
◪ Loyalists claim the "food has improved" at this Tarrytown
casual American and scores support that opinion; they say
"sitting outside with a view of the Hudson" is "delightful
for lunch" and a "good value", but to a number of others
it's just a place to snack on "pub grub" while enjoying the
excellent live music on weekends.

Jade Palace (Scarsdale) S   20 13 17 $22
694 Central Park Ave. (south of A&P), 914-472-8888
■ "Too many people know" this is the place for "first-rate
Cantonese in Westchester"; "the menu is fairly typical",
but "some of the specials are different and interesting",
and the kitchen is "responsive to diners' wishes"; the one
quibble is that there's nothing palatial about the decor.

Jaipore Royal Indian Cuisine   23 21 19 $32
(Brewster) S
Rte. 22 (2 mi. north of Rte. 100), 914-277-3549
■ A "beautiful Victorian house" is the setting for this
"elegant and comfortable" Brewster Indian, which is
considered "one of the best around"; the lunch buffet "gives
a good sampling" of the "fresh and interesting" ethnic fare;
surveyors are less happy with the "inconsistent service";
N.B. on Friday nights there's live sitar and tabla music.

Japan Inn (Bronxville) S   20 13 20 $27
28 Palmer Ave. (Lawrence Hospital), 914-337-1296
■ There's "surprisingly special sushi", "friendly and warm
service" and "simple decor" at this sometimes "crowded
and noisy" Bronxville Japanese; to most it's "dependable",
but a few are "not impressed", calling it "uneven."

Jason's Ltd. (Eastchester) S   19 16 20 $31
478 White Plains Rd. (Mill Rd.), 914-961-5717
■ "What's not to like?" ask regulars of this Eastchester
Continental veteran that's fine for "big portions" of "staples
like steaks"; popular for "business lunches" and with "an
older crowd", it can be "much too crowded"; as for service,
some say "you are well treated when they know you."

John Richard's (Dobbs Ferry) **S**   16 | 14 | 17 | $23 |
39 Chestnut St. (Main St.), 914-693-6404
☑ "Good beer and burgers" are the draws at this "friendly"
Dobbs Ferry Traditional American "neighborhood hangout"
that's apt for "spur of the moment" moods; those who find
the eating merely "reasonable not memorable" advise "go
for the music" – there's jazz and blues on weekends.

K. Fung's (Hartsdale) **S**   22 | 17 | 21 | $24 |
222 E. Hartsdale Ave. (opposite RR station), 914-472-3838
■ Not "run of the mill", this Hartsdale contemporary Chinese
is "innovative" and "excellent"; relying on nontraditional
"high-quality ingredients" and a wide selection of vegetarian
dishes, the results are "healthy and different"; "very trendy"
and "sophisticated", it "doesn't look like a Chinese
restaurant"; the "good fast service" is another plus.

Khan's Mongolian (Rockland) **S**   16 | 12 | 15 | $20 |
21 N. Rte. 303 (Palisades Pkwy., exit 5N), 914-359-8004
■ "Kids love" choosing and cooking their own ingredients –
selected "from a 'salad bar' of shrimp, beef, noodles, spices,
etc." – at this Rockland County Mongolian BBQ; though "a
fun experience", some assert "it all tastes the same after
a while"; so whether this is "a once a year experience" or
a place to go once is your call.

King and I, The (Nyack) **S**   20 | 17 | 18 | $27 |
93 Main St. (Franklin St. & Broadway), 914-353-4208
■ Loyalists (and royalists) love the "extremely friendly"
service and "tasty", "well-priced" Thai cuisine that "delights
the eye" here, calling it "a great place to go with a group
of friends"; the restaurant is suitably close to Nyack's
Broadway and offers pre-theater and early-bird menus.

Kit 'N Caboodle (Mount Kisco) **S**   15 | 15 | 16 | $24 |
443 Lexington Ave. (Rte. 117), 914-241-2440
☑ Fans of this Mount Kisco New American "great value
neighborhood restaurant" believe it's "best for salads";
dissenters say while it's "ok for lunch", it's "disappointing
for dinner" and just "not as good as it used to be", asserting
"a more innovative kitchen" is in order.

Kozel's (West Ghent) ◖**S**   ▽ 14 | 12 | 15 | $23 |
*1006 Rte. 9H (1 mi. south of Columbia County Airport),
518-828-3326*
■ "Remember the relish tray?" well, "it still lives" at this
old-style Traditional American that has been a Columbia
County fixture since the '30s – and some complain that not
much has changed since then; today it caters largely to
"an older crowd" that appreciates the reasonable prices.

La Camelia (Mount Kisco) S 23 21 21 $42
234 N. Bedford Rd. (Rte. 117), 914-666-2466
■ "A classy Mount Kisco Spanish" set "high on a hill" in a "romantic", "pleasant country atmosphere"; this is an "always good, never cheap" venue for fare that is "usually wonderful and well presented", like the "super tapas", paella and white sangria; there's also a "good Spanish wine list", but both the kitchen and service can be "slow."

LA CRÉMAILLÈRE (Banksville) S 27 27 25 $56
46 Bedford-Banksville Rd. (4 mi. north of Merritt Pkwy.), 914-234-9647
■ It's "the crème de la crème" of "beautifully presented" Contemporary French fare and ratings continue to climb at this "bastion of fine food"; there's "excellent service" and the "old country house adds to the leisurely charm" so it's "perfect for celebrations"; a few regard it as "a bit stuffy" and "pretentious", but they're vastly outvoted by those who say it's "pricey" but "worth it."

La Duchesse Anne ▽ 22 23 22 $33
(Mount Tremper) S
1564 Wittenberg Rd. (Rte. 212), 914-688-5260
■ For a "romantic trip to provincial France", try this "charming", "low-key" Ulster County inn where "classic country French cooking with an occasional twist" is served by "hospitable hosts."

La Fonda del Sol ▽ 15 13 15 $25
(Wappingers Falls) S
100 Old Rte. 9 (State Rd. 28), 914-297-5044
☑ "There's better", but this Wappingers Falls veteran offers decent Mexican-Spanish food and "good service"; the downstairs bar pours a mean margarita and has a full menu in addition to live music and karaoke.

La Foresta Restaurant ▽ 18 15 18 $29
(Dobbs Ferry) S
92 Main St. (Broadway), 914-674-0517
■ "Hospitable service" and "heartwarming Italian food" with "rich, well-spiced sauces" and homemade breads and pastas are found at this Dobbs Ferry "standby"; it's "not fancy, but it is tasty and prices are fair."

Lago di Como (Tarrytown) S 21 18 21 $36
27 Main St. (John & Washington Sts.), 914-631-7227
☑ "Just like being back in Milano" say fans of this understated Tarrytown Northern Italian who appreciate the "very welcoming service and interesting menu"; critics agree it's like being in Italia alright – they detect a "little imported attitude" and also complain that although the food is "great", there's "not enough of it" for the price.

La Griglia Ristorante (Windham) S _ | _ | _ | E |
Rte. 296, 518-734-4499
Few reviewers have tried this Windham veteran, but we hear
it's the place to go in Greene County for solid Northern
Italian fare; as there's a limited reservations policy, there
can be waits on weekends in ski season or at summer's
peak; the addition of a new bakery/gourmet shop means
all breads and pastries are made on the premises.

L'Air de Paris (New Windsor) S   _ | _ | _ | E |
617 Little Britain Rd., 914-567-6628
A "French gem that's worth the trip" rave the handful who've
tried this small, chic New Windsor newcomer owned by
chef Laurent Ceron, who worked at the renowned Lucas
Carton in Paris, and his wife; surveyors savor the "real
bistro flavor", saying his cooking is a treat "both for the
eyes and the taste buds"; the prix fixe lunch is a deal.

La Lanterna (Yonkers) S   18 | 15 | 19 | $31 |
23 Grey Oaks Ave. (Barney & Hearst Sts.), 914-476-3060
◪ Fans of this Yonkers "good Italian with a Swiss twist"
praise the "large portions" of "good pasta" and the "best
fried calamari ever", calling it "a real bargain" and awarding
the "well-informed staff" kudos; but others feel the food is
"bland" and criticize the "curious location in a former
freight depot" and "deafening noise on Saturday night."

La Manda's (White Plains) S⇗   18 | 8 | 16 | $19 |
251 Tarrytown Rd. (I-287), 914-684-9228
■ A "home away from home" for many White Plains
families, this venerable "terrific value" Italian with "an
accommodating staff" just celebrated its half century; the
brick-oven pizza and "no-frills home cooking" are in demand
with regulars who try to ignore the fact that there's "not
much to look at" and it can be "crowded" and "loud."

LA PANETIÈRE (Rye)   28 | 26 | 26 | $57 |
530 Milton Rd. (Oakland Beach Ave.), 914-967-8140
■ "It just doesn't get any better than this" say the legions of
loyalists who adore this "elegant, classy" Rye Contemporary
French; "ethereal food", "exquisite service" and a "lovely
country setting" make "this gem" a "fine French treasure"; if
a few find it "pretentious", more maintain that it's "wonderful
and worth the money" – the "perfect place to propose."

La Parmigiana (Rhinebeck)   _ | _ | _ | M |
37 Montgomery (Livingston St.), 914-876-3228
This Rhinebeck Northern Italian housed in a "charming,
renovated church" with soaring ceilings serves "special"
brick-oven pizza, "great foccacia" and pastas that are
made fresh daily; since the price is right, and there are
live bands on weekends, there can be crowds and long
waits in the summer.

Laredo Southwestern Grill
| 15 | 14 | 16 | $24 |

(Ardsley) **S**

Ardsley Town Mall, 875 Saw Mill River Rd. (Ashford Ave. & Rte. 119), 914-693-1111

▣ The owner and staff at this "welcome addition" to Ardsley are "anxious to please"; many call the casual Southwestern fare "innovative" and "creative", citing the "delicious" fish and homemade muffins, but others claim the sometimes "odd combinations" can make for an inconsistent experience.

La Riserva Trattoria (Larchmont) **S**
| 19 | 18 | 20 | $32 |

2382 Boston Post Rd. (Winans Rd.), 914-834-5584

■ Newly renovated (it's "not so old and stuffy") and with a revised menu, this Larchmont Italian is "still a favorite"; the "upscaled prices" are less popular, but regulars depend upon the "helpful staff" and "always good food" and advise ordering the specials for a "home run"

La Rive (Catskill) **S**
▽ | 27 | 18 | 21 | $42 |

141 Dedrick Rd. (Old King's Rd.), 518-943-4888

■ This beloved but "hard to find" Catskill Contemporary French veteran has reopened after repairs and devotees who missed the "unique, unadorned farmhouse where dining is a memorable experience" say it's still "worth finding"; "it makes you think you are back in France" and there's "terrific service"; N.B. open May–October only.

Las Brisas II (Port Chester) **S**
▽ | 18 | 6 | 10 | $16 |

173 Westchester Ave., 914-939-2360

■ "Good homestyle Mexican" that's "cheap" and "real" report those who've weathered the "grumpy service" to sample the "delicious" fare at this plain Port Chester spot.

La Scala (Armonk) **S**
| 17 | 14 | 19 | $32 |

386 Main St. (¼ mi. south of Rte. 684), 914-273-3508

▣ Supporters sing the praises of this "lively and warm" Armonk Italian "neighborhood staple" where there is "hearty food" and "every diner is treated like someone special"; however, detractors shriek the food is just "so-so" and it's "way, way overpriced."

Latin American Cafe
| 17 | 9 | 15 | $19 |

(White Plains) **S**

134 Post Rd. (Mamaroneck Ave.), 914-948-6606

■ "No ambiance" and "no frills in a nondescript location" might not sound appealing, but they "get crowds of folks who know quality" at this White Plains Cuban; there are "humongous portions" and insiders insist the food is "more inventive" than you'd expect; all in all it's "a bargain and a cultural delight."

Le Canard Enchaîné   ▽ 22 | 20 | 20 | $32 |
(Kingston) S
276 Fair St. (John & Main Sts.), 914-339-2003
■ Though it's named after owner Jean-Jacques Carquillat's favorite satirical newspaper, there's nothing tongue in cheek about the "excellent" French fare at this new, "very typical bistro", which brings a Gallic flair to Downtown Kingston; for a real Parisian feel, try the sidewalk cafe.

LE CHAMBORD   24 | 25 | 23 | $46 |
(Hopewell Junction) S
2075 Rte. 52 (Carpenter Rd.), 914-221-1941
☑ Dining at this "most elegant" Classic French is a "special experience to be savored" at this "romantic" Dutchess County inn and rising ratings support their point of view; but a few curmudgeons counter "outdated" and "overrated."

LE CHATEAU (South Salem) S   25 | 27 | 24 | $51 |
Rte. 35 (Rte. 123), 914-533-6631
☑ This South Salem castle, actually a "glorious old baronial home", makes a "simply regal" setting for "fine" Classic French food (including "the best dessert soufflés") and "excellent service"; do try it for a "festive occasion", but "don't go on Saturday nights" or "when there's a function" since "it can get too crowded and noisy"; wallet watchers warn that it's "best enjoyed on someone else's tab."

LE PAVILLON (Poughkeepsie)   27 | 21 | 24 | $40 |
230 Salt Point Tpke./Rte. 115 (N. Grand Ave.), 914-473-2525
■ "Consistently excellent" cuisine courtesy of chef-owner Claude Guermont and the "best wine list at the best prices" make this Poughkeepsie Classic French a "great experience" and rising food ratings reflect that opinion; it's "not pretentious but still fancy enough for mom" although some say the decor "needs updating"; oenophiles should take note of the special Sunday wine dinners.

Le Petit Bistro (Rhinebeck) S   24 | 19 | 24 | $37 |
8 E. Market St. (Rtes. 308 & 9), 914-876-7400
■ "Just as the name suggests", this Rhinebeck French bistro is "small and intimate" with "crowded tables" and "charming, delicious" "traditional" fare; "service is top-notch" and owner "Yvonne is a great hostess."

Le Provençal (Mamaroneck) S   ▽ 25 | 21 | 24 | $32 |
436 Mamaroneck Ave. (across from the RR station), 914-777-2324
■ A "small and cozy" Mamaroneck newcomer that scores for its "authentic French dining"; chef-owner Derrick Dikkers has created "one of the better dining experiences in Westchester" say early samplers who've discovered that this "true treat" has "good potential.

195

Les Pyrenées (Canaan) ⑤✄ | – | – | – | E |
15 Queechy Lake Dr., 518-781-4451
Closer to the Berkshires than any French mountain range,
this pricey Columbia County veteran has Classic French
food; it's relatively unknown and only a handful of city
dwellers rate it for "Sunday dinner on the way home."

L'EUROPE RESTAURANT | 24 | 21 | 23 | $47 |
(South Salem) ⑤
*407 Smithridge Rd./Rte. 123 (½ mile from CT border),
914-533-2570*
☑ The "gracious dining" at this "upscale" South Salem
French-Continental inn attracts an "older, wealthy-looking"
crowd that appreciates the "attentive", "unpretentious"
service and "tables well-spaced for privacy"; a few feel
the "menu needs to be updated", but most assert that its
"combination of service, food and ambiance is tough to
beat" and the Sunday brunch is a "great value."

Lexington Square Cafe | 21 | 21 | 19 | $31 |
(Mount Kisco) ⑤
510 Lexington Ave. (Rte. 117), 914-244-3663
☑ "NYC dining at NYC prices" is found at this Mount Kisco
New American putting "interesting new spins on saloon
food"; while some say the "creative" "eclectic menu" is
"consistently good", others caution that it "can rise to
superb heights or be very ordinary"; the "modern urban
decor" and "noisy, trendy" scene lead one reviewer to
conclude it's "yuppie heaven – pass the cigars."

Lia's Mountain View Restaurant ▽ | 14 | 13 | 16 | $22 |
(Pine Plains) ⑤
Rte. 82 S. (Rte. 199), 518-398-7311
☑ This Northern Dutchess County consistent "casual
Italian" is "ok if you're in that neck of the woods"; it's a
"warm", friendly place for a good pizza or pasta.

Lisboa A Noite (Ossining) ⑤ | 19 | 16 | 17 | $31 |
107-109 Main St. (bet. State & Spring Sts.), 914-941-4132
■ Many regard this "fancy Portuguese" as "Ossining's
treasure"; "large portions" make it a "good value", but
with "such good food it's too bad they can't get their act
together" when it comes to keeping customers waiting.

LOCUST TREE INN, THE | 21 | 25 | 21 | $34 |
(New Paltz) ⑤
215 Huguenot St. (Rte. 299), 914-255-7888
■ "Very cozy and historic", this 1759 New Paltz stone
house provides a "beautiful setting" for "good", solid
American-Continental cooking; the patio overlooking a
lush golf course, the working fireplaces and the "great
seasonal decorations", including an enormous collection
of Santas, add to the ambiance.

Loft, The (New Paltz)   – – – M
46 Main St. (off Rte. 32), 914-255-1426
This new casual Contemporary American has garnered rave
reviews from New Paltz locals and weekenders who say a
lot of care goes into the cooking of chef-owner William
Loughlin, who relies on local organic produce whenever
posssible; the upstairs dining room is actually a loft.

Louie's Italian Restaurant   17 11 15 $24
(Yonkers) S
187 S. Broadway (Herriot St.), 914-969-8821
■ Regulars come for the "hearty Italian food", reasonable
prices and warm family atmosphere at this "noisy" Yonkers
veteran; despite the fact that the "neighborhood is bad",
"the food is good" and the sauces are "delicious."

Louisana Cajun Cafe   16 13 16 $26
(Dobbs Ferry) S
25 Cedar St. (½ block west of Broadway/Rte. 9), 914-693-9762
◪ Fans of this Dobbs Ferry Cajun feel it's "interesting for a
change", praising the "fun" food and citing the "very good
gumbo"; foes snipe it's "a far cry from the French Quarter"
with its "gimmicky decor" and only "decent down-home
cooking"; there's live Dixieland on Saturday nights.

Luna Restaurant (Mount Kisco) S 20 18 18 $37
*251 Main St. (½ mile north of Rtes. 117 & 172 intersection),
914-242-5151*
◪ "Good for when you are feeling too suburban", David
Liederman's Mount Kisco New American "feels like NYC",
with "Manhattan prices and lines"; supporters say it's
worth it for "interesting dishes" like the "excellent duck"
and "incredible chicken", the "casual but chic setting" and
the "accommodating" service; however, naysayers find
it's "up and down", adding it's too "noisy" and "expensive."

Luna 61 (Red Hook)   – – – I
61 E. Market St. (Rte. 9), 914-758-0061
Vegetarian organic cafe where food, service and ambiance
all appeal; the futomaki (veggy sushi) and a shot of
wheatgrass will give you a Zen holliday; you don"t have to
be a vegetarian to enjoy this.

LUSARDI'S (Larchmont) S   23 20 21 $40
*1885 Palmer Ave. (Chatsworth Ave. & Weaver St.),
914-834-5555*
■ "It's wonderful to have a real sophisticated Northern
Italian restaurant in Westchester" declare devotees of
this "Manhattan spin-off" with "excellent food" and
"great style"; of course "the place to be" is also "noisy",
"crowded" and "impossible to get into", so make your
reservations now; while inside "tables are cramped",
outside you'll find "cute sidewalk seating in the summer."

Maddalena Ristorante　21　19　20　$38
(Armonk) **S** (CLOSED)
61 Old Rte. 22 (Rte. 128), 914-273-1644
■ "Off the beaten path", this Armonk "upscale Northern
Italian" has "excellent food and service" and a "genteel"
ambiance aided by a "lovely dining room with fireplaces";
while a few carp that it's "overpriced" and there are "small
portions", many others enthuse "bring money and someone
to have a romantic evening with."

Madrid (Palisades) **S** (CLOSED) ▽ 18　14　16　$28
779 Rte. 340 (2 blocks west of Rte. 9W), 914-359-7227
■ There's "Spanish food and lots of it" at this "noisy,
family-oriented" Rockland County restaurant with "great
green sauce and shrimp"; there's a "pleasant atmosphere",
though some say some spiffing up is in order.

Main Course (New Paltz)　–　–　–　M
232 Main St. (Rte. 229, off NY State Twy.), 914-255-2600
Simple diner-style decor and a casual atmosphere keep the
focus on the food at this New Paltz Contemporary American;
chef-owner Bruce Kazan adds a variety of accents – from
Central American to Asian – to the cooking, while also
keeping an eye on fat and salt to suit his health-conscious
patrons; in contrast, his homemade desserts are decadent.

Main Street Cafe (Tarrytown) **S**　17　13　16　$23
24 Main St. (Rte. 9), 914-524-9770
■ "They try hard" at this "cutesy" Tarrytown New American
where "tasty" "unusual" fare and "amiable service" make it
a "good lunch and light dinner spot."

Maison Lafitte (Briarcliff Manor) **S**　19　21　18　$39
Chappaqua Rd. (Rte. 9A), 914-941-5787
◪ Briarcliff Manor's "beautiful" "Tara-like" setting provides
a "gracious" backdrop for Continental cooking; though it
has its adherents who find it "charming and friendly", others
sigh that "it has seen better days."

Malabar Hill (Elmsford) **S**　22　16　17　$25
145 E. Main St./Rte. 119, 914-347-7890
■ The "excellent lunch buffet" at this "palace-like" Elmsford
Indian is widely praised as a "best buy"; fans consider the
food "excellent" with "wonderful breads"; a few say the
staff is "unfriendly" and consider it "expensive for dinner",
but to most it's "elegant in every way."

Manzi's Restaurant　17　14　16　$26
(Hastings-on-Hudson) **S**
17-19 Main St. (Warburton & Farragut Aves.), 914-478-0404
◪ This "old-style" Hastings Italian has a dedicated following
among "older locals" who like the "humongous portions"
and "reasonable" prices; but critics counter the fare is
"uninspired" and the "service is slow."

MARCELLO'S RISTORANTE   25 21 24 $41
(Suffern) S
21-3 Lafayette Ave. (Rte. 59 & Orange Ave.), 914-357-9108
■ At what many call the "best Italian in Rockland County"
and a "must for serious diners", chef-owner Marcello
Russodivito and his staff "really have their act together":
the "formally presented" food "is prepared with love" and
"always delicious"; reviewers have only one quibble: "this is
still the suburbs and we expect the prices to match."

Marcel's (West Park) S   ▽ 24 21 22 $33
Rte. 9W (Floyd Ackert), 914-384-6700
■ Though "tiny", this "friendly" Ulster County French bistro
has garnered a big reputation for "great food" over the
years; it's often "crowded", but there's a "cozy, inviting
ambiance" replete with fireplaces; regulars suggest "try
to make it the night they have jazz" (one Sunday a month
year-round); N.B. open for dinner only Friday–Monday.

Mardino's (Mount Kisco) S   ▽ 15 9 16 $26
473 Lexington Ave. (Rte. 117), 914-666-2428
✓ "Your parents' favorite Italian restaurant" sums up the
appeal of this "reliable and genial" Mount Kisco veteran
for some; but dissenters dis it's "nothing special" and it's
in a "time warp."

Marichu Restaurant (Bronxville) S 24 20 22 $37
*104 Kraft Ave. (Pondfield Rd., opposite RR Station),
914-961-2338*
■ This Basque in Bronxville, with an offspring in Manhattan,
serves "unusual", "excellent" Northern Spanish fare
including "wonderful tapas", a "great vegetarian dinner"
and "the best fish in Westchester"; it's a "darling", "pretty
place" with "nice people" and "expensive" prices.

Mariner's Harbor Inn (Red Hook) S 13 16 14 $27
Rte. 9G (opposite Bard College), 914-876-1331
✓ Loyalists claim "the critics complain, but the people
love" this Red Hook seafood and steak sibling of the
Highland original, which has since closed; but detractors
say the food is "poorly prepared" and point out that the
new location, directly opposite Bard College, does not
offer river views to distract patrons from the fishy fare.

Martindale Chief Diner   ▽ 11 11 16 $12
(Craryville) S ⊘
1000 Rte. 23 (Taconic Pkwy.), 518-851-2525
■ For those heading north on the Taconic, this Columbia
County pit stop pioneer is mainly a respite from the road
and "will do if you gotta eat"; locals value it as a decent
"breakfast and lunch place" for "no nonsense reliable fare",
and nostalgia buffs admire the '50s classic dining car.

199

Maruzzella Due (Scarsdale) S   17 17 16 $28
754 White Plains Rd. (Wilmot Rd.), 914-725-0566
☑ An "upscale" Northern Italian with seafood specialties and a handy Scarsdale location "near Lord & Taylor"; fans relish the "generous portions" of "delicious specials" and like the "airy" interior, but others say "the menu is average" and "overpriced for so-so pasta and pizza."

Mary Ann's (Port Chester)   – – – M
275 Boston Post Rd. (Rte. 1), 914-939-8700
The new Port Chester branch of this popular Manhattan minichain Mexican draws favorable write-in responses for its "very good" food and "unusual low-fat entrees."

Maud's Tavern   17 16 18 $25
(Hastings-on-Hudson) S
149 Southside Ave. (Spring St.), 914-478-2326
■ "A pleasant place with decent fare at a reasonable price", this Hastings-on-Hudson International has a "welcoming" "pub-style" ambiance and a staff that "likes kids"; a few sniff they offer "no more than fancy bar food" and all agree it's "somewhat noisy."

MAXIME'S (Granite Springs) S   28 27 27 $56
Old Tomahawk St. (Rtes. 118N & 202), 914-248-7200
■ "Everything a French restaurant should be", this is "the place for that really special occasion" rave those who've savored chef-owner Maxime Ribera's "exquisite" Classic French with its "delectable sauces"; the "beautiful", "parklike Northern Westchester setting", "extraordinary atmosphere" and "gracious, warm" service make for "a perfect evening"; it may be "pricey, but it's worth it."

Max Memphis BBQ (Red Hook)   – – – I
138 S. Broadway (bet. Rtes. 199 & 9G), 914-758-6297
David Weiss, owner of Tivoli's trendy Santa Fe, brings a taste of the south to northern Dutchess; slow, wood-smoked meats, pulled pork and ribs dominate at this Red Hook barbecue joint, plus all the sides your mammy used to make.

MCKINNEY & DOYLE   25 19 22 $33
FINE FOODS CAFE (Pawling) S
10 Charles Colman Blvd., 914-855-3875
Corner Bakery, The (Pawling)
10 Charles Collman Blvd., 914-855-3707
■ "Everything is well-done" at these "jewels", which share owners and an "out of the way" Pawling location; the "short menu" of New American food served at the cafe is "terrific, tasty and interesting" and the brunch "is top-notch", though some find the portions "small for a man at dinner"; the bakery is renowned for its breads and pastries and there's a cappuccino bar where you can sit and sample the blends.

Mediterraneo (Pleasantville) **S**   18 | 20 | 16 | $31 |
75 Cooley St. (Bedford Rd. & Rte 117), 914-773-1020
■ This new Pleasantville Italian is truly "pleasant" with its
elegant faux marble walls and columns and live music;
the "stylish, clean food", including "unique pastas", leads
reviewers to say it "feels like we're in Italy"; as it's often
"busy", for "lower decibels go later at night."

Michael's Tavern (Pleasantville) **S**   13 | 11 | 14 | $19 |
150 Bedford Rd. (Rtes. 117 & 141), 914-769-9849
■ A Pleasantville veteran "sports bar" where the "great
college scene" happily distracts you from the quality of
the food; you'll be fine if you stick to the "beer and burgers",
but it's "too noisy at night for us older folks."

Mill House Panda **S**   19 | 16 | 17 | $24 |
289 Mill St. (Garden St.), Poughkeepsie, 914-454-2530
19-21 W. Market St. (Garden St.), Rhinebeck, 914-876-2399
☑ Surveyors seem to see these Dutchess County Chinese
pandas in black and white: fans like the "fresh-tasting"
food, "friendly service" and "big bang for the buck", while
foes say they're just "ok."

Milliway's at the   – | – | – | E |
Hasbrouck House (Stone Ridge) **S**
Inn at Stone Ridge, Rte. 209, 914-687-0736
A beautiful 1750 inn on the National Register of Historic
Places provides a luxurious setting for this upscale Ulster
County American; the few reviewers who've tried the
monthly changing menus report "they try hard": the terrace
and garden offer enticing outdoor dining.

Miraggio (Yorktown Heights) **S** ▽ 18 | 16 | 16 | $25 |
Yorktown Triangle Shopping Ctr., 90 Triangle Ctr. (Rte. 35),
914-248-6200
■ The latest addition to the Eclisse-Brezza family, this
Yorktown Heights Italian set in a shopping center serves
"large portions" of "good food" in a "big, nice-looking"
space; though some say it's loud, others report it's "on a
par with Eclisse but not as noisy."

Mitty's of Westchester   18 | 17 | 19 | $29 |
(Hartsdale) **S**
Hartsdale Plaza, 149 S. Central Ave. (½ mile south of Four
Corners), 914-682-7310
◪ Fans of this Hartsdale steakhouse with a wide selection
of seafood cite the "attractive fixed-price dinner menu for
the budget-conscious" as well as the "huge portions" "at
a fair price" offered by a "very hospitable" owner, Mitty
Carpenito, but critics call it a "food factory" where the
tables are "very close", the menu is "overpriced" and
there's "too much Mitty."

Mohonk Mountain House | _ | _ | _ | M |
Dining Room (New Paltz) S
Mohonk Mt. House, 1000 Mountain Rest Rd. (Rte. 299),
914-256-2056
A venerable New Paltz mountain resort catering to a wide
range of tastes with everything from a children's buffet to
formal afternoon tea and Traditional American dinners; if
some consider the menu to be of the same vintage as the
1869 restaurant, others argue it's a place for "solid fare."

Mona Trattoria (Croton Falls) S | 22 | 21 | 20 | $43 |
592 Rte. 22 (Hardscrabble Rd.), 914-277-4580
☑ This veteran Croton Falls Northern Italian has a
Bolognese accent and "a real old-world feel"; though it
still has many loyal patrons who praise the "idyllic food"
and "gorgeous old house", detractors maintain that it has
"has lost some character over the years" and the cooking
can be "inconsistent", which "at these prices is a no-no."

Monteverde at Oldstone | 20 | 22 | 19 | $34 |
(Peekskill) S
28 Bear Mt. Bridge Rd. (Rtes. 6 & 202W), 914-739-5000
☑ "Inspirational views of the Hudson" are the major appeal
at this Peekskill Continental; most say the food, while
"good", takes second place to the setting, so they advise
making it "a day's outing", not an after-dark dinner; since
the interior "decor is definitely tacky", it's best to opt for
"outdoor seating."

Mountain Brook (Hunter) S | _ | _ | _ | M |
Main St. (entrance to Hunter Mtn.), 518-263-5351
Location, location, location – this casual Contemporary
American is situated at the entrance to Hunter Mountain,
attracting skiers, summer residents and locals; the menu
emphasizes fresh, local food, portions are generous and
wood stoves add to the warm, friendly atmosphere.

Mountain Gate Indian S | _ | _ | _ | I |
Mountain Gate Lodge, 10 McKinley Hollow Rd. (Rte. 28W,
Oliverea exit), Oliverea, 914-254-6000
4 Diming St. (Rte. 212), Woodstock, 914-679-5100
For "inspired Indian food" in an "unpretentious" setting,
Ulster County diners say unlock the gates; these spicy
siblings offer bargain prix fixe dinner menus that provide
a great bang for the buck.

Mount Fuji (Hillburn) S | 20 | 24 | 19 | $32 |
Rte. 17N (2 mi. north of Mahwah, NJ), 914-357-4270
■ "The chefs are very entertaining and the kids love the
show" at this Rockland County Japanese steakhouse with
"very good" "fresh, fresh" food and hibachi-style
cooking; the "beautiful", "colorful" interior also appeals and
there's a great view from the "atop-the-hill" location; with
so much "fun" and activity, some advise "bring earplugs."

Mulino's of Westchester   22 | 22 | 22 | $44
(White Plains) ◐

99 Court St. (bet. Quarropas St. & Martine Ave.), 914-761-1818

☑ "Like Arthur Avenue but prettier", this "welcome addition to White Plains" is a "top-notch", "stylish" Northern Italian offering "consistently high-quality food" and "wonderful service"; foes say "it's excellent if you are a regular" and label it "a bit pretentious"; all agree it's "pricey", but fans urge it's "worth it."

Nanuet Hotel (Nanuet) ⑤   17 | 8 | 15 | $17
Nanuet Hotel, 132 S. Main St. (Rte. 59), 914-623-9600

■ This Italian-American veteran is "known for its thin-crust pizza without peer", which is acclaimed by fans as "the best in Rockland county", but "don't bother with anything thing else on the menu" they warn; as to ambiance, let it be known there is none.

New World Home Cooking   ▽ 22 | 18 | 20 | $27
(Woodstock) ⑤

424 Zena Rd., Box 874 (Sawkill Rd.), 914-679-2600

■ "What you'd expect to find in Woodstock", the "unusual, hip" New American–International menu offers "interesting" food from "a chef who loves to make people happy"; other pluses are "friendly service" and "great ambiance."

Noda's Japanese Steakhouse   19 | 15 | 19 | $25
(White Plains) ⑤

White Plains Mall, 200 Hamilton Ave. (Grove St.), 914-949-0990

■ Expect "flying knives, flying food and group seating" at this White Plains "entertaining Japanese grill" where the "chefs put on a good show at the table"; though "not for purists", it's "worthwhile if you are 12 years old and having a birthday party."

Northern Spy Cafe (High Falls)   – | – | – | M
Rte. 213 (exit 19, off NY State Twy.), 914-687-7298

Named after the variety of apple that once grew widely in the High Falls area, this Eclectic-American is known for its creative vegetarian cooking but also offers the likes of shell steak; owners Tim Celuch and George Nagle grow their own produce in season and, not surprisingly, some of their signature desserts feature juicy Northern Spies.

Northgate at Dockside Harbor   ▽ 19 | 19 | 21 | $31
(Cold Spring) ⑤

1 North St. (Main St.), 914-265-5555

■ With its "sunset Hudson River views" and "outdoor patio", this Cold Spring New American is a "very good place to drink", though there's also an "ample" menu offering "good food at good prices."

Off Broadway Restaurant | 22 | 16 | 20 | $33 |
(Dobbs Ferry) **S**
17 Ashford Ave. (Broadway), 914-693-6170
■ The "creative dishes" at this "innovative", "ambitious"
and "consistently delicious" Dobbs Ferry New American win
wide applause; while most say there's "pleasant service in a
comfortable setting", a number moan about the "deafening
noise" and suggest "the rear room for quiet dining."

Old Chatham Sheepherding ▽ | 26 | 27 | 25 | $53 |
Company Inn (Old Chatham) **S**
99 Shaker Museum Rd., 518-794-9774
■ This "exquisite", "expensive" Columbia County relative
newcomer has won kudos for the Contemporary American
cooking of chef Melissa Kelly; her "wonderful" daily
changing menu includes the farm's own lamb and cheeses,
plus ewe's milk ice creams and sorbets; the "lovely" 18th-
century inn, which is on the National Register of Historic
Places, offers overnight accommodation.

OLD DROVERS INN | 23 | 26 | 22 | $48 |
(Dover Plains) **S**
Old Drovers Inn, Old Rte. 22 (E. Duncan Hill Rd.), 914-832-9311
■ You're transported to "another world" when you enter this
18th-century Dover Plains Relais & Châteaux inn, which
fans regard as "absolutely first-rate across-the-board";
there's a new chef presiding over the "excellent" New
American fare and a "wonderful wine list and sommelier";
on the downside, a few complain that service can be "slow"
and "snotty" and add it's "expensive for what you get."

Old '76 House, The (Tappan) **S** | 18 | 23 | 19 | $32 |
110 Main St. (Palisades Pkwy., exit 5S), 914-359-5476
☑ The oldest tavern in the Hudson Valley, this Tappan
Traditional American serves "homey", "comfortable food" in
a "charming" 1755 inn, making it a "great place to go for
Thanksgiving dinner"; but foes find the atmosphere "fake"
and call the food "not too memorable."

Old Stonehouse Inn ▽ | 18 | 22 | 17 | $31 |
(Orangeburg) **S**
15 Kings Hwy. (Rte. 303), 914-359-5665
☑ There's suitably "old-fashioned decor" at this 18th-
century Rockland County inn; the Traditional American–
Continental fare draws mixed reviews: for some it's "good",
but for others it's only "a place for lunch if you're in the area."

Olliver's (White Plains) ◗**S** | 14 | 12 | 13 | $21 |
15 S. Broadway, Rte. 22 (Main St.), 914-761-6111
■ A "young after-work crowd" calls this White Plains
American home, making it a "very loud" "meat market" ("I
felt I was the prime cut of the day"); the food is secondary
to the scene, so stick to the nachos and burgers.

Onda Blu Restaurant (Armonk) ⑤ 18 | 12 | 17 | $35
Elide Plaza, 111 Bedford Rd. (Business Park), 914-273-4186
◩ "Generous portions" of "decent" Italian food draw locals
to this Armonk "diamond in the rough" with a "great prix
fixe" dinner; others find the food "nothing special" but
admit it's "reliable"; regulars who always complained of
the "tired decor" will be happy to hear the dining room
has been renovated post-*Survey*.

Osaka (Rhinebeck) ⑤   ▽ 21 | 14 | 22 | $27
18 Garden St. (W. Market St.), 914-876-7338
◼ Northern Dutchess diners praise this Rhinebeck
newcomer for its "good value" Japanese fare, including
fresh sushi; they also appreciate the efficient service and
conclude that this is a delicious taste of the land of the
rising sun sampled "way north of New York City."

O'Sho (Poughkeepsie)   – | – | – | E
763 South Rd. (exit 13, Rte. 84), 914-297-0540
This large and often bustling Japanese steak and sushi
house is a perennial favorite with Dutchess County diners;
hibachi entrees, cooked tableside, are a draw, as is the
highly rated sushi; and regulars report it's a great place to
take someone for their first taste of Japanese cooking.

Osteria Xe Sogni (Amenia)   – | – | – | M
Rte. 44, 914-373-7755
A "nice hideaway" on Route 44, just west of Amenia, this
Italian has developed a good local reputation, keeping
it hopping on weekends; however, it's easier to get a
reservation during the week and you may get the chance
to talk to the chef through his open kitchen; N.B. though
still on Route 44, a new locale means the addition of a
fireplace and a full bar.

Pagoda   ▽ 18 | 17 | 18 | $22
(Eastchester) ⑤ **(CLOSED)**
*701 White Plains Rd. (bet. California & Wilmot Rds.),
914-472-1600*
◩ There's a towering discrepancy of opinion about this
Eastchester veteran: some residents count on it for "good,
local Chinese", but cynics claim it's more out of "the '50s
than the '90s in terms of food and service."

Painter's   ▽ 19 | 20 | 19 | $27
(Cornwall-on-Hudson) ⑤
266 Hudson St. (Ave. A & Idelwild Ave.), 914-534-2109
◼ "Go for the art, stay for the food" say frequenters of
this popular Cornwall-on-Hudson Eclectic; the "casual
and friendly ambiance" and an ever-changing show of
work by local artists provide a "lovely" if "noisy" setting
for "good food", with the Sunday brunch getting special
mention; if you consume too many mimosas, you can check
into one of the five new rooms they've added.

205

Pane E Vino,   23 | 23 | 22 | $37
A Culinary Journey (Bronxville) **S**
124 Pondfield Rd. (Cedar St.), 914-337-3330
■ For "a culinary journey through Italy", try this "pretty",
"trendy" Bronxville newcomer where the "changing
regional menu is a treat" that gets transformed four times
a year; while "sometimes quirky", the food is generally
"terrific" and the service is "excellent."

Pantanal (Port Chester) **S**   ▽ 20 | 13 | 19 | $25
29 N. Main St. (bet. Adee St. & Westchester Ave.),
914-939-6894
■ "A meat eater's paradise", the rodizio at this Port Chester
Brazilian offers an "endless" array of "succulent meats,
rice and beans" brought to the table by "nice waiters";
it's an "eating adventure" that's "fun with a group",
though there's "no decor"; to avoid the "long waits",
savvy diners suggest "go early – the natives eat late."

Papa Razzi (White Plains) **S**   16 | 16 | 16 | $24
1 N. Broadway (bet. Main & Hamilton Sts.), 914-949-3500
☑ For those looking for "a good and relaxing spot for early
eating with kids" or a "popular" "after-work bar", this White
Plains Italian fills the bill for "peppy pastas" and pizzas; but
critics carp this "crowded, noisy" "T.G.I.Friday's Italian-
style" serves "so-so" food that's "overpriced."

Paramount Grill, The (Hudson)   – | – | – | M
225 Warren St. (bet. 2nd & 3rd Sts.), 518-828-4548
While Hudson is an antiques lover's paradise, it sure
isn't a food lover's, so this New American–Eclectic with a
"gracious staff" is seen as "an oasis."

Pasta Cucina **S**   21 | 15 | 17 | $25
261 Little Tor Rd. (Middletown Rd.), New City, 914-638-4729
8 Airmont Rd. (NY Twy., exit 14B), Suffern, 914-369-1313
☑ The "lines start by 5 PM" at this very popular Rockland
County Italian offering a "warm welcome" and a "large
selection" of "creative and consistently good food" at
"wonderful prices"; but detractors sniff "it's quite adequate
but nothing special" and say watch out for the "service
with attitude"; for fans, perhaps the opening of the Suffern
branch will ease the wait.

Pas-Tina Restaurant (Hartsdale) **S**   20 | 15 | 19 | $25
Hartsdale Plaza, 155 S. Central Ave. (½ mi. south of
Four Corners), 914-997-7900
■ Both the "good value" and the "fresh, tasty pastas"
attract patrons to this "lively, bustling" Hartsdale Italian;
the early-bird special is "excellent" and there's always a
"friendly welcome" from the "accommodating" staff;
yes, it's "too noisy" and "always packed", but you simply
"can't beat the price."

Peabody's Cafe (Chappaqua) **S**   15 | 12 | 15 | $25 |
61 N. Bedford Rd. (Rtes. 117 & 120), 914-238-6416

■ "Every town needs a good, simple place and this is it" for Chappaqua; a "relaxed" Traditional American that is "great for kids" (though one wag warns "not if they're not yours") and is "adequate" for "casual meals."

Penfield's (Rye Brook)   19 | 22 | 20 | $37 |
Rye Town Hilton, 699 Westchester Ave. (I-287, exit 10), 914-939-6300

■ This "ritzy" Rye Brook hotel provides a "classy formal setting" for New American cooking that's "a surprise and a good one", particularly the "excellent prix fixe dinner."

Peppino's Ristorante   ▽ 15 | 15 | 18 | $28 |
(Katonah) **S**
116 Katonah Ave. (Rtes. 35 & 117), 914-232-3212

◪ Located in a "former railroad station", this old-fashioned Katonah Northern Italian "neighborhood spot" is frequented more for the convenience of its location than its cuisine.

Per Voi (Port Chester) **S**   17 | 17 | 18 | $31 |
23 N. Main St. (Westchester Ave.), 914-937-3200

◪ While some find "clouds in the ceiling but sun in the food", others call this Port Chester "family-style Italian" "pedestrian" and slipping food ratings support this point of view; the service can be "spotty" and some add the experience is "better when you're a regular."

Peter Pratt's Inn   _| _| _| E |
(Yorktown Heights) **S**
673 Croton Hts. Rd. (Rte. 118), 914-962-4090

Ye "olde inn ambiance" of this 18th-century Yorktown Heights colonial farmhouse provides a nice contrast to the New American–Eclectic cooking from a "short, varied menu" with "fair prices"; fans say that while it's "hard to find", this family-run veteran is "worth the effort"; for those who want to explore culinary cyberspace, the inn even has its own Web site.

Pickling Station, The   ▽ 15 | 14 | 17 | $23 |
(Valhalla) **S** **(CLOSED)**
2 Cleveland St. (Bronx River Pkwy.), 914-949-3386

■ The dining rooms of this Valhalla Traditional American are composed of "real rail cars"; since it's located right beside the tracks, the locomotives "rattle your food", but it's a fun place for "the kids to watch the trains go by."

Piemonte (Ardsley) **S**   23 | 17 | 23 | $36 |
473 Ashford Ave. (Rte. 9A), 914-693-2500

■ The "nice twist" to this Ardsley Northern Italian is that the cuisine is prepared by a Japanese chef who creates food that's "delicious", "interesting" and "imaginative"; surveyors adore this "lovely, low-key" "fusion" spot that has a "warm host"; N.B. children under 12 are not permitted.

Pinocchio (Eastchester) S   24 | 18 | 20 | $42
309 White Plains Rd. (Highland Ave.), 914-337-0044

▣ Fans of this "excellent" Eastchester Italian insist it's altogether "top of the line", with "delicious gourmet" food, "restful decor" and "soothing service"; but naysayers maintain it's "overrated and too expensive", and even regulars warn "watch out for the price of specials."

Pizza & Brew S   15 | 11 | 14 | $18
747 N. Bedford Rd. (Green Ln.), Bedford Hills, 914-666-9222
440 S. Riverside Ave. (Rte. 9A, Croton Point exit),
Croton-on-Hudson, 914-271-6608
85 Knollwood Rd. (Rtes. 100A & 100B), Greenburgh, 914-946-5211
1272 Boston Post Rd. (Weaver St.), Larchmont, 914-834-5088
416 Nanuet Mall S. (Rte. 59), Nanuet, 914-624-2530
136 S. Ridge St. (Rte. 287E, exit 10), Rye Brook, 914-937-2511
851 Central Ave., Scarsdale, 914-472-1033
Shop Rite Shopping Ctr., 1020 Broadway (Saw Mill River Pkwy.,
exit Marble Ave.), Thornwood, 914-747-1505

▣ This Italian chain of "good family formula restaurants" has "lots of red sauce and low prices"; boosters say "the pizza's great" and "big portions" mean you "always go home with leftovers", but critics counter "why bother?" – you're in the "land of chronically undercooked pizza"; both friends and foes agree the decor "needs a face-lift"; and with reservations only for seven or more, there are always "long lines."

Pizza Beat (Yonkers) S   14 | 10 | 14 | $17
2575 Central Park Ave. (Jackson Ave.), 914-961-4456

■ If you "don't expect much" of this "cheap" Yonkers "family pizza place", you'll be pleasantly surprised by the "big menu" and "cheerful", "fast service."

Pizza Pizzazz (Mount Kisco) S   16 | 11 | 12 | $12
153 Main St. (Green St.), 914-241-1200

▣ "Put the kids in the game room, pick a pizza and put in your earplugs" at this Mount Kisco Italian where small-fry slurp down subs, pasta and "pies with every topping under the sun"; but while it's great for parents and their charges, those minus offspring growl "intolerable."

PLUMBUSH (Cold Spring) S   23 | 25 | 24 | $41
Rte. 9D (¾ mi. south of Rte. 301), 914-265-3904

■ "If there's only one restaurant left on earth, let it be Plumbush"; this Cold Spring Victorian mansion has "wonderful ambiance", with "individual dining rooms, fireplaces" and an "exquisite bar"; "superb service" adds to the appeal of the "rich" Swiss-Continental cuisine; though a few feel it's "old-fashioned and slightly stodgy" most believe this "unique inn" has "classic flair."

Portofino Pizza & Pasta   ▽ | 19 | 9 | 18 | $13 |
(Goldens Bridge) S ⌿
A&P Shopping Ctr., Rtes. 22 & 138, 914-232-4363
■ Supporters say the "best pizza in Westchester" and "the largest slices in the USA" are served at this Goldens Bridge favorite where the "crowds on Friday nights" queue up for the "great value" fare.

Portofino Ristorante   ▽ | 21 | 15 | 20 | $26 |
(Staatsburg) S
57 Old Post Rd. (River Rd.), 914-889-4711
■ "Best area Italian" cheer boosters of this Dutchess County spot with "cheap" food and "good management"; if the decor is lackluster, live jazz on Fridays adds atmosphere.

Postage Inn, The (Tillson) S   ▽ | 18 | 16 | 18 | $27 |
838 Rte. 32 (Grist Mill Rd.), 914-658-3434
☒ Located in a renovated post office, this Ulster County American-Continental offers what a few call a "routine" menu of steak, seafood and chicken; but until we know more, we can't stamp this one with approval.

Priya Indian Cuisine (Suffern) S ▽ | 18 | 11 | 19 | $23 |
36 Lafayette Ave. (bet. Rte. 202 & Chestnut St.),
914-357-5700
☒ Rockland County regulars praise the "surprisingly good" Indian fare at this Suffern staple; whether the food is "very spicy" or "toned down to American tastes" is open to debate, but no one has good words for the "dark decor."

Provare (Rye Brook) S | 18 | 20 | 18 | $34 |
Doral Arrowwood, Anderson Hill Rd. (bet. King St. &
Lincoln Ave.), 914-939-4554
☒ "The rooms are the star" at this Italian-Mediterranean housed in a hotel/conference center with "expense-account prices"; patrons say the cooking is "inventive" with "good pastas" and "nice personal pizzas", but detractors maintain the "food's gone downhill and the noise level's gone up."

Raccoon Saloon (Marlboro) S   ▽ | 21 | 16 | 18 | $22 |
1330 Rte. 9W (Western Ave.), 914-236-7872
■ "A find in the sticks", this Ulster County pub has "the best beer list and burgers in the Hudson Valley"; it's "very colorful" and "lots of fun" for families or for those who enjoy perusing the selection of over 100 brews.

Rainbow (Monroe) S | – | – | – | M |
16 Rte. 17M (Rte.32), 914-783-2670
Though not well known to our reviewers, this Monroe Italian is loved by locals for its generous portions of good value, "homey, old-time fare"; but be warned that the decor is "shabby", there's "no atmosphere" and service can be hit or miss.

Ray's Cafe (Larchmont)   23 11 19 $24
1995 Palmer Ave. (Larchmont Ave.), 914-833-2551
■ "The place for Shanghai cuisine", this "tiny", "hole-in-the-wall" Larchmont Chinese uses "fresh ingredients" and serves "amazing dumplings" and "delicate sauces"; the "light", "healthful, somewhat limited menu" is "fabulous" rave fans, who also appreciate the "courteous service" and try to overlook the "spare luncheonette environment."

Red Hook Inn, The (Red Hook) S   18 16 18 $31
Red Hook Inn, 31 S. Broadway (Rte. 199W), 914-758-8445
■ "The owner is making a big improvement" at this "charming" 1842 inn in northern Dutchess County; in addition to an American menu, there's an extensive wine list and an "excellent selection of single-malt scotches"; overnight accommodations make it "perfect for parents visiting students at nearby Bard and Vassar colleges"; N.B. new chef Melicia Phillips (ex Stoney Creek) is expected to be another asset.

Red Rooster Drive-In   17 12 15 $10
(Brewster) S⟰
Rte. 22 (3 mi. north of I-684 & I-84), 914-279-8046
■ One of the "last of the '50s-style drive-ins", this "comforting" Brewster "landmark" strikes supporters as the "perfect" venue for a "burger, fries and ice cream"; it's "busier than McD's", but with good reasons – "great prices and good service."

Reka's Thai Restaurant   19 14 19 $29
(White Plains) S
2 Westchester Ave. (Main St. & N. Broadway), 914-949-1440
◪ Boosters say this White Plains pioneer offers "Thai food at its best" and "great lunch specials" served by a "gracious" staff; but detractors say it's "nothing special" and "there's much better Thai to be found"; even enthusiasts concede that the "portions are small for the price" and advise chef-owner Reka to "hire a new decorator."

Ricky's Seafood Restaurant   18 16 18 $30
(Yonkers) S
1955 Central Park Ave. (Heights Dr.), 914-961-8284
■ "A new chef has revitalized" this veteran Yonkers seafooder that features a raw bar, "the best steamed clams in Westchester" and soft-shell crabs, which "are a must"; the "drab" decor has been "renovated nicely."

River Club, The (Nyack) ●S   16 19 17 $27
11 Burd St. (on the Hudson), 914-358-0220
■ "Best on a nice summer day" when you can see and "hear the mighty Hudson", this Nyack American offers "substantial portions" of "average food with no surprises", although the "salads are recommended"; however, a new chef and a new dining room may make waves.

Riverview Restaurant   ▽ 19 | 19 | 22 | $27
(Cold Spring) S
45 Fair St. (Northern Ave.), 914-265-4778
■ This "typical" Cold Spring New American has expanded its repertoire with wood-fired brick-oven pizza; Hudson views and patio dining also add appeal.

Rockwell's   11 | 12 | 13 | $21
77 Knollwood Rd. (100B), Greenburgh, 914-287-0091
105 Wolfs Ln. (Hutchinson Pkwy., exit 10), Pelham, 914-738-5881
16 Depot Sq. (Main St.), Tuckahoe, 914-961-7744
◪ While these "loud" American "neighborhood joints" are "a step above Bennigan's and Friday's", the majority dismisses the food as "substandard"; but supporters relish the "big portions" of "burgers, fries and apple pies."

Rolling Rock Cafe ●S   14 | 17 | 16 | $20
46 Rte. 9N (3 mi. south of Rte. 199), Rhinebeck, 914-876-7625
1239 Rte.9 (4 mi. north of I-84), Wappingers Falls, 914-297-7625
◪ These "noisy" Dutchess County siblings rock with a "swinging young crowd" who claim the American menu offers "something for everyone"; no reservations mean there often are "long lines", and critics comment that the "wonderful" decor is "much more original than the formula food" served in an atmosphere of "uncontrolled chaos."

Romolo's Restaurant (Congers) S   22 | 19 | 22 | $35
77 Rte. 303 (Tremont St.), 914-268-3770
■ "Still one of the best", this Rockland County "classic Italian" is a fave "for food and romance"; the "wonderful" cooking is "done with flair" and the "service is obliging."

Royal Siam (Pearl River) S   ▽ 15 | 16 | 14 | $23
22 E. Central Ave. (bet. Main & Williams Sts.), 914-735-5906
◪ While a few find the food at this Rockland County Thai "very good", most give it a middling rating and criticize the "very small portions" and "slow and inattentive" service.

Rudy's Beau Rivage   10 | 17 | 14 | $30
(Dobbs Ferry) S
19 Livingston Ave. (Broadway), 914-693-3192
■ The Continental fare "does not live up to the great view" at this Dobbs Ferry veteran, which is a good place to enjoy a "beautiful" sunset if you "eat home first"; critics conclude there's "nothing beau about it."

Rustico Ristorante (Scarsdale) S   23 | 19 | 19 | $30
753 Central Park Ave., 914-472-4005
■ This "trendy" Scarsdale Southern Italian is an "excellent new local" offering "fresh, authentic food", including special pastas that are "to die for"; there's "a lively European bistro ambiance" and a "dedicated staff"; the only quibbles are it's "noisy on weekends" when there are "long waits" for the tables, which are "on top of one another."

Ruth's Chris Steak House
(Tarrytown) S | 23 | 22 | 22 | $45 |
*Westchester Marriott, 670 White Plains Rd.-Rte. 119
(I-287), 914-631-3311*
▣ "Good but not Peter Luger's" say carnivorous
connoisseurs who appreciate the "huge steaks" at the
Tarrytown branch of this "classic chain"; but carpers
counter it's "overrated, overpriced and overbuttered."

Ryan O'Leary's (Middletown) S | – | – | – | M |
6 Evergreen Dr. (Rte. 17M & North St.), 914-343-3020
This newish Middletown American-Eclectic is set in a circa
1860 colonial house filled with period antiques; the few
surveyors who are familiar with it agree "it's an excellent
value for good food and comfortable surroundings."

Rye Grill & Bar (Rye) S | 19 | 16 | 17 | $27 |
1 Station Plaza (Purchase St. & Purdy Ave.), 914-967-0332
■ "The world's best mashed potatoes" are but one of the
attractions of this "trendy", "noisy" Rye Traditional American
whose train station location makes it "crowded after work"
with "a great yuppie bar scene"; the "high-quality" food
offers "the most flavor for the buck" in an "upgraded pub
setting" with "good service."

Saigon Cafe (Poughkeepsie) S | – | – | – | M |
6A La Grange Ave. (Raymond Ave.), 914-473-1392
The few who know this Poughkeepsie Vietnamese
appreciate it as a "best buy" and praise the "charming
husband-and-wife team" of owners.

Sakura (Scarsdale) S | 18 | 14 | 16 | $27 |
56 Garth Rd. (Bronx River Pkwy.), 914-723-7767
▣ Supporters of this "solid neighborhood" Scarsdale spot
serving "good basic" Chinese and Japanese praise the
"fresh, delicious sushi" and the "wide variety of hot dishes";
however, foes contend the food is only "fair at best",
adding the "atmosphere is dinerlike."

Salerno's Old Town
Coach House (Tuckahoe) S   ▽ | 20 | 16 | 19 | $36 |
100 Main St. (Terrace St.), 914-793-1557
▣ Loyalists love the "good, hearty" fare at this Tuckahoe
steak and seafooder; but foes call the veteran "a throwback
to another era" and say it "needs a shot in the arm."

Sam's (Dobbs Ferry) S | 15 | 11 | 17 | $19 |
128 Main St. (Oak St.), 914-693-9724
▣ While the "food isn't fabulous" at this Dobbs Ferry Italian
family favorite, the pizza wins praise and it's "solid for a
hamburger"; in addition, regulars report they "make you
feel at home" and "they'll make you anything you want";
with such a friendly atmosphere "there are sometimes
long waits" on weekends.

Santa Fe Restaurant (Tarrytown) S 18 | 18 | 18 | $25 |
5 Main St. (Broadway), 914-332-4452
◪ There's "consistently good" Mexican and Southwestern food at this Tarrytowner, which also offers a number of vegetarian options; "excellent margaritas," "reasonable" prices and a staff that is "child and baby friendly" explain why this "fun" place is frequently "crowded."

Santa Fe Tivoli (Tivoli) S 21 | 18 | 18 | $27 |
52 Broadway (Montgomery St.), 914-757-4100
■ Some say the "awesome", "always tasty" fare at this "noisy", popular Tivoli Southwestern-Mexican "has slipped recently" and a slip in ratings since our last *Survey* supports that opinion; the "fascinating decor" makes for a "festive, raucous setting" with "charming" service; N.B. it's "very busy on weekends."

Satsuma-Ya (Mamaroneck) S 22 | 13 | 19 | $29 |
576 Mamaroneck Ave. (RR station), 914-381-0200
■ There's "something for everyone" at this "low-key" Continental-Japanese; "one can have serious sashimi and sushi here or excellent meat and fish with, of all things, mashed potatoes"; the "interesting" "fusion cuisine" is "a nice change from the typical Westchester restaurant", if "a bit pricey."

Scaramella's (Dobbs Ferry) S 20 | 14 | 19 | $30 |
1 Southfield Ave. (Ashford Ave. & Saw Mill River Pkwy.), 914-693-6024
■ This Dobbs Ferry Italian offers such "gargantuan portions" of "great food" that it leads locals to hope it "keeps its low profile."

Scarborough Fair (Bronxville) S 22 | 19 | 20 | $30 |
65 Pondfield Rd. (Garden Ave.), 914-337-2735
■ The "tasty, creative cuisine" at this Bronxville Eclectic makes it "a true find" for a "fabulous brunch and ladies' lunch"; the "charming", "newly remodeled" space, "lovely garden" and "eager-to-please staff" add up to an "easygoing atmosphere."

Schemmy's Ltd.   ▽ 13 | 14 | 15 | $14 |
(Rhinebeck) S 🍴
19 E. Market St. (Rtes. 9 & 9G), 914-876-6215
■ By day this "charming, authentic ice cream parlor" and luncheonette is a "favorite homebase for Rhinebeck breakfasts and lunches" and a "great place for kids" as well; but now with the addition of candlelit dinners featuring seafood, meats and pastas in an antiques-filled atmosphere, maybe adults will start to take the food more seriously.

Schneller's Restaurant   19 | 12 | 18 | $22
(Kingston) S
61 John St. (bet. Crown & Wall Sts.), 914-331-9800
■ Loyalists lament that there are "not many authentic
family places left like this" Kingston veteran for "good,
basic German" fare, which has its own excellent "attached
butcher shop"; while the interior is "slightly seedy"
everyone's enthused about the "nice summer beer
garden" offering local brews.

Seafood Peddler (Yonkers) S   13 | 13 | 15 | $22
*High Ridge Shopping Ctr., 1789 Central Park Ave.
(Tuckahoe Rd.), 914-779-8007*
☑ "Always busy", this "ordinary fish house" in Yonkers is
popular for its "great cheap lunch" and "early-bird special,
which is a huge deal"; there's a "large variety of other
entrees for nonseafood eaters", but what many feel
they're peddling is "unremarkable" "franchise food."

Seasons Cafe & Restaurant   17 | 12 | 17 | $21
(Harrison) S
*Harrison Shopping Ctr., 385 Halstead Ave. (Oakland Ave.),
914-835-3434*
■ This Harrison New American "treasure" may look
like a "glorified luncheonette" "hidden" in "a local shopping
center", but insiders praise the "creative menu" with its
"wonderful food" and many "healthy choices" and like
the "concerned service."

76 Main   – | – | – | M
(Cold Springs) S **(CLOSED)**
76 Main St. (Rte. 9D), 914-265-7676
A "local favorite", this Cold Spring Continental cooks
"simple" standards including "serious pizza"; on the
downside, we hear the "kitchen falls apart with more than
a few tables filled"; but if you're waiting in the charming
garden, it won't seem so bad.

Shipwrecked (Port Chester)   – | – | – | M
23½ N. Main St. (Westchester Ave.), 914-937-9524
The owners of Port Chester's Per Voi opened this seafood
house right next door and their new baby is anything but
beached; early write-in votes indicate the modestly priced
food "is always good" and the live jazz and blues is another
reason this place should stay afloat.

Shuji's (New Lebanon) S   – | – | – | E
Rtes. 20 & 22 (I-295), 518-794-8383
This "old standby" for "good, somewhat Americanized"
Japanese in Columbia County is housed in an enormous,
"lovely" Victorian mansion; N.B. open for dinner only
from April–October.

Siam Orchid I (Scarsdale) **S**   20 | 12 | 18 | $26
750 Central Park Ave. (Ardsley Rd.), 914-723-9131
◼ The "decor may be nothing to write home about", but most agree the food at this "excellent" Scarsdale Thai is "pretty and tasty", "like the whole cooked fish", and is served by "an extremely friendly" staff; but naysayers call the fare "pedestrian" and even admirers admit "it's expensive for a storefront."

Siam Sea Grill   21 | 15 | 17 | $30
(Port Chester) **S** **(CLOSED)**
134 N. Main St. (Willet Ave.), 914-939-0477
◼ This "terrific Thai is spicy and interesting" according to fans who consider it "the best Thai food in Westchester"; while the room is "ordinary", there is "pleasant" service and it's only "crowded on weekends"; those who say the "fab food" is served in "tiny" amounts should heed the advice of regulars who say you get "better, bigger portions for takeout."

Simmons' Way Village   – | – | – | E
Inn & Restaurant (Millerton) **S**
33 Main St., 518-789-6235
Those reviewers who know this northern Dutchess County inn, which dates back to 1854, tell us the Eclectic-International cooking makes it a venue for "great food"; though they consider it "pricey", the charms of this casual, antiques-filled inn make it worth visiting; N.B. dinner served Wednesday–Sunday.

Skytop (White Plains) **S**   ▽ 11 | 11 | 14 | $22
Westchester Cty. Airport, Main Terminal, 2nd Floor (Hwy. 684, exit 2), 914-428-0251
◼ A "notch or two above airport fare", the Continental cuisine at this unusual White Plains restaurant overlooking the runway comes with "great views if you're into planes"; otherwise it's "only for the kids."

Slattery's (Nyack) **S**   13 | 13 | 15 | $23
9 N. Broadway (Main St.), 914-358-1135
◼ "Local and convenient", this "popular" Downtown Nyack Traditional American has a "good ole pub" atmosphere; the best thing about the "average to mediocre" fare is the "awesome, more-than-you-can-eat brunch."

Sonoma Restaurant & Cafe   ▽ 20 | 18 | 19 | $31
(Croton-on-Hudson) **(CLOSED)**
1 Baltic Pl. (Rte. 9A), 914-271-2600
◼ This "stylish" Croton-on-Hudson New American with a California accent is a "quiet" place for "interesting good food"; a handful report that it "tries hard but doesn't always succeed."

Spaccarelli's Restaurant   22 16 19 $36
(Millwood) **S**
Millwood Plaza, 230 Saw Mill River Rd. (Rtes. 100 & 133),
914-941-0105
■ A local "standby", this small Millwood restaurant
specializes in the food of the Italian region of Abruzzi and
surveyors claim it's so "wonderful" they've "died and
gone to Italy"; though they say the "decor needs some
work", they like the "professional service."

Spiga (Scarsdale) **S**   17 18 16 $25
718 Central Park Ave. (Ardsley Rd.), 914-725-8240
◪ There's "plenty of food and plenty of noise" at this
"brightly colored, cavernous family-style" Scarsdale
Northern Italian; while most regard it as "a fun place to
eat and look, especially on weekends", a vocal minority
pipes up "large portions do not mean great food" and
there's "lots of nothing" here.

Spotted Dog Firehouse   _ _ _ M
Restaurant, The
(Mount Tremper) **S**
5340 Rte. 28 (NY State Twy., exit 19), 914-688-7700
Part of the new Catskill Corners complex, this Mount
Tremper Traditional American has a creative children's
menu and bright, "charming" Victorian firehouse theme
decor that's sure to appeal to would-be firefighters.

Squires (Briarcliff Manor) **S**   ▽ 17 10 18 $20
94 N. State Rd. (opposite A&P Shopping Ctr.), 914-762-3376
■ Fans of "the ultimate neighborhood joint" declare that
a "better hamburger has yet to be invented", but caution
"don't order anything else" at this Briarcliff Manor pub,
which has "no decor" but sterling service.

St. Andrew's Cafe (Hyde Park)   23 23 23 $31
Culinary Institute of America, 433 Albany Post Rd./Rte. 9
(north of E. Dorsey Ln.), 914-471-6608
■ "Healthy dining at its finest" is found at this Hyde Park
Contemporary American cafe with a wood-fired grill; CIA
students provide "impeccable table service" in "plush
surroundings" and the "delicious, nutrition-conscious
food" leads fans to rave "who would guess it could be this
good?"; only a few counter it's "so healthy we leave hungry."

Stefini Trattoria   _ _ _ E
(Irvington) (CLOSED)
50 South Buckhout St., 914-591-7208
"Tucked away in historic Irvington", this "virtually unknown"
Northern Italian is a "hidden jewel" where the "food and
service are first-class"; regulars say it's "easy to relax" at
this "quiet restaurant" and their only quibble is that the
"exceptional dishes" "could be a touch cheaper."

Stella D'Mare
17 | 13 | 15 | $31 |

(Yonkers) S (CLOSED)

High Ridge Shopping Ctr., 1791A Central Park Ave. (NY Twy., exit 5), 914-337-0491

◪ Devotees of this "crowded" Yonkers Northern Italian ignore the "shopping center setting" and "cramped, tacky decor" for "consistently good" "fish and pasta"; but foes respond it "used to be much better" and now it's just "fair."

Stewart House (Athens) S
– | – | – | E |

2 N. Water St. (2nd St.), 518-945-1357

It's "the only game in town" and Greene County diners delight in this "interesting", historic 1883 inn right on the Hudson offering Contemporary American cuisine; if you choose you can spend the night in one of the inn's rooms and if you prefer to sail in rather than drive up, there are docking spaces available at the park across the street.

Stoney Creek (Tivoli) S
▽ 21 | 14 | 17 | $30 |

76 Broadway (next to post office), 914-757-4117

◪ "A great local bistro" with a "gracious" chef-owner formerly of Manhattan's prestigious Chanterelle; customers caution the "excellent food" at this Tivoli New American–French can be "uneven", but overall it's a "pleasant" place that just got more appealing with the addition of a garden.

Stoutenburgh House
▽ 19 | 20 | 18 | $24 |

(Hyde Park) S

564 Albany Post Rd. (Rte. 9), 914-229-0909

■ "A place to linger over dinner by the fireplace and listen to the piano music", this Hyde Park inn has a new menu that blends Eclectic and Continental cuisines as well as offering steak and seafood; the prices are still "from another era", as is the "1770 colonial atmosphere."

Striped Bass (Tarrytown)
– | – | – | M |

236 W. Main St. (next to RR station), 914-366-4455

For waterfront dining, this brand new Tarrytown casual seafood house is set right on the Hudson; it has a bright, almost-Caribbean decor replete with indoor koi pond, reasonable prices and, considering the proprietors also have a wholesale fish company, what should be some of the freshest fish around.

Susan's (Peekskill)
21 | 17 | 22 | $29 |

12 N. Division St. (bet. Main & Park Sts.), 914-737-6624

■ A New American "charming little place" in historic Downtown Peekskill that is applauded for using "fresh ingredients" in its "innovative, imaginative" fare; the "owners know most of their customers" and display work by local artists on the walls of this "jewel."

Sushi Raku (North Tarrytown) S　22 15 19 $30
279 N. Broadway (Beekman Ave.), 914-332-8687
■ The "eminently fresh and good" sushi, the "interesting boxed meals" and the "friendly service", but not the "ordinary decor", keep devoted diners coming to this "small" North Tarrytown Japanese; regulars say it's a "clean, cheery place."

Swaddee House of Thai Food　▽ 20 15 19 $27
(Thornwood) S
886 Franklin Ave. (Marble Ave.), 914-769-8007
■ Compared to other Westchester Thai restaurants, this Thornwood spot is a "bit pricey but worth it" for the "delicious", nicely different food, "friendly owners" and "comfortable, pleasant room."

Sweet Sue's (Phoenicia)　▽ 22 13 18 $12
Main St. (Rte. 214), 914-688-7852
■ Catskill Mountains visitors and residents alike declare this "local legend" delivers the "world's best breakfasts" with "pancakes and French toast in every flavor you can imagine"; soups, salads and pastas are available at lunch and dinner, but it's breakfast and brunch that send diners into a sugary swoon; not surprisingly there's "a killer wait for a table on weekends."

Sweetwaters　18 17 18 $27
(North White Plains) S
577 N. Broadway (Fisher Ln.), 914-328-8920
■ "The kind of place you'll put on your list of regulars" say those who frequent this North White Plains Continental; its location, "convenient to the train", means it's "often crowded and there is a high noise level", but the food is "consistent" and "fairly priced", and the staff is "helpful"; for "eating outside on a warm day", it's "very sweet."

Swiss Hutte (Hillsdale) S　22 20 20 $37
Rte. 23 (MA & NY border), 518-325-3333
☑ This veteran Columbia County inn nestled beneath a Berkshires mountain has a "pleasant" "alpine-like setting" and attracts après-skiers with Continental fare prepared by the Swiss chef-owner; out of ski season, it's also "great for an outdoor summer lunch."

Taconic Diner (Chatham) S　12 10 14 $14
309 Rigor Hill Rd. (Taconic State Pkwy.), 518-392-5005
■ Just about "the only place if you're driving on the Taconic", this "classic diner" is "very mediocre" but "very clean"; if you need a "pit stop", it offers a "good brunch."

Taco's Don Pancho
(Mount Vernon) ◗ S ⊄   _ | _ | _ | I |
166 Gramatan Ave. (Lincoln Ave.), 914-664-1111
Unusual dishes like pozole and goat in parchment give
this Mount Vernon Mexican an authentic feel as does the
revolving crowd of patrons from south of the border; the
decor is a holdover from the restaurant's previous Italian
incarnation and is best ignored; it's better to focus on the
good value, fresh fare that's more than just typical tacos.

Taj, The (Mount Kisco) S   18 | 14 | 16 | $24 |
15 Main St. (N. & S. Mojer Aves.), 914-242-2004
◪ It's the "great bargain lunch buffet and not much
more" at this Mount Kisco Indian, which locals describe
as "decent", although they comment that this taj with
"dim" decor is no mahal.

Taro's NY Style Pizza   ▽ 14 | 4 | 10 | $15 |
(Millerton) S ⊄
Main St., 518-789-6630
◪ To fans, this "down-to-earth" Millerton Northern Italian
serves up "huge portions of solid home-cooked" food as
well as the signature New York–style pizzas; but foes say
service is "bad" and there's "better pizza elsewhere"; as
for decor, scores suggest it's nonexistent.

Tarrytown Diner (Tarrytown) ◗ S   13 | 12 | 14 | $18 |
460 S. Broadway (opposite Hilton Hotel), 914-332-5838
◪ The best thing about this "kitschy" but "clean" diner is the
"convenient location"; however, opinions about the food
vary: some say it's "adequate and fresh" and "reasonably"
priced for such "enormous portions", while others complain
it's just "mediocre" and "overpriced for an ordinary menu."

Tastings (Suffern) S (CLOSED) ▽ 24 | 21 | 23 | $38 |
100 Orange Ave. (Lafayette Ave.), 914-368-3551
■ The "interesting food combinations" and "novel menu"
appeal at this Rockland County Contemporary American
located in a spacious storeront that's handy to the train
station and Downtown Suffern; regulars praise the "warm
welcome", but point out "the wine list needs major help."

Temptations Cafe (Nyack) S   18 | 10 | 14 | $17 |
80 ½ Main St. (Broadway), 914-353-3355
■ Sweet tooths rave that this small Nyack Eclectic is "a
dessert delight" with many "fabulous" and "irresistible"
enticements; since it's a "bargain for dinner" and "lunch
is lovely", who cares about the "bland decor."

Tequila Sunrise (Larchmont) S   15 | 17 | 16 | $25 |
145 Larchmont Ave. (Post Rd.), 914-834-6378
◪ "It might not be authentic but it tastes good and it's fun"
say fans of this "basic" Larchmont Mexican; however, foes
find the food "watered down" and this "festive" spot "noisy."

219

Texas Grill (Yonkers) **S** (CLOSED)▽ 15 | 13 | 15 | $23
Cross County Shopping Ctr., 1 West Dr. (Rte. 87, exit 4),
914-963-7427
▪ If you "need a rib fix, this is the place" say barbecue
boosters of this Yonkers shopping center newcomer; less
enamored patrons counter it's "run-down" and "noisy."

T.G.I. Friday's ◐**S**   13 | 14 | 14 | $19
825 Central Park Ave. (Ardsley Rd.), Scarsdale, 914-722-4088
240 White Plains Rd. (Rte. 119), Tarrytown, 914-332-0960
▪ "Been to one been to them all" say those of this chain's
Westchester outposts; it's a "cookie-cutter experience", but
they're ok for "average American food" and "good drinks."

Thierry's Relais   22 | 23 | 21 | $48
(Bedford Hills) **S** (CLOSED)
352 N. Bedford Rd. (Hill St.), 914-666-9504
▪ A "pretty country house dining room" provides a "romantic
setting" for the "beautifully presented" French-Belgian
cuisine at this Bedford Hills relais, which "has character
and a very decent wine list."

3B Off Broadway (Nyack) **S**   ▽ 21 | 16 | 24 | $33
(fka 3 Broadway)
117 Main St. (Burd St.), 914-358-2900
▪ Nyack natives praise the "superb food and very
professional service" at chef-owner Anthony Gerson's
storefront bistro; his Eclectic-French cooking with Japanese
influences is highly rated though "portions are smallish."

Tilly's Diner (Monticello) **S**⊉   – | – | – | I
5 Raceway Rd. (near race track), 914-791-9848
Close to Route 17, this classic stainless steel diner car is a
popular stopping place for travelers as well as locals who
relish the homemade pies; just "don't expect too much."

Tin Horn (Millbrook)   – | – | – | M
Franklin Ave., 914-677-5600
Opened this past summer, this innovative, attractive
American bistro specialist is winning over local diners
with good fresh food grown in the Hudson Valley.

Tomaso's Bedford Village Inn   21 | 18 | 20 | $37
(Bedford Village) **S**
Rte. 22 (Rte. 172), 914-234-3343
▪ "Ask to sit near the fireplace" at this "warm, cozy"
northern Westchester inn and enjoy the "surprisingly
good" Northern Italian food, which is "getting better all
the time" and "is worth a visit"; but whether the service is
"wonderful" or "indifferent" and "amateurish" is your call.

Tony La Stazione (Elmsford) 🟥   17 | 15 | 16 | $32
15 Saw Mill River Rd. (Rtes. 9A & 119), 914-592-5980

🔳 The "satisfying" Northern Italian food at this "casual" Elmsford veteran makes it a good place for "friendly family dining"; those less impressed label it "ordinary"; located in a former train station, the "large open room" is "noisy but nice", leading those in the know to caution "don't go there on a Saturday night."

Tony May's Hostaria   20 | 19 | 18 | $38
(Port Chester) 🟥
25 S. Regent St. (Westchester Ave.), 914-939-2727

🔳 "Like eating in NYC in Westchester", meaning Tony May's Port Chester Italian offers "pricey, authentic food" in an "attractive modern room"; fans praise the "great antipasti bar", "wonderful" brick-oven pizza and "super breads"; however, many complain there's "a lot of hype but no performance" and it's "not as good as it should be."

Tony's Lobster & Steakhouse   19 | 17 | 17 | $34
(Sparkhill)
Rte. 340 (1 mi. southeast from Palisades Pkwy.), 914-359-7380

🔳 Loyalists cite the "huge portions" of "good" surf 'n' turf at decent prices "considering what you are getting" at this 100-year-old Sparkill establishment; however, even though there is a retail fish store attached, others carp the "quality of the food has steadily declined" over the years, adding "don't go for the atmosphere" either.

Torchia's Ristorante   14 | 11 | 14 | $21
(Briarcliff Manor) 🟥
516 N. State Rd. (Rte. 9A), 914-762-2963

🔳 Locals lament that "nothing is the same" at this one-time Briarcliff Manor Italian "standby"; while a few loyalists maintain it's "reliable and basic", critics counter it's for "pizza only" and the "food and service show they don't care."

Toscana   – | – | – | E
(Port Chester) 🟥 (CLOSED)
163 N. Main St. (Highland Rd.), 914-937-2727

Umberto Proserpio, the former chef-owner of the well-regarded Rye restaurant Umberto's, has moved to Port Chester for his "excellent" new Northern Italian venture.

Toscani & Sons (New Paltz)   – | – | – | M
119 Main St. (exit 18, 1 mi. east of NY State Twy.), 914-255-2272

The popular new offspring of the well-known New Paltz deli, this warm, friendly and sometimes noisy restaurant has pretty decor replete with a stone fountain and faux grapevines; on the menu is hearty, casual Italian fare that makes the most of the deli's delicious homemade mozzarella, sausages and fresh-baked semolina bread.

Towne Crier Cafe (Pawling) **S**   ▽ 19 | 19 | 19 | $28
62 Rte. 22 (Rte. 311), 914-855-1300
■ A "fun place to go for dinner and a show", you'll also
be "pleasantly surprised by the food" at this Pawling
Southwestern veteran, which is considered "the best
place to see live music"; the "improved menu" gets
improved ratings, though a few caution that there can be
very "long waits for the food."

Travelers Rest (Ossining) **S**   20 | 22 | 20 | $37
Rte. 100 (2 mi. north of Taconic Pkwy.), 914-941-7744
■ "Can't be beat at Christmas", this Ossining German-
Continental "jewel" with "exceptional service" is also lovely
in the summer when you can enjoy "the view overlooking
the garden"; while the majority says it serves "huge
portions" of "decent value", "consistently good" food, a
minority contends "it used to be much better."

Trio's Cafe (Scarsdale) **S**   18 | 14 | 17 | $25
*Golden Horseshoe Mall, 1096 Wilmot Rd. (Weaver St.),
914-725-8377*
☑ Supporters of this Scarsdale "shopping center" "great
luncheon place filled with women" praise it for "wonderful
salads" and "good pastas" and say it's swell for "a quick
bite"; but detractors declare the spot "has lost steam",
the experience is "nothing special" and the space is so
"small" it's like "dining in a fishing boat."

TROUTBECK (Amenia) **S**   23 | 27 | 25 | $48
Troutbeck Inn, Leedsville Rd. (Rte. 343), 914-373-9681
■ "Pricey but irresistible", this Amenia inn does double duty
as a conference center and restaurant with a "genteel,
rustic" ambiance and "lovely service"; while ratings for
the American fare have slipped, most maintain the "classic"
food is "fine" and though the "rooms cost a fortune", this
"wonderful" country house is well worth a stay.

Tulip Tree (Rye Brook) **S**   ▽ 11 | 13 | 13 | $24
*Rye Town Hilton, 699 Westchester Ave. (I-287, exit 10),
914-939-6300*
■ This Rye Brook "casual hotel restaurant" has a "nice
setting" that's "best for a good Sunday brunch" and
"unimaginative but totally reliable" Traditional American fare.

Turning Point Restaurant   18 | 17 | 18 | $29
(Piermont) **S**
468 Piermont Ave. (Rte. 9W), 914-359-1089
■ "When you can't get into the Freelance Cafe, walk down
the block" to this casual Piermont "Greenwich Village–type
place" that's so far known more for the folk and blues music
and bar downstairs (where light fare is offered) than the
"fairly good" New American cooking served above.

Tuscan Oven   18 | 16 | 18 | $26 |
(South Salem) **S** **(CLOSED)**
Oak Ridge Shopping Ctr., Rte. 123, 914-532-2600
Tuscan Oven Trattoria (Mt. Kisco)
360 N. Bedford Rd., 914-666-7711
◪ These Westchester Northern Italian siblings decidedly
draw a mixed response: boosters praise the "affordable"
and "wonderful, innovative pizzas", "always good pastas"
and "solid service", claiming these places are "improving
with age"; but critics counter they're just "ok for a quick
bite with the kids", adding they're "expensive for glorified
pizza joints" with "tacky decor" and "too noisy and
crowded" an atmosphere.

TWO MOONS (Port Chester) **S**   23 | 24 | 20 | $36 |
179 Rectory St. (Willett Ave.), 914-937-9696
■ "Two moons gets three stars" for its "beautiful Native
American decor" and "creative", "masterful meals"; this
"excellent" "eclectic" Port Chester New American with a
Southwestern bent is "fresh" and "full of surprises for the
taste buds"; and though "some dishes are uneven", it's "a
winner" with "friendly service."

Underhill Inn, The   ▽ 19 | 18 | 19 | $35 |
(Hillsdale) **S** **(CLOSED)**
3 Underhill Rd./Rte. 22 (Anthony St.), 518-325-5660
◪ A 200-year-old farmhouse with views of the Berkshires
is the bucolic backdrop for this Columbia County Continental;
but whether the "food is beguiling – from pastas to fish and
chicken" – or whether "it started out great but has slipped
as prices have gotten higher", will have to be your call.

Underhills Crossing Restaurant   18 | 19 | 18 | $31 |
(Bronxville) **S**
74 ½ Pondfield Rd. (Park Pl.), 914-337-1200
◪ This "elegant" Bronxville New American offers
"inventive" "lighter choices" and has a "perfect location
around the corner from the movies"; but others call it an
"Upper West Side wanna-be in the 'burbs" that's "trendy",
"noisy" and "overpriced."

Uno Chicago Bar & Grill **S**   15 | 13 | 14 | $17 |
*4 Martine Ave. (S. Lexington Ave.), White Plains,
914-684-7040*
(fka Pizzeria Uno)
*Central Plaza, 2650 Central Park Ave. (Jackson Ave.),
Yonkers, 914-779-7515*
◪ A "notch above fast food", the Westchester branches
of this chain are "ok as a standby" if you "steer clear of
anything but the deep-dish pizza"; supporters call them
"typical family-style" spots with a "fun atmosphere", but
foes hiss "go back to Chicago."

Valentino's (Yonkers) ⑤   22 12 19 $29
*Key Food Shopping Ctr., 132 Bronx River Rd. (2 blocks
north of McLean Ave.), 914-776-6731*
■ "What Carmine's pretends to be in NYC, Valentino's
really is" enthuse fans of this "old-fashioned" Yonkers
Italian that's "a home away from home" for a "mostly
regular" crowd; "huge family portions of terrific food" and
"attentive" service in a basic shopping center setting that's
"always mobbed" make this "an experience."

Via Appia Restaurant   18 12 18 $22
(White Plains) ⑤
9 E. Taylor Sq. (Underhill Ave.), 914-949-5810
■ Boosters of this "great mom and pop Italian" with
"consistently good" food, "nice thin-crust pizza" and
"service with a smile" make this White Plains institution
"a family tradition"; but critics carp it's "tired."

Via Emilia Ristorante (Pelham) ⑤   22 16 21 $34
115 Wolfs Ln. (RR station), 914-738-3008
■ Regulars are happy this "very comfortable Pelham nook"
"continues to be a well-kept secret" so they can keep the
Italian fare, which includes "pasta that can be sublime",
and the "gracious host" to themselves; but others object
to the "inconsistent" food, saying "at times it's excellent,
at other times it's very average."

Villagio Sereno   _ _ _ M
(Hastings-on-Hudson)
(fka Devin Anthony)
14 Main St. (Warburton Ave.), 914-478-4105
There's a new name, but you'll find the same chefs, menu
and decor at this family-style Italian; while some find
the food "good, if predictable", others dismiss it as "ok,
but nothing special."

Vinny's (Pleasantville)   14 11 16 $22
468 Bedford Rd. (Marble Ave.), 914-769-5710
■ "Still the same" after all these years, this "good value"
Pleasantville veteran is "a hometown favorite" with "pizza
for the masses" and "big portions" of "standard Italian
dishes"; though lacking in decor, there are three dining
rooms – one for fast food, one for families and one for adults.

Westchester Brewing Company   17 17 16 $23
(White Plains) ⑤
179 Mamaroneck Ave. (Post Rd & Maple Ave.), 914-997-0001
■ This cavernous White Plains microbrewery is a "favorite
hot spot" that "everyone is checking out"; but opinion
about the "upscale pub fare" (steaks, seafood, burgers) is
decidedly divided, with some saying it "isn't as good as
the beer" and others claiming it's "better"; so it's up to
you whether you want to get into a stew over this brew.

Weston's Country House   _ _ _ M
(Irvington) ⌔
45 Main St. (Dutcher), 914-591-7406
This Irvington tearoom/gift shop is "a delightful spot to lunch" on the likes of homemade quiche and chicken salad; of course, they also serve a formal afternoon tea in a charmingly "relaxed atmosphere."

West Taghkanic Diner   ▽ 13 9 15 $13
(Ancram) S⌔
1016 Rte. 82 (Taconic Pkwy.), 518-851-7117
■ "A good rest stop en route to the Berkshires", this Columbia County veteran is just "the way diners used to be" with a "friendly staff" and "rice pudding and Jell-o for the restless kids in the back."

Wildflower Cafe (New Paltz) S⌔▽ 18 16 15 $18
18 Church St. (N. Front St.), 914-255-0020
■ Mostly vegetarian, this New Paltz cafe is abloom with healthy preparations but does include chicken and seafood on its menu; while sybarites snipe it's "too earthy", and even fans complain about the service, a dedicated band of diners is wild for the wholesome fare.

Willett House, The   22 20 21 $44
(Port Chester) S
20 Willett Ave. (Abendroth Ave.), 914-939-7500
■ "The best steakhouse in Westchester" is "expensive but worth it every time" for "you won't eat for a week" portions of "fine steaks"; the "huge old factory" has a "barnlike atmosphere" and regulars advise "ask for the main dining room, the other rooms are tacky"; with "entertaining waiters", it's "not quite Peter Luger, but then what is?"

Willow Inn, The (Armonk) S   18 14 17 $34
30 Old Rte. 22 (Main St.), 914-273-8737
◩ A "quaint and good" Armonk New American with "sophisticated food, but unsophisticated setting and service" say some; however, others are unbending about this willow, calling it "mediocre" and adding "don't look for ambiance" as the "restaurant needs a face-lift."

Would Bar & Grill (Highland)   _ _ _ M
120 North Rd. (off Rte. 9W), 914-691-9883
Though it's difficult to find, it's well worth the effort for this ambitious Highland New American; chef-owner Claire Winslow and partner Debra Dooley have carefully preserved the ambiance of a '50s Elk lodge – including a great pool room – but serve food that's very '90s; they use local ingredients whenever possible and offer an interesting and reasonable wine list.

XAVIAR'S (Garrison) ⑤⇗   28 | 26 | 27 | $58

Highlands Country Club, Rte. 9D (Rte. 403), 914-424-4228

■ "The best of the best", this "romantic" Garrison gem is only open on weekends, but scores of surveyors say it's "perfect in every way"; chef-owner Peter Kelly's "excellent", "creative" New American cuisine is served in a "lovely" "country club setting" with live harp music; while Friday and Saturday the six-course prix fixe dinners are $75, if you "go for the Sunday brunch, you'll get a taste of the great food at a much reduced price."

XAVIAR'S AT PIERMONT   28 | 25 | 27 | $57
(Piermont) ⑤⇗

506 Piermont Ave. (Ash St.), 914-359-7007

■ "Small, romantic and special" devotees rave over this "elegant yet comfortable" New American in Rockland County, which is "more low-key than its Garrison" sibling; with "impeccable service" and "as good as it gets" prix fixe tasting menus, the experience may be "very expensive but it's worth it."

Yobo (Newburgh) ⑤   ▽ 22 | 21 | 20 | $25

1061 Union Ave./Rte. 300 (next to Ramada Inn), 914-564-3848

■ This "great for the area" Newburgh Asian offers a wide variety of culinary choices – from Chinese, Japanese, Korean and Indonesian to Thai dishes – in an "engaging" setting that includes a rocky indoor waterfall; but note it "can be expensive for what it is."

ZEPHS' (Peekskill) ⑤   25 | 18 | 23 | $38

638 Central Ave. (bet. Nelson Ave. & Water St.), 914-736-2159

■ This Eclectic "culinary delight" is "worth a trip to Peekskill" to dine on "excellent, innovative" fare prepared by "creative" chef-owners and served in the "simple setting" of an "old factory building"; surveyors say it's "much better than the location would suggest."

Indexes to Southern New York Restaurants

Special Features and Appeals

TYPES OF CUISINE

American (New)

Allyn's
Amity Bakery
An American Bistro
Armonk Crossings
Bear Cafe
Bear Cafe Catering
Black Bass
Blue Heron
Bois d'Arc
Bridge St.
Cafe Mozart
Cafe Tamayo
Calico
Central Square
Christopher's
Church St. Cafe
Cobble Creek
Crabtree's
Cripple Creek
Crossroads
Crystal Bay
DePuy
Dudley's
Equus
Farm Country
Foundry Cafe
Freelance Cafe
Gedney Grille
Goldie's
Grande Centrale
Hudson Hse./Country
Hudson Hse./Nyack
Inn/Osborne Hill
Inn/Pound Ridge
Kit 'N Caboodle
Lexington Sq.
Locust Tree
Loft
Luna Rest.
Main Course
Main St. Cafe
McKinney & Doyle
Milliway's
Mountain Brook
New World
Northgate
Off Broadway
Old Chatham Sheep
Old Drovers Inn
Paramount Grill

Penfield's
Peter Pratt's
Red Hook Inn
Riverview
Seasons
Sonoma
St. Andrew's
Stewart Hse.
Stoney Creek
Susan's
Tastings
Trio's Cafe
Troutbeck
Turning Point
Two Moons
Underhills Crossing
Westchester Brewing
Willow Inn
Would B&G
Xaviar's
Xaviar's/Piermont

American (Regional)

American Bounty
An American Bistro
Beekman 1766
Bois d'Arc
Cascade Mtn
Central Square
Charleston
Dominick's
Happiness Is
Laredo
Ryan O'Leary's
Westchester Brewing

American (Traditional)

Allie s
Ardsley Ale Hse.
Armonk Crossings
Armonk Grill
Ashley's
Atrium
At the Reef
Aubergine
Backwater Grill
Banta's
Bear Mountain
Beechmont
Bird & Bottle
Black Bass
Blazer Pub

Le Chambord
Le Chateau
Le Pavillon
Le Petit Bistro
Le Provençal
Les Pyrenées
L'Europe
Maxime's
Thierry's Relais

French Bistro
Bistro Maxime
Blue Mountain
Le Canard
Le Petit Bistro
Marcel's
Stoney Creek

French (New)
Arch
Auberge Maxime
Aubergine
Bistro Twenty-Two
Buffet de la Gare
La Crémaillère
L'Air de Paris
La Panetière
La Rive
3B Off B'way

German
Breakneck Lodge
Cornucopia
Heidi's
Schneller's
Travelers Rest

Hamburgers
Beechmont
Blazer Pub
Candlelight Inn
Horsefeathers
Michael's
Raccoon
Red Rooster
Sam's
Schemmy's Ltd.
Squires
T.G.I. Friday's
Westchester Brewing

Health Food
Foundry Cafe
Wildflower

Hungarian
Schneller's

Indian
Abhilash
Bengal Tiger
Dawat
India House
Jaipore Royal
Malabar Hill
Mountain Gate
Priya Indian
Taj

Indonesian/Malaysian
Yobo

Irish
Nanuet Hotel

Italian
(N=Northern; S=Southern;
N&S=Includes both)
Abatino's (N&S)
Albanese's (N&S)
Alba's (N)
Amalfi (N&S)
Amendola's (N&S)
Angelina's (N&S)
Antonio's (N&S)
Baci (N)
Belvedere Inn (N)
Blue Dolphin (N&S)
Brezza (N)
B'way Pizza/Diamante's (N)
Cafe Antico (N)
Cafe Morelli (N)
Cafe Portofino (N&S)
Caffe Strega (N&S)
Capriccio (N&S)
Caputo's (N)
Casa Mia (N&S)
Caterina de Medici (N)
Chef Antonio (S)
Ciao! (N&S)
Claire's (N&S)
Conca D'Oro (S)
Coppola's (N&S)
Cosimo's (N&S)
Defemio (N&S)
DiNardo's (N&S)
Dominick's (N&S)
Eclisse (N)
Eduardo's (N&S)

Emilio (N)
Enzo's (N&S)
Giorgio's (N)
Giulio's (N)
Gregory's (N&S)
Guida's (N&S)
Guidetti's (N)
Hilltop (N&S)
Il Cenàcolo (N)
Il Cigno (N)
Il Portico (N)
Il Sorriso (N&S)
La Foresta (N&S)
Lago di Como (N)
La Griglia (N)
La Lanterna (N&S)
La Manda's (N&S)
La Parmigiana (N)
La Riserva (N)
La Scala (N&S)
Lia's (N&S)
Louie's (N&S)
Lusardi's (N)
Maddalena (N)
Manzi's (N&S)
Marcello's (N&S)
Mardino's (N&S)
Maruzzella Due (N)
Mediterraneo (N&S)
Miraggio (N)
Mona (N)
Mulino's (N)
Nanuet Hotel (N&S)
Onda Blu (N&S)
Osteria Xe (N&S)
Pane E Vino (N&S)
Papa Razzi (N)
Pasta Cucina (N&S)
Pas-Tina (N)
Peppino's (N)
Per Voi (N&S)
Piemonte (N)
Pinocchio (N&S)
Pizza & Brew (N&S)
Pizza Pizzazz (N&S)
Portofino Pizza (N&S)
Portofino Rist. (N&S)
Provare (N)
Rainbow (N)
Romolo's (N&S)
Rustico (N&S)
Sam's (N&S)
Scaramella's (N&S)
Spaccarelli's (S)

Spiga (N)
Stefini (N)
Stella D'Mare (N)
Taro's NY (N)
Tomaso's (N)
Tony La Stazione (N)
Tony May's (N&S)
Torchia's (N&S)
Toscana (N)
Toscani & Sons (N&S)
Tuscan Oven (N)
Uno Chicago B&G (N&S)
Valentino's (N&S)
Via Appia (N&S)
Via Emilia (N)
Villagio Sereno (N&S)
Vinny's (N&S)

Japanese
Abis
Ajiyoshi
Azuma
Cherry Blossom
Fujinoya
Gasho of Japan
Golden Ginza
Gyosai
Ichi Riki
Japan Inn
Mount Fuji
Noda's
Osaka
O'Sho
Sakura
Satsuma-Ya
Shuji's
Sushi Raku
3B Off B'way
Yobo

Jewish
Epstein's

Korean
Aria
Yobo

Kosher
Epstein's*

Mediterranean
Baci
Blue Mountain
Cafe Mez
Café 32

Dominick's
Provare

Mexican/Tex-Mex
Armadillo B&G
Camino Real
Casa Miguel
Charleston
Corridos
El Coyote
La Fonda
Las Brisas II
Mary Ann's
Santa Fe Rest.
Santa Fe Tivoli
Taco's
Tequila Sunrise

Mongolian
Khan's

Pizza
Angelina's
Broadway Pizza
B'way Pizza/Diamante's
Pizza & Brew
Pizza Beat
Pizza Pizzazz
Portofino Pizza
Taro's NY
Uno Chicago B&G
Vinny's

Portuguese
Aquario
Caravela
Lisboa A Noite

Seafood
Amendola's
Aquario
At the Reef
Benny's Landmark
Black Bass
Brass Anchor
Caravela
Casa Mia
Chart House
Conte's
Cornetta's
Crab Shanty
Crystal Bay
Eastchester Fish
Gus's
Hilltop

Hudson's Ribs
Il Portico
Il Sorriso
Mariner's
Maruzzella Due
Mitty's
Ricky's
Salerno's
Seafood Peddler
Shipwrecked
Stoutenburgh Hse.
Striped Bass
Tony's Lobster

South American
Latin American

Southern/Soul
Max Memphis

Southwestern
Casa Miguel
Laredo
Santa Fe Rest.
Santa Fe Tivoli
Towne Crier

Spanish
Café 32
España
La Camelia
La Fonda
Madrid
Marichu

Steakhouses
At the Reef
Banta's
Charlie Brown's
Chart House
Gasho of Japan
Hudson's Ribs
Mariner's
Mitty's
Mount Fuji
Noda's
Ruth's Chris
Salerno's
Stoutenburgh Hse.
Tony's Lobster
Westchester Brewing
Willett House

Swiss
Brasserie Swiss
La Lanterna

Plumbush
Swiss Hutte

Thai
King & I
Reka's
Royal Siam
Siam Orchid I
Siam Sea Grill
Swaddee Hse.
Yobo

Vegetarian
(Most Chinese, Indian and
Thai restaurants)
Brickhouse
Foundry Cafe
K. Fung's
Luna 61
Santa Fe Rest.
Wildflower

Vietnamese
Saigon Cafe

NEIGHBORHOOD LOCATIONS

Airmont
Citrus Grille

Amenia
Cascade Mtn.
Osteria Xe
Troutbeck

Ancram
West Taghkanic

Ardsley
Ardsley Ale Hse
Golden Wok
Laredo
Piemonte

Armonk
Armonk Crossings
Armonk Grill
Brezza
Broadway Pizza
David Chen
La Scala
Maddalena
Onda Blu
Willow Inn

Athens
Stewart Hse.

Banksville
La Crémaillère

**Bear Mountain
State Park**
Bear Mountain

Bearsville
Bear Cafe
Bear Cafe Catering

**Bedford/
Bedford Village**
Bistro Twenty-Two
Hoppfield's
Tomaso's

Bedford Hills
Pizza & Brew
Thierry's Relais

Brewster
Arch
Capriccio
Jaipore Royal
Red Rooster

Briarcliff Manor
Amalfi
Maison Lafitte
Squires
Torchia's

Bronxville
Japan Inn
Marichu
Pane E Vino
Scarborough Fair
Underhills Crossing

Canaan
Backwater Grill
Les Pyrenées

Catskill
La Rive

Central Valley
Gasho of Japan

Chappaqua
Bistro Maxime
Crabtree's
Peabody's

Chatham
Taconic Diner

Cold Spring
Breakneck Lodge
Foundry Cafe
Hudson Hse./Country
Northgate
Plumbush
Riverview
76 Main

Congers
Grande Centrale
Romolo's

Cornwall-on-Hudson
Painter's

SPECIAL FEATURES AND APPEALS

Breakfast
(All hotels and the following standouts)
Allie's
Amity Bakery
Cafe Pongo
City Limits
Crumpets
Daily Planet
Eveready Diner
Gager's Diner
Grandma's
Martindale Chief
McKinney & Doyle
Sweet Sue's
Taconic Diner
Tilly's Diner
West Taghkanic

Brunch
(Best of many)
Abis
An American Bistro
Ashley's
Atrium
Bear Mountain
Beekman 1766
Bengal Tiger
Bird & Bottle
Brickhouse
Cafe Antico
Cafe Pongo
Central Square
Charleston
Chart House
City Limits
Crabtree's
Jaipore Royal
La Griglia
L'Europe
Marcello's
Maxime's
McKinney & Doyle
Milliway's
Mountain Brook
Old '76 Hse.
Old Stonehse. Inn
Rockwell's
Scarborough Fair
76 Main
Spiga

Sweetwaters
Troutbeck
Underhill Inn
Xaviar's
Xaviar's/Piermont

Buffet Served
(Check prices, days and times)
Abis
Atrium
Bear Mountain
Beekman 1766
Bengal Tiger
Caravela
Central Square
Crabtree's
Crystal Bay
Dawat
Dominick's
España
Il Sorriso
Jaipore Royal
K. Fung s
La Griglia
Malabar Hill
Manzi's
Milliway's
Mountain Gate
Old '76 Hse
Priya Indian
Rolling Rock
Ryan O'Leary's
Scaramella's
Schneller's
Skytop
Spiga
Stoutenburgh Hse.
Sweetwaters
Taj
Taro's NY
Tulip Tree
Xaviar's

Business Dining
Allyn's
Atrium
Bridge St.
Escoffier
Freelance Cafe
Il Portico
Lago di Como

Le Chateau
Mitty's
Old '76 Hse.
Reka's
Rustico
Ryan O'Leary's
Sweetwaters
Tony La Stazione
Tony May's
Troutbeck
Willett House
Xaviar's
Xaviar's/Piermont

BYO
Il Cenàcolo
Ile de France
Mohonk Mtn.
Sweet Sue's
Weston's

Caters
(Best of many)
Albanese's
Allyn's
Amendola's
Amity Bakery
An American Bistro
Angelina's
Aquario
Armadillo B&G
Armonk Grill
Bear Cafe Catering
Beekman 1766
Blue Dolphin
Blue Heron
Blue Mountain
Bois d'Arc
Brodie's Pub
Cafe Mozart
Cafe Pongo
Caffe Strega
Calico
Cascade Mtn.
Christopher's
Citrus Grille
City Limits
Clove Valley
Cornetta's
Cornucopia
Crab Shanty
Crabtree's
Crystal Bay

Daniel's
Dawat
DiNardo's
Dominick's
Dynasty
Eastchester Fish
Epstein's
Gregory's
Guida's
Hope & Anchor
Hudson Cafe
Hudson's Ribs
Hunan Village
Il Cenàcolo
Ile de France
Il Portico
Il Sorriso
Imperial Wok
India House
Inn/Osborne Hill
King & I
La Duchesse
La Foresta
La Griglia
L'Air de Paris
La Manda's
La Panetière
La Parmigiana
Laredo
La Rive
Le Canard
Le Pavillon
Le Provençal
Lia's
Lisboa A Noite
Louisana Cajun
Lusardi's
Malabar Hill
Marcello's
Marcel's
Mary Ann's
Max Memphis
McKinney & Doyle
Mediterraneo
Mill House
Mountain Brook
New World
Northern Spy
Off Broadway
Osaka
Osteria Xe
Painter's
Pane E Vino
Pantanal

Papa Razzi
Pas-Tina
Pinocchio
Pizza & Brew
Pizza Beat
Pizza Pizzazz
Priya Indian
Rainbow
Rustico
Santa Fe Rest.
Santa Fe Tivoli
Scaramella's
Schneller's
Spiga
Susan's
Tastings
Tony May's
Toscani & Sons
Turning Point
Tuscan Oven
Weston's
Would B&G
Xaviar's
Xaviar's/Piermont

Cigar Friendly

Allie's
Arch
Ardsley Ale Hse.
Armonk Grill
Auberge Maxime
Aubergine
Baci
Backwater Grill
Bear Cafe Catering
Belvedere Inn
Black Bass
Bois d'Arc
Brickhouse
Cafe Antico
Central Square
Clermont
Clove Valley
Cobble Stone
Crabtree's
Crystal Bay
Dominick's
Eclisse
Emilio
Equus
Gregory's
Hudson Hse./Country
Inn/Osborne Hill
Jaipore Royal

La Griglia
L'Europe
Lexington Sq.
Lia's
Louisana Cajun
Lusardi's
Maruzzella Due
Max Memphis
Milliway's
New World
Old '76 Hse.
Penfield's
Per Voi
Peter Pratt's
Pizza & Brew
Provare
Red Hook Inn
Ricky's
Ryan O'Leary's
Shipwrecked
Stoney Creek
Thierry's Relais
Tony May's
Tuscan Oven
Underhills Crossing
Westchester Brewing
Willett House

Dancing/Entertainment
(Check days, times and
performers for entertainment;
D=dancing)

Alex & Henry's (D)
Armadillo B&G (blues/jazz)
Armonk Crossings (D/bands)
Armonk Grill (jazz)
Atrium (D/jazz)
Banta's (varies)
Blue Mountain (jazz/piano)
Box Tree (piano)
Brodie's Pub (D/bands)
Cafe Mozart (varies)
Cafe Pongo (varies)
Cafe Portofino (classical guitar)
Charleston (varies)
Ciao! (keyboard)
Clarksville Inn (piano)
Clermont (blues/jazz)
Clove Valley (band)
Coppola's (piano)
Crab Shanty (D/bands)
Crabtree's (jazz)
Cripple Creek (jazz)
Crossroads (piano)

Crystal Bay (D/varies)
Defemio (jazz)
DePuy (varies)
Dominick's (jazz)
Dudley's (jazz)
Hudson Hse./Country (folk)
Inn/Pound Ridge (piano)
Isabel's Cafe (bands/jazz)
Jaipore Royal (sitar)
La Fonda (bands/karaoke)
La Griglia (D/varies)
La Parmigiana (bands/jazz)
Louisana Cajun (jazz)
Mary Ann's (mariachi)
Max Memphis (bands)
Mediterraneo (varies)
Mohonk Mtn. (classical music)
Northgate (guitar/piano)
Old '76 Hse. (jazz/piano/singer)
Old Stonehse. Inn (varies)
Painter's (jazz)
Papa Razzi (varies)
Penfield's (piano)
Pickling Station (bands)
Portofino Rist. (jazz)
Red Hook Inn (jazz)
Ricky's (jazz)
Ryan O'Leary's (piano/violin)
Santa Fe Tivoli (D/bands)
Scarborough Fair (jazz)
Shipwrecked (varies)
Slattery's (bands)
Spotted Dog (dinner theater)
Stoutenburgh Hse. (piano)
Swiss Hutte (D/jazz)
Towne Crier (varies)
Turning Point (varies)
Vinny's (D)
Westchester Brewing (blues)
Willett House (piano)
Willow Inn (piano)
Xaviar's (harp)

Delivers*/Takeout

(Nearly all Asians, coffee
shops, delis, diners and
pasta/pizzerias deliver or do
takeout; here are some
interesting possibilities;
D=delivery, T=takeout)
Abatino's (D,T)
Abhilash (T)
Abis (T)
Ajiyoshi (T)

Albanese's (T)
Alba's (T)
Allyn's (T)
Amalfi (T)
Amendola's (T)
Amity Bakery (T)
Angelina's (D,T)
Aquario (D,T)
Armonk Grill (T)
Ashley's (D,T)
At the Reef (T)
Azuma (T)
Baci (T)
Backwater Grill (T)
Bear Cafe (T)
Bear Cafe Catering (T)
Beechmont (T)
Bengal Tiger (T)
Black Bass (T)
Blazer Pub (T)
Blue Heron (D,T)
Blue Mountain (T)
Brezza (D)
Bridge St. (T)
Broadway B&G (T)
Cafe Antico (T)
Cafe Mozart (T)
Caffe Strega (T)
Calico (T)
Caputo's (T)
Carl's (T)
Casa Mia (T)
Casa Miguel (T)
Cascade Mtn. (D)
Charleston (T)
Chef Antonio (T)
Cherry Blossom (T)
Christy's (T)
Church St. Cafe (T)
Ciao! (T)
Citrus Grille (T)
Claire's (T)
Clarksville Inn (D,T)
Clermont (D,T)
Clove Valley (T)
Coppola's (T)
Cornucopia (T)
Corridos (T)
Cosimo's (T)
Crab Shanty (D,T)
Crabtree's (T)
Cripple Creek (T)
Crossroads (D,T)
Crumpets (T)

Dessert/Ice Cream

Dining Alone

(Other than hotels, coffee
shops, sushi bars and places
with counter service)

Martindale Chief
Mountain Brook
Osaka
Rainbow
Reka's
Schneller's
Taconic Diner
Tilly's Diner
Turning Point
Weston's
West Taghkanic

Fireplaces

Alex & Henry's
Allie's
Arch
Aubergine
Banta's
Bear Cafe
Bear Cafe Catering
Beekman 1766
Belvedere Inn
Bird & Bottle
Black Bass
Blue Mountain
Cafe Tamayo
Capriccio
Cascade Mtn.
Christy's
Citrus Grille
Clermont
Crab Shanty
Crabtree's
Crumpets
Crystal Bay
DePuy
Equus
Gentleman Jim's
Giulio's
Goldie's
Gregory's
Guidetti's
Harralds
Hudson Hse./Country
Hudson's Ribs
Huff House
Inn/Osborne Hill
Inn/Pound Ridge
La Foresta
La Griglia
Le Chateau
L'Europe
Lia's
Locust Tree

Lusardi's
Maddalena
Marcel's
Mariner's
Maxime's
Mill House
Milliway's
Mountain Gate
Old Chatham Sheep
Old Drovers Inn
Painter's
Penfield's
Peter Pratt's
Plumbush
River Club
Rolling Rock
Ryan O'Leary's
Seafood Peddler
Simmons' Way
Stoutenburgh Hse.
Swiss Hutte
Tomaso's
Tony's Lobster
Travelers Rest
Troutbeck
Tuscan Oven
Xaviar's

Game In Season

Arch
Auberge Maxime
Aubergine
Baci
Beechmont
Beekman 1766
Belvedere Inn
Black Bass
Blue Mountain
Bois d'Arc
Box Tree
Breakneck Lodge
Buffet de la Gare
Caffe Strega
Calico
Capriccio
Cascade Mtn.
Central Square
Charleston
Christy's
Citrus Grille
Cobble Creek
Country Manor
Crabtree's
Daniel's

1883 Stewart Hse.*
1890 Emilio*
1896 Pickling Station*
1897 Tony's Lobster*
1900 Jason's Ltd.
1900 Willow Inn*
1903 Willett House*
1907 Le Chateau*
1914 Bear Mountain
1926 Charleston*
1926 Guidetti's*
1934 Gager's Diner
1953 West Taghkanic
1958 Martindale Chief
(*Building)

Hotel Dining
Bear Mountain Inn
  Bear Mountain
Beekman Arms
  Beekman 1766
Bird & Bottle Inn
  Bird & Bottle
Box Tree Inn
  Box Tree
Crabtree's Kittle House
  Crabtree's
Doral Arrowwood
  Atrium
  Provare
Inn at Stone Ridge
  Milliway's
La Duchesse Anne
  La Duchesse
Locust Tree Inn
  Locust Tree
Nanuet Hotel
  Nanuet Hotel
Old Chatham Sheep
  Sheepherding Company Inn
  Old Chatham Sheep
Old Drovers Inn
  Old Drovers Inn
Plumbush Inn
  Plumbush
Red Hook Inn
  Red Hook Inn
Rye Town Hilton
  Penfield's
  Tulip Tree
Simmons' Way Village Inn
  Simmons' Way
Troutbeck Inn
  Troutbeck

Westchester Marriot
  Allie's
  Ruth's Chris

"In" Places
Bear Cafe Catering
Bridge St.
Cobble Stone
Conte's
Eclisse
Freelance Cafe
Lexington Sq.
Malabar Hill
Mediterraneo
Off Broadway
Pasta Cucina
Rye Grill & Bar
Santa Fe Tivoli
Westchester Brewing

Jacket Required
Alex & Henry's
Arch
Auberge Argenteuil
Bird & Bottle
Box Tree
Buffet de la Gare
Emilio
Equus
España
Giorgio's
Harralds
Hudson Hse./Country
La Panetière
Le Chateau
L'Europe
Mohonk Mtn.
Plumbush
Portofino Pizza
Xaviar's
Xaviar's/Piermont

Late Late – After 12:30
(All hours are AM)
Candlelight Inn (3)
Defemio (1)
Eveready Diner (1)
Rolling Rock (1)
T.G.I. Friday's (1)

Meet for a Drink
(Most top hotels and the following standouts)
Ardsley Ale Hse.
Armadillo B&G

Bear Cafe Catering
Bridge St.
Broadway B&G
Caffe Strega
Chart House
Corridos
Gentleman Jim's
Hudson Hse./Nyack
Il Cenàcolo
Isabel's Cafe
La Fonda
Michael's
Mountain Brook
Off Broadway
Raccoon
Rolling Rock
Turning Point
Westchester Brewing

Noteworthy Newcomers (15)

Belvedere Inn
Blue Mountain
Bridge St.
Equus
Ile de France
L'Air de Paris
Le Canard
Loft
Mountain Brook
Mountain Gate
Striped Bass
3B Off B'way
Toscana
Toscani & Sons
Would B&G

Noteworthy Closings (5)

Bully Boy
Jake Moon
Sorrel
Thymes
Vintage

Offbeat

An American Bistro
Bear Cafe
Cafe Pongo
China Rose
Conte's
Cripple Creek
Hope & Anchor
New World
Yobo

Outdoor Dining

(G=garden; P=patio;
S=sidewalk; T=terrace;
W=waterside; best of many)
Amity Bakery (P)
Angelina's (P)
Arch (P)
Ardsley Ale Hse. (P)
Armadillo B&G (P)
Armonk Crossings (P)
Armonk Grill (P)
Atrium (P)
Auberge Maxime (G,T)
Baci (S)
Bear Cafe (G,W)
Bear Cafe Catering (P)
Bear Mountain (P)
Beekman 1766 (P)
Belvedere Inn (P)
Bird & Bottle (P)
Bistro Maxime (T)
Bois d'Arc (P)
Box Tree (P)
Brass Anchor (P,W)
Breakneck Lodge (W)
Brickhouse (P)
Bridge St. (P)
Brodie's North Pub (P)
Cafe Antico (P)
Cafe Mez (P)
Cafe Pongo (P,S)
Cafe Portofino (W)
Cafe Tamayo (P)
Caputo's (S)
Caravela (S,T)
Casa Mia (G,P)
Cascade Mtn. (P)
Central Square (P,T)
Chart House (P,W)
China Rose (P,W)
Christy's (P)
Church St. Cafe (S)
Claire's (P,W)
Clermont (P,T)
Cornetta's (P)
Cosimo's (P)
Country Manor (P,T)
Crab Shanty (T)
Crabtree's (G)
Cripple Creek (P)
Crossroads (S)
Crumpets (P)
Crystal Bay (G,P,T,W)
DiNardo's (P)

Parties & Private Rooms
(Any nightclub or restaurant charges less at off-times; * indicates private rooms available; best of many)

Schemmy's Ltd.*
Schneller's*
Shipwrecked
Siam Sea Grill*
Simmons' Way
Skytop
Spotted Dog
St. Andrew's*
Stefini
Stewart Hse.
Stoutenburgh Hse.*
Susan's*
Sweetwaters
Swiss Hutte
Taj*
Tastings
Thierry's Relais*
Tomaso's*
Tony La Stazione
Tony May's*
Toscani & Sons*
Travelers Rest*
Troutbeck*
Tuscan Oven*
Two Moons*
Underhill Inn
Vinny's*
Westchester Brewing*
Weston's
Willett House*
Would B&G*
Xaviar's*
Yobo*

People-Watching
Bear Cafe
Bear Cafe Catering
Bois d'Arc
Cafe Antico
Cafe Tamayo
Caffe Strega
Eclisse
Epstein's
Il Portico
Le Canard
Stoney Creek
Tony May's
Westchester Brewing

Power Scenes
Allyn's
Freelance Cafe
Le Chateau
Tony May's

Xaviar's
Xaviar's/Piermont

Pre-Theater/ Early-Bird Menus
(Call to check prices, days and times)
Banta's
Beechmont
Benny's Landmark
Cafe Mez
Central Square
Cobble Creek
Crab Shanty
Daniel's
Defemio
Gentleman Jim's
King & I
La Griglia
Maddalena
Marcello's
Mariner's
Pas-Tina
Pizza & Brew
Satsuma-Ya
Seafood Peddler
Stefini
Stoney Creek

Prix Fixe Menus
(Call to check prices, days and times)
Abis
Allyn's
Arch
Armadillo B&G
Atrium
Auberge Maxime
Bear Mountain
Beechmont
Bengal Tiger
Bird & Bottle
Breakneck Lodge
Capriccio
Central Square
Citrus Grille
Cobble Creek
Dynasty
Emilio
Equus
Goldie's
Grande Centrale
Harralds
Hoppfield's

257

India House (L)
Jaipore Royal (L)
K. Fung's (L)
King & I (L)
La Crémaillère (L)
Lago di Como (L)
La Griglia (L)
La Manda's (L)
La Parmigiana (L)
Las Brisas II (L)
Le Canard (L)
Le Provençal (L)
L'Europe (L)
Lexington Sq. (L)
Locust Tree (L)
Loft (L)
Luna Rest. (L)
Madrid (L)
Main Course (L)
Malabar Hill (L)
Mary Ann's (B,L)
Maxime's (L)
McKinney & Doyle (B)
Michael's (L)
Milliway's (L)
Mohonk Mtn. (L)
Mountain Brook (L)
Nanuet Hotel (L)
Old Drovers Inn (L)
Onda Blu (L)
Osaka (L)
Painter's (L)
Pantanal (L)
Paramount Grill (L)
Pickling Station (L)
Plumbush (L)
Raccoon (L)
Rainbow (L)
Red Hook Inn (L)
Red Rooster (L)
Riverview (L)
Rustico (L)
Rye Grill & Bar (L)
Sam's (L)
Santa Fe Rest. (L)
Satsuma-Ya (L)
Scarborough Fair (L)
Schemmy's Ltd. (B,L)
Schneller's (L)
Seafood Peddler (L)
Seasons (B,L)
76 Main (L)
Spaccarelli's (L)
Spiga (L)

Spotted Dog (L)
Squires (L)
Stoney Creek (L)
Stoutenburgh Hse. (L)
Susan's (L)
Sweet Sue's (L)
Sweetwaters (B,L)
Taco's (L)
Temptations (L)
Thierry's Relais (L)
3B Off B'way (L)
Tilly's Diner (L)
Toscani & Sons (L)
Towne Crier (B)
Trio's Cafe (L)
Troutbeck (L)
Turning Point (L)
Underhills Crossing (L)
Valentino's (L)
Westchester Brewing (L)
Weston's (L)

Sunday – Best Bets
(B=brunch; L=lunch;
D=dinner; plus most hotels
and Asians)
Abatino's (L,D)
Abis (B,D)
Ajiyoshi (L,D)
Alba's (L,D)
Allie's (L,D)
Allyn's (B,L,D)
Amity Bakery (L,D)
An American Bistro (B,D)
Aquario (L,D)
Arch (B,D)
Armadillo B&G (B,L,D)
Auberge Maxime (L,D)
Aubergine (D)
Azuma (D)
Baci (B,D)
Bamboo Garden (D)
Bear Cafe (D)
Bear Cafe Catering (B,D)
Bear Mountain (B,D)
Beechmont (B,L,D)
Beekman 1766 (B,D)
Belvedere Inn (D)
Bengal Tiger (B,L,D)
Benny's Landmark (L,D)
Bird & Bottle (B,D)
Bistro Twenty-Two (D)
Black Bass (B,D)
Blazer Pub (L,D)

Blue Heron (L,D)
Blue Mountain (D)
Bois d'Arc (B,D)
Box Tree (B,D)
Brass Anchor (L,D)
Brasserie Swiss (D)
Brezza (D)
Brickhouse (B,D)
Bridge St. (D)
Brodie's North Pub (L,D)
Cafe Mozart (L,D)
Cafe Pongo (D)
Cafe Portofino (D)
Cafe Tamayo (B,D)
Caffe Strega (D)
Calico (B,L,D)
Capriccio (B,D)
Carl's (L,D)
Cascade Mtn. (L)
Central Square (B,D)
Charleston (L,D)
Chart House (L,D)
Cherry Blossom (L,D)
China Rose (D)
Church St. Cafe (L,D)
Citrus Grille (D)
City Limits (L,D)
Claire's (L,D)
Clermont (L,D)
Clove Valley (L,D)
Cobble Creek (D)
Cornetta's (L,D)
Cosimo's (D)
Crabtree's (B,D)
Cripple Creek (L,D)
Crossroads (B,D)
Crumpets (L)
Daniel's (D)
Dawat (L,D)
DePuy (D)
Dominick's (B,D)
Dudley's (D)
Eduardo's (D)
Egg's Nest (L,D)
Epstein's (L,D)
Equus (L,D)
España (D)
Farm Country (L,D)
Fernwood (D)
Foster's (L,D)
Foundry Cafe (L)
Freelance Cafe (L,D)
Fujinoya (D)
Gasho of Japan (L,D)

Gedney Grille (D)
Gentleman Jim's (D)
Giulio's (D)
Goldie's (B,D)
Grande Centrale (D)
Grandma's (L,D)
Gyosai (D)
Hartsdale Garden (D)
Heidi's (D)
Horsefeathers (B,L,D)
Hudson Cafe (L,D)
Hudson Hse./Country (L,D)
Hudson Hse./Nyack (B,D)
Hunan Village (L,D)
Ichi Riki (D)
Il Cenàcolo (D)
Il Cigno (D)
Il Portico (D)
Imperial Wok (L,D)
India House (L,D)
Inn/Pound Ridge (B,L,D)
Jaipore Royal (L,D)
K. Fung's (L,D)
King & I (L,D)
La Camelia (L,D)
La Crémaillère (L,D)
La Duchesse (L,D)
La Foresta (D)
Lago di Como (L,D)
La Griglia (B,L,D)
L'Air de Paris (D)
La Lanterna (D)
La Manda's (L,D)
La Parmigiana (L,D)
La Riserva (B,D)
La Rive (D)
Le Canard (B,L,D)
Le Chambord (D)
Le Chateau (D)
Le Petit Bistro (D)
Le Provençal (L,D)
Les Pyrénées (D)
L'Europe (B,D)
Lexington Sq. (L,D)
Lisboa A Noite (L,D)
Locust Tree (B,L,D)
Loft (L,D)
Lusardi's (L,D)
Maddalena (D)
Madrid (L,D)
Main Course (B,L,D)
Main St. Cafe (L,D)
Malabar Hill (L,D)
Marcello's (B,D)

Senior Appeal

Singles Scenes

Cafe Pongo
Casa Miguel
China Rose
Clermont
Cobble Stone
Conca D'Oro
Hudson Hse./Nyack
Isabel's Cafe
La Fonda
Lexington Sq.
Louisana Cajun
New World
Olliver's
Rolling Rock
Rye Grill & Bar
Santa Fe Tivoli
Stoney Creek
Turning Point
Westchester Brewing

Sleepers
(Good to excellent food,
but little known)
Ajiyoshi
Amity Bakery
Aubergine
Backwater Grill
Belvedere Inn
Blazer Pub
Bois d'Arc
Brickhouse
Cafe Pongo
Cafe Tamayo
Caffe Strega
Calico
China Rose
Conte's
Cosimo's
Cripple Creek
Crossroads
Dynasty
El Coyote
España
Fujinoya
Grande Centrale
Guida's
Guidetti's
Gyosai
Il Cenàcolo
Il Portico
India House
Jaipore Royal
Japan Inn
La Duchesse

La Griglia
L'Air de Paris
La Rive
Le Canard
Le Pavillon
Le Provençal
Locust Tree
Marcel's
Max Memphis
Milliway's
New World
Old Chatham Sheep
Osaka
Portofino Rist.
Raccoon
Santa Fe Tivoli
Shuji's
Simmons' Way
Stoney Creek
Susan's
Sushi Raku
Swiss Hutte
Tastings
3B Off B'way
Via Emilia
Yobo

Teflons
(Get lots of business, despite
so-so food, i.e. they have
other attractions that prevent
criticism from sticking)
Boston Market
Pizza & Brew
T.G.I. Friday's

Smoking Prohibited
(May be permissible at bar or
outdoors; N.B. county
regulations prohibit smoking
in Westchester restaurants)
Abatino's
Abhilash
Ajiyoshi
American Bounty
Amity Bakery
Atrium
Azuma
Bear Mountain
Bengal Tiger
Bistro Maxime
Blue Dolphin
Boston Market
Box Tree

Escoffier
Freelance Cafe
Inn/Osborne Hill
Inn/Pound Ridge
La Camelia
L'Europe
New World
Peter Pratt's
Red Hook Inn
Stoney Creek
Troutbeck
Xavier's
Xavier's/Piermont

Worth a Trip
Armenia
  Cascade Mtn.
Bearsville
  Bear Cafe
  Bear Cafe Catering
Bedford
  Bistro Twenty-Two
Brewster
  Arch
Catskill
  La Rive
Chappaqua
  Crabtree's
Dover Plains
  Old Drovers Inn
Elmsford
  Malabar Hill
Fishkill
  Inn/Osborne Hill
Garrison
  Bird & Bottle
  Xavier's
Granite Springs
  Maxime's
High Falls
  DePuy
Hillsdale
  Aubergine
Hunter
  Mountain Brook
Hyde Park
  American Bounty
  Caterina de Medici
  Escoffier
Irvington
  Bridge St.
Mount Kisco
  Conte's

Mount Temper
  La Duchesse
North Salem
  Auberge Maxime
North Tarrytown
  Goldie's
  Sushi Raku
Nyack
  Hudson Hse./Nyack
  3B Off B'way
Piermont
  Freelance Cafe
Pine Plains
  Church St. Cafe
Port Chester
  Tony May's
Pound Ridge
  Inn/Pound Ridge
Red Hook
  Bois d'Arc
Rhinebeck
  Beekman 1766
  Cripple Creek
Saugerties
  Cafe Tamayo
Scarsdale
  Eastchester Fish
South Salem
  L'Europe
Staatsburg
  Belvedere Inn
Stormville
  Harralds
Suffern
  Marcello's
Tuckahoe
  An American Bistro
White Plains
  Westchester Brewing
Wingdale
  Guidetti's
Woodstock
  New World

Young Children
(Besides the normal fast food places; *indicates children's menu available)
Abis
At the Reef*
Bear Cafe Catering*
Blue Heron*
Cafe Pongo
Calico*

Wine Vintage Chart 1985-1996

This chart is designed to help you select wine to go with your meal. It is based on the same 0 to 30 scale used throughout this *Survey*. The ratings (prepared by our friend Howard Stravitz, a law professor at the University of South Carolina) reflect both the quality of the vintage and the wine's readiness for present consumption. Thus, if a wine is not fully mature or is over the hill, its rating has been reduced. We do not include 1987 because, with the exception of '87 cabernets, those vintages are not recommended.

	'85	'86	'88	'89	'90	'91	'92	'93	'94	'95	'96
WHITES											
French:											
Burgundy	27	28	20	29	24	18	26	19	25	25	26
Loire Valley	–	–	–	25	24	15	19	22	23	24	24
Champagne	28	25	24	26	28	–	–	24	–	25	26
Sauternes	22	28	29	25	26	–	–	–	18	22	24
California:											
Chardonnay	–	–	–	–	23	21	26	25	22	23	22
REDS											
French:											
Bordeaux	27	26	25	28	28	–	19	23	24	25	24
Burgundy	24	–	26	27	29	21	23	25	22	23	24
Rhône	26	20	26	28	27	26*	16	23*	23	24	22
Beaujolais	–	–	–	–	–	22	13	21	22	24	21
California:											
Cab./Merlot	27	26	16	22	28	26	25	24	24	23	22
Zinfandel	–	–	–	–	–	20	20	20	22	20	21
Italian:											
Tuscany	27	16	25	–	26	19	–	20	19	24	19
Piedmont	26	–	24	27	27	–	–	19	–	25	25

*Rating and recommendation is only for Northern Rhône wine in 1991 and Southern Rhône wine in 1993.

Bargain sippers take note: Some wines are reliable year in, year out, and are reasonably priced as well. These wines are best bought in the most recent vintages. They include: Alsatian Pinot Blancs, Côtes du Rhône, Muscadet, Bardolino, Valpolicella and inexpensive Spanish Rioja and California Zinfandel.